CULTURALLY COMPETENT

A Framework for Growth and Action

CULTURALLY COMPETENT PRACTICE

A Framework for Growth and Action

DOMAN LUM

California State University–Sacramento

BROOKS/COLE PUBLISHING COMPANY

I(T)P® **An International Thomson Publishing Company**

Pacific Grove • Albany • Belmont • Bonn • Boston • Cincinnati • Detroit • Johannesburg • London
Madrid • Melbourne • Mexico City • New York • Paris • Singapore • Tokyo • Toronto • Washington

Acquisitions Editor: *Lisa Gebo*
Marketing Team: *Steve Catalano, Donna Shore, Aaron Eden*
Editorial Assistants: *Susan Wilson*
Production Editor: *Majorie Z. Sanders*
Manuscript Editor: *Lorraine Anderson*
Permissions Editor: *May Clark*
Design Editor: *Roy R. Neubaus*

Interior and Cover Design: *EllenPettengell*
Interior Illustration: *Jennifer Mackres*
Cover Illustration: *Stephan Daigle/The Stock Illustration Source*
Art Editor: *Jennifer Mackres*
Typesetting: *CompuKing*
Printing and Binding: *Webcom*

For more information, contact:

BROOKS/COLE PUBLISHING COMPANY
511 Forest Lodge Road
Pacific Grove, CA 93950
USA

International Thomson Publishing Europe
Berkshire House 168-173
High Holborn
London WC1V 7AA
England

Thomas Nelson Australia
102 Dodds Street
South Melbourne, 3205
Victoria, Australia

Nelson Canada
1120 Birchmount Road
Scarborough, Ontario
Canada M1K 5G4

International Thomson Editores
Seneca 53
Col. Polanco
11560 México, D. F., México

International Thomson Publishing GmbH
Königswinterer Strasse 418
53227 Bonn
Germany

International Thomson Publishing Asia
60 Albert Street
#15-01 Albert Complex
Singapore 189969

International Thomson Publishing Japan
Hirakawacho Kyowa Building, 3F
2-2-1 Hirakawacho
Chiyoda-ku, Tokyo 102
Japan

Printed in Canada

10 9 8 7 6 5 4 3 2 1

Library of Congress Cataloging-in-Publication Data
Lum, Doman, [date]
    Culturally competent practice : a framework for growth and action
/ Doman Lum.
        p.   cm.
    Includes bibliographical references and index.
    ISBN 0-534-35686-9
    1. Social work with minorities.   2. Social work with minorities-
United States. I. Title
HV3176.L89   1998
362.84'00973—dc21   98-17046
                                                              CIP

Credits continue on page 201.

To the persons and groups who have influenced the development of this book:

Herbert Aptekar and Herman Stein,
who brought me into social work education

The Cultural Diversity Committee of the Board of Directors, Council on Social Work Education,
who are advocates of cultural competency programs

The multicultural counseling psychology movement leaders,
who are pioneers in cultural competency publications,

and

My wife, Joyce, and children: Lori, Jonathan, Amy, and Matthew Lum

Contents

CHAPTER FOUR

Knowledge Acquisition 79

CHAPTER FIVE

Skill Development 111

Competency Studies

Foreword

This timely text represents the culmination of serious dialogues, curriculum workshops, classroom instruction, and extensive research on multiculturalism. In particular, it provides the reader with a solid framework for the development and measurement of cultural competency in social work practice with people of color. The essential components of culturally competent social work practice include cultural awareness, knowledge acquisition, skill development, and inductive learning.

With respect to cultural awareness, it is posited that before cultural sensitivity and ultimately cultural competence can develop, there must be cultural awareness. This awareness must take place in an environment of trust and openness—as in a classroom.

Outside the classroom on the national policy level, President Clinton introduced the "Initiative on Race," which calls for a series of "Dialogues on Race." The goal of these dialogues or cultural awareness sessions is to find the mutual understanding that can somehow lead to a stronger sense of community. The assumption here, which I believe is a good one, is that you care more about neighbors you understand than about strangers who you perceive to be different. True cultural awareness, like successful dialogue, must include opportunities for exchange and interaction with persons with different backgrounds and ideologies. Regardless of background, it is imperative that all persons—whether they are students, practitioners, educators, or community representatives—be responsible, honest, and willing to search for the kernel of truth or validity in what the other side is saying or doing.

Although nationwide surveys have documented significant declines in whites' overt racism toward blacks, substantial differences persist in the social, economic, and physical well-being of blacks and whites. Blacks continue to report greater distrust of government and other people than do whites. Similar empirical data for other minority groups suggest that race remains a critical issue in our society. Further case examples can be seen in the experiences of golfer Tiger Woods, who, despite his accomplishments, still bears the brunt of a racial joke; and former

Virginia governor, L. Douglas Wilder, who, despite his achievement as the first black elected governor since Reconstruction, was harassed by airport security guards.

If we as social work educators are serious about preparing our students to become culturally competent in this increasingly multicultural world, we must have our own dialogue in a race or cultural awareness session. The time is now right for social work practice and social work education to address the racial divide. Without such a dialogue to "clear the air" in the profession and clarify the issues and perspectives on how race matters, we will miseducate even those students with the highest level of aptitude and commitment.

It is no secret that our country is becoming increasingly more multicultural and diverse. While it must be acknowledged that the ethnic groups from European countries have contributed to the diversity in America and that such groups were often met with hostility and discrimination upon immigration, the focus of this text is on people of color. While each cultural group, whether a white European ethnic group or a racial minority, had imposed upon it the dominant group's culture (White Anglo-Saxon Protestant) in the forms of the English language, religious values, work ethic, and music and art, people of color have had the additional burden of racism undergirding discrimination. Some, such as those who were brought to this country from Africa against their will, were slow to acculturate because families were split and human rights were denied due to slavery and servitude. However, each group, despite its voluntary or involuntary departure from its homeland, contributes to the richness of the multicultural fabric of our society.

The Nondiscrimination and Human Diversity Evaluative Standard of the Council on Social Work Education (CSWE) clearly states that: "The program must make specific, continuous efforts to provide a learning context in which understanding and respect for diversity (including age, color, disability, ethnicity, gender, national origin, race, religion, and sexual orientation) are practiced.

Culturally Competent Practice undoubtedly addresses the Council standard on nondiscrimination and human diversity by solidly equipping students with the awareness, knowledge, skills, and inductive learning to practice in a culturally competent manner on both the generalist and advanced levels. As we move into the next millennium, cultural sensitivity without cultural competency in practice with people of color is doomed to failure. An understanding and utilization of the components of Lum's framework and accompanying behavioral assessment will prepare the practitioner for work in a multicultural America as well as the global marketplace that will increasingly become commonplace in the next millennium.

Moses Newsome, Jr., Ph.D.
President, Council on Social Work Education, and Dean,
The Ethelyn R. Strong School of Social Work, Norfolk, VA

Preface

As we begin the 21st century it is fitting for culturally diverse social work practice to begin a new chapter in its development. Cultural competency is an important innovation in social work practice with people of color. The new and emerging field of multicultural social work seeks to craft cultural abilities with clients and measure behavioral learning outcomes. The development of cultural competency begins with multicultural counseling psychology, which developed a competency framework and a system of competencies or performance characteristics during the early nineties. This book helps the social work student to understand the pioneering multicultural counseling competency literature and to build from this foundation a culturally competent perspective on social work.

I have sought to break new ground in cultural competency in this text. It has not been an easy task, as I have found myself piecing together various strands of cultural competency mentioned by a few social work educators and practitioners. The seed for this book was planted when I taught a social work curriculum workshop on cultural competency with my good friend and colleague Yuhwa Eva Lu, an associate professor of social work at New York University. We prepared a paper on cultural competency that covered basic concepts, a framework model, and research trends in this new field. At the 1997 Council on Social Work Education Annual Program Meeting in Chicago, we met with 50 curious and enthusiastic participants who asked many questions about cultural competency an eagerly interacted with us during our presentation. They were excited about teaching cultural competency to their students.

As a result of this wonderful peak experience in March 1997, I spent the next months working day and night to turn the framework presented in Chicago into a manuscript on culturally competent practice. It reminded me of my work in the early eighties when I was writing *Social Work Practice and People of Color* with a minimum of material to draw on and a maximum of creativity required. However, with contributions from V. Eva Lu of New York University and Andrew Bein of California State University, Sacramento, I put together a working draft of this book. Then during the fall 1997 semester, students in my multicultural social work classes read chapters and reacted to several of the exercises, which gave me a positive sense of how students might respond to this material.

I have entitled the text *Culturally Competent Practice: A Framework for Growth and Action*. The culturally competent practice (CCP) model is a framework for understanding, measuring, and evaluating cultural competency in the social work student's learning. The text places cultural competency in the context of outcome measurement and practice performance. I hope that students will discuss and debate what the appropriate cultural competencies are and how these competencies are measured to ensure outcome effectiveness. Moreover, there is room for formulating some basic definitions from the student perspective. The social work cultural competencies framework helps the student to conceptualize a structural model that addresses the unique areas of social work competency. I also was aware of the different learning needs of BSW and MSW degree students and sought to address these needs in the generalist and advanced levels of the framework.

At the Chicago Annual Program Meeting, my colleague, Rowena Fong from the University of Hawaii mentioned to me the need for an instrument to measure cultural competency. I saw the strategic importance of this and designed a 44-item cultural competency instrument using a Likert-type scale. At the beginning and end of the semester, students are asked to take a pretest and a posttest of the social work cultural competency instrument to determine and compare their levels of cultural competency before and after the course. Janet B. W. Williams of Columbia University College of Physicians and Surgeons, Department of Psychiatry and Neurology, helped me with the revision of this instrument. Phyllis N. Black of Marywood College School of Social Welfare gave helpful feedback on the instrument and on a sample chapter of the book. I am grateful to these colleagues.

This text builds on my earlier book, *Social Work Practice and People of Color: A Process-Stage Approach* as a companion text. Running throughout both books is a case study that views the Hernandez family through the lens of generalist and advanced practice. This case follows the social worker as he or she masters the knowledge and skills necessary to lead the clients through the process stages (contact, problem identification, assessment, intervention, and termination) and develops cultural competency (cultural awareness, knowledge theory, skill development, and inductive learning).

Along with the Hernandez family case study are special sections throughout the text entitled "Tools for Student Learning." These sections are strategically placed to assist the reader in the development of cultural competency and are springboards for small group discussion in the classroom. In many instances there are questionnaires designed to help the student with the application of concepts in his or her personal and professional lives.

I want to thank Larry Ortiz, professor of social work and program director at Westchester University, who invited me to give the workshop on cultural competency in Chicago and started me on the road to writing this book; Moses Newsome, president of the Council on Social Work Education and dean of the

Ethelyn R. Strong School of Social Work, Norfolk State University; and the manuscript reviewers: Sally Alonzo Bell, Azusa Pacific University; Linda F. Crowell, University of Akron; Emelicia Mizio, Indiana Sate University; Janice Matthews Rasheed, Loyola University of Chicago; and Maria E. Zuniga, San Diego State University. Special thanks are due to Lisa Gebo, social work editor of Brooks/Cole Publishing Company, who recognized the importance of this book and offered valuable suggestions for improvement; and to the staff at Brooks/Cole: Marjorie Sanders, production editor; Roy Neuhaus, design editor; Jennifer Mackres, art coordinator; May Clark, permissions editor; Donna Shore, advertising coordinator; and Steve Catalano, marketing manager.

Doman Lum

CULTURALLY COMPETENT PRACTICE

A Framework for Growth and Action

CHAPTER ONE

Culturally Competent Practice

This chapter begins by discussing the meaning of culture and cultural competency, traces the development of multicultural social work, raises questions about cultural competency, and ends with an exploration of beliefs about cultural competency. It has one Tool for Student Learning: a self-assessment instrument.

This book is an introduction to cultural competency that explores how to become a culturally effective social worker in the 21st century. It is a guide to and a resource for culturally competent social work practice with clients of color. The emphasis is not so much on how to be culturally competent with clients; that outcome will occur in the course of working with culturally diverse people. Rather, the starting point is your self-development in learning the areas of cultural competency, which will eventually make for client effectiveness.

This text defines major terms and themes of cultural competency, constructs a social work cultural competencies framework, and focuses on cultural awareness, knowledge acquisition, skill development, and inductive learning as important tools of cultural competency. Interspersed in the various chapters are Tools for Student Learning, which are exercises around the important themes of the book, and a continuous case study of the Hernandez family, which illustrates how to apply cultural competency in dealings with the client. I hope these materials will help you in continuous cultivation of cultural competency.

At the same time it is crucial to blend in an understanding of how our experiences shape our interactions with other populations, particularly African, Latino, Asian, and Native American, and how as practitioners we need to accept other experiences. This is the true mark of cultural competency on our part as social workers. It is our goal to learn the competency areas of cultural awareness, knowledge acquisition, skill development, and inductive learning so that we can understand ourselves as cultural individuals and experience our own sense of cultural competency. In turn we can accept clients as cultural people, increase our understanding of their cultural perspectives, and affirm cultural competency in their lives.

The purpose of this chapter is to introduce the concept of cultural competency and describe the scope of this book. We begin with the meaning of culture and cultural competency. Next we survey trends in cultural competency, explore questions and beliefs about cultural competency, and ask you to test yourself with the Social Work Cultural Competency Self-Assessment instrument.

THE MEANING OF CULTURE

A starting point in our understanding of cultural competency is the concept of culture. What is culture? Culture is the way of life of multiple groups in a society and consists of prescribed ways of behaving or norms of conduct, beliefs, values, and skills (Gordon, 1978). Culture is the sum total of life patterns passed on from generation to generation within a group of people and includes institutions, language, religious ideals, habits of thinking, artistic expressions, and patterns of social and interpersonal relationships (Hodge, Struckmann, & Trost, 1975). Cultural pluralism is a reality confronting our current society. It involves the coexistence of multicultural communities that tolerate and acknowledge each other's styles, customs, languages, and values (Pantoja & Perry, 1976). At times, bicultural tension and conflict occur when there are differences between an individual's family values and behavior and those of the society at large (Galan, 1992).

A number of related cultural concepts are familiar to us. Culture shock (Draguns, 1996) involves cognitive disorientation and personal helplessness due to an abrupt immersion in a different cultural environment, particularly when there is minimal or no preparation. Culture shock occurs when there is a confrontation with a physically remote and dramatically different culture, such as experienced by rural Hmong refugees of the Laos highlands relocated to metropolitan areas of the United States. Culture accommodation (Higginbotham, West, & Forsyth, 1988) is a process that involves social workers in exploration, data gathering, and negotiations before developing culturally appropriate programs in new cultural settings. Local needs expressed by indigenous leaders and conflicts, insecurities, and preferences are taken into account in the process, prior to the introduction of new services in an ethnic community. Cultural empathy (Ridley & Lingle, 1996) involves the learned ability of social workers to gain an accurate understanding of the self-experience of clients from other cultures based on the interpretation of cultural data. It involves culturally empathic understanding and responsiveness based on cultural perception, sensitivity, and interpretation along with cognitive, affective, and communicative processes between workers and client communities.

Culture is a key factor in the social work helping process. Pinderhughes (1989) asserts that culture defines the problem perspective, the expression of the problem, the treatment provider, and the treatment options. Social work practice must be culturally relevant to clients. Cultural factors may contribute to the problem situation, impact the interaction between the worker and the client, and influence cultural interventions related to the extended family, the ethnic church, and ethnic community resources.

THE CONCEPT OF CULTURAL COMPETENCY

In the field of social work, there has been an emphasis on understanding of and sensitivity to ethnic and cultural differences within the context of oppression of and racism toward people of color. The culture of the client is an important factor in her or his psychosocial well-being. Culture is a strength that empowers the individual and enhances family functioning.

The term *cultural competency* describes the set of knowledge and skills that a social worker must develop in order to be effective with multicultural clients. The culturally competent person has the task of bringing together elements from his or her culture of origin and the dominant culture to accomplish bicultural integration and competency.

LaFromboise, Coleman, and Gerton (1993) suggest that a culturally competent individual possesses a strong personal identity, has knowledge of the beliefs and values of the culture, displays sensitivity to the affective processes of the culture, communicates clearly in the language of the cultural group, performs socially sanctioned behavior, maintains active social relations within the cultural group, and negotiates the institutional structures of that culture. Cultural competency is part of a continuum of social skill and personality development. This concept addresses an individual's sense of self- sufficiency and ego strength; cultural identity related to culture of origin and cultural context; knowledge, appreciation, and internalization of basic beliefs of a culture; positive attitudes about a cultural group; bicultural efficacy, or ability to live effectively within two groups without compromising one's sense of cultural identity; ability to communicate, verbally and nonverbally, ideas and feelings to members of one's own or another culture; possession of a role repertoire, or range of culturally appropriate behaviors or roles; and belonging to stable social networks in both cultures.

From an education and training perspective, cultural competency may also be understood as the development of academic and professional expertise and skills in the area of working with culturally diverse clients. A starting point is the fostering of cultural self-awareness. The social worker become culturally effective with the client when the worker develops cultural awareness through an exploration of his or her own ethnic identity, cultural background, and contact with ethnic others. Next the social worker must develop a knowledge acquisition perspective and a set of skills in order to work with multicultural clients. Knowledge acquisition provides a body of facts and principles that serve as boundary guidelines. Skill development applies knowledge acquisition to actual practice with clients from a culturally competent perspective. It also addresses the service delivery structure that ought to be in place for client services. Finally, cultural competency must constantly uncover new facts about multicultural clients through an inductive learning process.

So cultural competency involves the areas of cultural awareness, knowledge acquisition, skill development, and continuous inductive learning. The social work student reaches a point of comprehension and relative mastery of multicultural knowledge and skills in the classroom, the field placement, and the research project. Cultural competency is a learning outcome that integrates cultural dimensions of social work. It is a continuous, lifelong process that involves new learning to maintain.

Manoleas (1994) presents a preliminary social work cultural competency model that categorizes cultural competency according to three dimensions: knowledge base, skill base, and value base. The knowledge base for cultural competency explains how culture affects basic developmental events such as gender role development, rites of passage, sexuality development, mate selection, child-rearing practices, development of social networks, aging. and mourning; different cultural care-giving patterns within families, kinship networks, and communities, such as caring for the young, infirm, aged, and mentally ill; non-European ways of relating to nature, metaphysical harmony, time, and spirituality; and patterns of interdependency, mutuality, and obligations between individuals, their families, and their communities that exist in various cultures.

According to Manoleas, the skill base necessary for cultural competency includes assessment of health, illness, functional and dysfunctional behavior, and psychopathology, taking into account the cultural relativity of categories and modes of expression; culturally appropriate interviewing techniques that consider level of intrusiveness, directness, social distance, formality, and forms of address; evaluation of the client family's world view and level of acculturation or biculturality; cultural self-assessment on how the worker's cultural amalgam complements or contrasts with the client's cultural modes of expression; and development of professional relationships across cultures with the appropriate level of intimacy and proper timing. The values necessary for cultural competency involve acknowledgment and acceptance of the following: cultural differences and their impact on service delivery and utilization; heterogeneity within and diversity between cultures; cultural relativism or different ways of viewing and interpreting phenomena, particularly non-Western and traditional as well as neo-European views; and the clash and complementary nature of professional social work and client cultural values.

Miley, O'Melia, and DuBois (1998) view cultural competence on three levels: practitioner, agency, and community. On the practitioner level, the worker must know about self-awareness in terms of his or her own personal values and cultural heritage, values differences and conflicts regarding assimilation and cultural pluralism, and awareness of the cultures of others, especially clients. The authors suggest that the social worker take a cultural self-inventory on personal identity, spiritual beliefs, knowledge of others, and cross-cultural skills, and study cultural groups through observational community research. They state:

> In summary, learning to be a competent cross-cultural practitioner is an evolutionary process that begins with awareness and increases with each interaction with clients. Workers first attempt to understand their own cultural filters. Next, they build a knowledge base of other perspectives through literature reviews and field research. Third, workers analyze the impact of cultural identities on the power dynamics of the worker-client partnership. Finally, practitioners continue to fine tune their cultural sensitivity through their ongoing practice experiences with unique client systems. (Miley, O'Melia, & DuBois, 1998, pp. 72–73)

They point out that there is agency-level cultural competence, in which workers are trained in necessary skills for diversity sensitive practice and multicultural awareness and functioning is promoted in organizational structure and program delivery. Cultural competence permeates agency policies on hiring and training staff, program evaluation, and criteria for eligibility: programs and procedures that focus on client strengths; culturally sensitive assessment instruments; culture as a resource; and ethnically oriented indigenous helping networks. Structures are designed for multicultural interchanges between agency, worker, and client; worker control over practice; and client influence on services. The desired physical environment is an accessible neighborhood location, outreach services, and cultural decor and setting. Culturally competent agencies have resource networks that include institutions and individuals in the ethnic community such as churches, schools, clubs, local healers, neighborhood leaders, and culturally oriented media.

Finally Miley, O'Melia, and DuBois (1998) discuss community-level cultural competence, which portrays the context for discrimination, segregation, and distinct boundaries or for pluralism, celebration of diversity, promotion of cross-cultural interaction, and social justice. The model for practitioner, agency, and community cultural competence sets a new benchmark for this field.

MEASURING LEARNING OUTCOMES RELATED TO CULTURAL COMPETENCY

Outcome measures and measurement methods are essential for social work education. The Council on Social Work Education's *Handbook of Accreditation Standards and Procedures* (4th ed.) has emphasized outcome measures and measurement methods on the undergraduate and graduate levels in Evaluative Standard 1. The purpose of this standard is to help the program, the faculty, and the student in their quest to determine whether adequate learning has occurred in a course area. Six components of the social work education program must be addressed: mission/goals, objectives statements, outcome measures/measurement methods, program implementation, actual outcomes, and systematic program evaluation (see Figure 1.1).

Regarding outcome measures and measurement methods, Evaluative Standard 1.4 states: "The program must specify the outcome measures and measurement procedures that are to be used systematically in evaluating the program, and that will enable it to determine its success in achieving its desired objectives" (Council on Social Work Education, 1994, p. 118). The emphasis is on the achievement of objectives, measurement instruments and statistical procedures, and program and curriculum evaluation. Examples of measurement instruments include pre- and posttests of knowledge and/or skill, student self-reports, evidence of contribution to professional knowledge-building, and student evaluations of courses and instructor performance.

This standard has created interest in measuring course learning, which leads to a discussion of cultural competencies. Cultural competencies are a series of

FIGURE 1.1 *The six components of the social work education program*

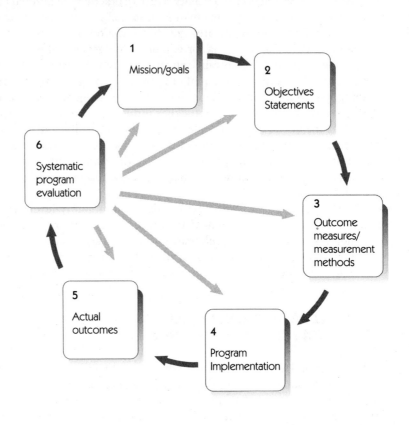

behavioral outcomes related to multicultural social work learning and professional practice. Cultural competencies are identified in a cultural competency framework that provides a basis for measuring the development and inclusion of abilities in the person. The framework translates the components of cultural competency into clear, measurable statements that can be used in a research instrument. Such an instrument could measure the degree of cultural competency before a multicultural social work course and on completion of the course in order to determine whether the knowledge and skills taught during the course have had an effect on the student.

As an example of cultural competencies, let us consider some competency statements developed in the field of child welfare. Title IV-E child welfare training grants heightened interest in the child welfare curriculum and social work graduate level education for child welfare specialists. The California Social Work Education Center at the University of California at Berkeley became the focal point for a statewide system of Master of Social Work child welfare training in all the California graduate social work programs. Among their many accomplishments was a strong six-section statement on competencies (California Social Work Education Center, 1996). Section 1, on ethnic sensitivity and multicultural practice, defines the knowledge, values, and skills necessary for culturally competent child welfare practice. The emphasis is on understanding of and sensitivity toward ethnic and cultural differences within the context of oppression and racism, the meaning of culturally competent practice, and the understanding of cultural norms and values. Fourteen cultural competencies are specified for student attainment.

On close examination these cultural competencies are teaching and learning outcomes that involve student mastery of ethnic and cultural knowledge and skills. The 14 cultural competencies are organized in three categories: population groups, child welfare knowledge, and practice skills.

The competencies having to do with population groups involve recognizing cultural and ethnic differences, ethnic group dynamics, cultural influence on behavior, socioeconomic and psychosocial issues facing immigrants/refugees, and the importance of client language. Cultural competencies in this category include the following:

1.1 Student understands and is sensitive to cultural and ethnic differences of clients.

1.6 Student has knowledge of the legal, socioeconomic, and psychosocial issues facing immigrants/refugees.

The competencies related to child welfare knowledge involve knowledge of child welfare services to cultural and ethnic populations and knowledge of relevant ethnic child welfare legislation. Cultural competencies in this category include the following:

1.9 Student understands and uses knowledge in the provision of child welfare services to cultural and ethnic populations.

1.12 Student has knowledge of and applies the Indian Child Welfare Act.

The competencies involving practice skills deal with relationship information and communication development, ethnic sensitivity assessment, evaluation of intervention models; community outreach collaboration, and resource and service advocacy. Cultural competencies in this category include the following:

1.3 Student is able to develop an ethnically sensitive assessment of a child and his family and adapt casework plans to that assessment in the provision of child welfare services and demonstrates an understanding of the continuum from traditional to acculturated values, norms, beliefs, and behaviors of major ethnic groups.

1.7 Student is able to evaluate models of intervention such as family preservation, family-centered services, family-centered crisis services for their application, possible modification, and relevance to cultural and ethnic populations.

Each statement centers on the student's grasp of a specific knowledge, value, or skill area related to cultural competency. Likewise, there are competency statements for 19 core child welfare skills, 25 social work skills and methods, 11 human behavior and the social environment items, 14 workplace management areas, and 12 child welfare policy, planning, and administration traits. Following is a sample of these competency statements.

Child welfare skills

2.2   Student is able to assess the interaction of individual, family, and environmental factors which contribute to abuse, neglect, and sexual abuse, and identifies strengths which preserve the family and protect the child.

2.4   Student gathers, evaluates, and presents pertinent information from informants, case records, and other collateral sources to support or refute an abuse or neglect allegation.

Social work skills and methods

3.6   Student is aware of his or her own emotional responses to clients in areas where the student's values are challenged, and is able to utilize the awareness to effectively manage the client-worker relationship.

3.22 Student is able to evaluate the need for removal and placement of a child and by weighing the risk to the child of continuing to remain in the home against the potential trauma of separation and placement.

Human behavior and the social environment

4.1   Student understands children's developmental needs and how developmental level affects a child's perception of events, coping strategies, and physical and psychological response to stress and trauma.

4.8   Student understands the interaction between environmental factors, especially in terms of racism, poverty, violence, and human development.

Workplace management

5.9   Student actively cooperates and collaborates with other community agencies and professionals in developing case plans and is an effective member of multi-disciplinary conferences.

5.10 Student demonstrates a working knowledge of the relationship process of accessing community resources available to families and children; utilizes them appropriately and updating as necessary.

Child welfare policy, planning, and administration

6.5   Student can demonstrate knowledge of how organizational structure and climate impact service delivery, worker productivity, and morale, and how students can contribute to improvements.

6.7   Student can identify how the legislative process impacts agency policies, procedures, and programs.

Each competency statement is related to the practice of child welfare on the state level. On the whole, the child welfare competencies are a uniform guideline that determines the social work education curriculum design, teaching and learning, and outcome measurement of child welfare student participants in Title IV-E training grant sites. Having this list of specific competencies helps Title IV-E staff, participating child welfare social work faculty, and students in the classroom and field placement.

In Competency Study 1.1, Hepworth, Rooney, and Larsen (1997) underscore the need for students to develop and update competent social work practice.

Competent Practice

COMPETENCY STUDY 1.1

Competent practice is defined as "fitting, suitable for the purpose; adequate; properly qualified; having legal capacity or qualification." To assess professional competency, however, is far from simple because competency in practice embodies knowledge, values, skills, and attitudes essential to fulfill one's professional role skillfully. Ingredients essential to perform one's role adequately vary according to the demands of each situation. A practitioner may thus be competent in providing certain types of service, such as marital or family therapy, and not in others, such as correctional services or protective services to children who have been abused or neglected. Furthermore, the elements of competent practice in various settings evolve as a result of expanding knowledge, emerging skills, and the changing demands of practice. Competency must thus be viewed within a temporal context, for a practitioner may achieve competence at one time only to suffer steady erosion of that competence by failing to keep abreast of ever-expanding knowledge and skills. (p. 15)

DEVELOPMENTS IN MULTICULTURAL SOCIAL WORK

During the mid-1990s, the Association for Multicultural Counseling and Development formulated a model of cultural competencies. The field of counseling psychology was concerned about multicultural content in clinical and counseling psychology doctoral programs. As a result this association formulated a three-characteristics, three-dimensional matrix of cultural competencies (Sue, Arredondo, & McDavis, 1995), identified a number of cultural competencies testing instruments (Pope-Davis & Dings, 1995), and generated two major texts (Ponterotto, Casas, Suzuki, & Alexander, 1995; Sue, Ivey, & Pedersen, 1996) that contributed to cultural competency studies.

At the 1997 annual program meeting of the Council on Social Work Education in Chicago, I was asked to conduct a curriculum workshop entitled "Developing Cultural Competency within a Culturally Sensitive Environment." The response before, during, and after the workshop was overwhelming and heartening. Social work colleagues from across the nation were discussing competencies and cultural competency, in particular, in small discussion and planning groups before the workshop. During the workshop there was a limit of 25 participants. Fifty social work educators showed up and raised a range of questions that reflected inquisitive interest. After Chicago there was a steady stream of requests for copies of the paper and e-mail messages that substantiated enthusiastic interest. I gradually realized that multicultural social work was reaching for a new milestone in developing cultural competency.

Leigh (1998) has written the first social work text on cultural competency and offers some words of wisdom for us in Competency Study 1.2.

Skill, Understanding, and Comprehension

A social worker can become culturally competent by gaining the skill of communicating competently with people of contrasting cultures. To rely on empathy alone is not enough. The social worker must strive for the degree of understanding that can derive only from information provided by a member of the contrasting cultural group. Failure to achieve this means the social worker cannot enter into the senses of the other. The social worker must comprehend the cultural context and meaning of these sensibilities. Only then will the social worker comprehend what it is that the person knows and how that knowledge is used in everyday life. Once meaning is revealed, meaning is known, and caring follows. (p. 15)

I have constructed a cultural competency framework for social workers that I call the culturally competent practice (CCP) model. I believe that cultural competency is an outcome goal, an end result, and a performance attainment related to mastery of cultural awareness, knowledge acquisition, skill development, and inductive learning. These four areas are the basic components of the framework, and I explain them in terms of generalist and advanced levels. I use these two concepts because they are familiar to undergraduate students in generalist practice and graduate students in generalist and advanced practice.

As a social work student, you are probably concerned about your grasp of the knowledge and skills of culturally diverse social work practice, and their application to a client. In the case of an individual cultural competency, the question becomes to what extent you have understood and integrated this competency into practice with a culturally diverse client.

Social work practice involves a helping relationship with individuals, families, small groups, communities, and organizations. Social work practice addresses these target groups, practice process stages, and knowledge and skill development on micro, meso, and macro levels. Cultural competency covers micro practice and later addresses meso and macro dimensions of cultural competency and practice evaluation. The Council on Social Work Education's Curriculum Policy Statement has emphasized the evaluation of one's own practice, particularly the relationship between practice and field. This is a necessary link to research-oriented practice. Cultural competency is a natural outgrowth of research-oriented practice, because cultural competencies are outcome measurement characteristics in culturally diverse social work.

This book will introduce you to cultural competency and involve you in a series of learning exercises that will deepen your cultural self-awareness, knowledge acquisition, development of skills, and orientation toward inductive learning.

QUESTIONS ABOUT CULTURAL COMPETENCY

The new field of cultural competency raises many questions from persons who are seeking to understand these concepts in a social work context. At the beginning of the workshop I conducted at the 1997 annual program meeting of the Council on Social Work Education, I asked the fifty social work educators who attended to identify questions related to the theme of cultural competency.

The questions they voiced are probably representative of what you might be wondering. Following is a sample of these questions.

The nature of cultural competency

What is the basic definition of cultural competency?

What is the knowledge theory behind cultural competency, and what skills must be developed?

What is the desired teaching/learning outcome with regard to cultural competency?

Is cultural competency a part of advanced practice?

What are the competency criteria (goal attainment standards) and the individual competencies (outcome measurement characteristics)?

Theme relationships

How is cultural competency related to the culture of origin and oppression by the dominant culture?

What is the relationship of cultural competency to cultural sensitivity, cultural awareness, and cultural diversity?

Course content integration and application

What does the client-worker relationship look like in a culturally competent helping process?

How is cultural competency integrated into multicultural social work?

How is cultural competency applied to fields of practice (such as child welfare), ethnic groups (for example, Asian Americans and Pacific Islanders), and community staff front line workers (such as indigenous paraprofessionals)?

Faculty and curriculum development, teaching techniques, and continuing education

How can social work faculty become culturally competent?

How can field placements incorporate cultural experiences with clients, agencies, and communities to build cultural competency?

How can we develop a cultural perspective for social work faculty, students, and field instructors—a total program perspective on culture?

What are some experiential exercises to foster cultural competency?

How can we update social work practitioners in social service agencies on cultural competency?

These questions on cultural competency prompted me to write this book. They sent me on a journey to explore the new and almost nonexistent literature on cultural competency, to piece together social work cultural competency in a creative manner, and to point to unresolved areas of cultural competency.

MY BELIEFS ABOUT CULTURAL COMPETENCY

I share some of my beliefs about cultural competency here in hopes that they will open up creative discussions among social workers in the classroom and agency.

Belief 1: Culturally competent practice is a major subject area for culturally diverse social work practice and a process of individual educational and professional growth.

Cultural competency is the subject area that relates to the social worker's experiential awareness of culture, ethnicity, and racism. Cultural competency is the result of a number of processes: individual and social reflection, academic education, career development, skill mastery, and continued contributions in multicultural practice. As a social work student, you will go through a reflection process that involves you as learner and thinker in the social environment of the classroom, in the field agency, and in life events and experiences. Acquiring a degree of cultural competency through an academic education will be an asset in the development of your career as a social worker. However, skill mastery is a continuous learning process, just like an exercise program. You must have regular exercise in order to maintain a fit and healthy body. In the same way, you should continue a cultural competency learning program with other social workers in your community. The outgrowth of cultural competency is the continued contribution, in papers and articles, of new information acquired with client cases and conceptual understanding.

Belief 2: We can trace a historical progress ion of related multicultural themes such as ethnic sensitivity, cultural awareness, cultural diversity, and now cultural competency. These concepts are not mutually exclusive. Rather, cultural competence serves as a rubric that embraces these areas of concern.

I have noticed that social workers often use interchangeably such terms as *cultural sensitivity, cultural awareness,* and *cultural diversity* when they discuss cultural competency. Devore and Schlesinger (1981) began culturally diverse social work practice with an emphasis on ethnic sensitivity. The main thrust of their work was to provide a practice structure for working with all ethnic groups. Green and associates (1982) introduced cultural awareness with an ethnographic approach to offering help. These authors wrote about the four major ethnic minority groups having common and specific patterns.

By the middle of the 1990s, multiculturalism and diversity were key concepts in ethnic studies literature. Lum (1996) conceptualized culturally diverse social work practice. About the same time, the Council on Social Work Education revised its evaluative standards to include the emphasis on outcome measurements. Social work educators began to speak about cultural competency, which influenced Lum and Lu (1997) to devise a social work cultural competency framework.

Belief 3: There is a concern about evaluating the competency of students through measurement instruments. Cultural competencies are outcome characteristics that can be measured to determine the extent to which social work students have attained teaching/learning objectives.

Students evaluate the teaching performance of instructors, while social work educators grade student performance in mid-terms and final examinations, term papers, and individual or group presentations. Now social work education is seeking to measure student acquisition of knowledge and skills. The competency movement is a reflection of this effort to measure individual student outcomes.

Social work programs may eventually devise outcome course competency instruments. Social work practice, behavior, research, and policy courses may follow the same evaluation intensity reflected in the field evaluation instrument that measures placement performance.

Belief 4: The applications of cultural competency to culturally diverse social work are legion and raise some interesting issues of how to foster the growth of cultural competency on the community practice level, with fields of practice, populations at risk, and particular ethnic groups.

At my workshop during the 1997 annual program meeting of the Council on Social Work Education, a social work educator asked me about the application of cultural competencies to indigenous community front-line paraprofessionals. These staff are often community outreach workers who work side by side with BSW and MSW practitioners. A related question is how field placements can build cultural competency into helping structures. A particular concern of social service agencies is the need to define cultural competencies as a part of their philosophy of services, program components, and program evaluation. On the job, a social worker could be evaluated according to cultural competency criteria along with related competency areas based on some continued education training in cultural competency.

At the state level, the state of Washington requires human service workers to complete training in multicultural practice with a cultural competency certificate as a part of the licensing process. The National Association of Social Workers should work toward such a requirement in every state of the union. This requirement would guarantee minimum standards for any mental health worker who works with a multicultural client and provide social work programs with continuing education workshops in multicultural social work for certification purposes.

Multicultural clients and communities should be brought into the discussion on cultural competency. These persons should advocate for culturally competent workers to assure themselves that the services they receive will be ethnically sensitive and culturally effective. There should be multicultural advisory consumer boards and consumer interns who graduate from client to paraprofessional helper in social service agencies. These groups should have strong ethnic community and culturally oriented perspectives and seek to have agency directors incorporate recommendations into the daily functioning of the agency.

Belief 5: Social work faculty members should become culturally competent. Many social work educators were self-learners of multicultural social work practice. They toiled by themselves or in groups, taught themselves culturally diverse practice principles, and singularly conducted multicultural research-oriented practices. It is time to formulate theory and concepts based on culturally sensitive research as part of a national social work education effort.

In 1996 the Council on Social Work Education Board of Directors, Cultural Diversity Subcommittee, presented a proposal for a multicultural social work curriculum conference that would assess past and present contributions and plan ten-year multicultural curriculum projects in practice, behavior, policy, research, field, and international social work. The result was that a conference entitled "Culturally Competent Social Work Education in the 21st Century" was scheduled for December 1998 at the University of Michigan, with the purpose of laying a foundation for developing a multicultural approach to practice that can more effectively address the social context of the 21st century. Selected social work educators who had made particular contributions in culturally competent social work were invited to present position papers, participate on response panels, and collaborate on five-year developmental plans for culturally competent social work theory and practice as a future blueprint for social work educators and practitioners.

The next step will be for a national task force to develop a culturally competent social work curriculum model and to disseminate social work practice knowledge to the wider social work education and practice audience.

THE SOCIAL WORK CULTURAL COMPETENCIES SELF-ASSESSMENT INSTRUMENT

The Social Work Cultural Competencies Self-Assessment instrument (Tools for Student Learning 1.1) is a 44-item Likert-type scale that measures your level of cultural competency. It is based on the framework in Chapter 2 and covers four competency areas (cultural awareness, knowledge acquisition, skill development, and inductive learning) and two levels (generalist and advanced). It is designed to satisfy the cultural diversity curriculum outcome requirement of the Council on Social Work Education's Evaluative Standard 1.

You are invited to take the self-assessment instrument as a pretest now. At this point you should be familiar with the idea of cultural competency, although you may have minimal comprehension of this field.

Your score is determined by counting the numbers circled and adding them together. There are four possible levels: Level 1 (score 43–95), Level 2 (score 96–128), Level 3 (score 129–171), and Level 4 (score 172 and over). You will score the instrument yourself and need not disclose the results to anyone else. Your scores at the beginning and at the end of the course will not affect your grade.

You are expected to score in the Level 4 range on the pretest unless you have had a strong multicultural life experience or extensive course work in ethnic studies, or both. It is normal to score at the lower levels when you are just beginning the course. You will master knowledge and skills during the semester. At the last class session, you will be asked to take the test again as a posttest outcome measurement and to score yourself. There should be a significant difference between your pretest and posttest scores. You should move into the Level 1, 2, or 3 categories.

I suggest that you write a two-page analysis comparing the results of the test before and after the course and sharing areas of growth and inquiry. The results provide excellent feedback for your instructor, who is concerned about teaching effectiveness in a culturally diverse practice course. These results will help your instructor determine which themes require more explanation in the next class.

TOOLS FOR STUDENT LEARNING 1.1

Social Work Cultural Competencies Self-Assessment

INTRODUCTION

This instrument measures your level of cultural competency at the beginning and end of the semester. The results of this self-assessment will be evaluated by your social work instructor. Strict confidentiality is observed regarding the results of the self-assessment.

Rate yourself on your level of competency on a scale of 1–4: 1= Definitely; 2=Likely; 3=Not very likely; and 4=Unlikely. Circle the appropriate number.

Name: *Course:*   *Campus:*

CULTURAL AWARENESS

1. I am aware of my life experiences as a person related to a culture (e.g. family heritage, household and community events, beliefs, and practices).

Definitely	*Likely*	*Not very likely*	*Unlikely*
1	2	3	4

2. I have contact with individuals, families, and groups of other cultures and ethnicities.

Definitely	*Likely*	*Not very likely*	*Unlikely*
1	2	3	4

3. I am aware of positive and negative experiences with persons and events of other cultures and ethnicities.

Definitely	*Likely*	*Not very likely*	*Unlikely*
1	2	3	4

4. I know how to evaluate the cognitive, affective, and behavioral components of my racism, prejudice, and discrimination.

Definitely	*Likely*	*Not very likely*	*Unlikely*
1	2	3	4

5. I have assessed my involvement with cultural and ethnic people of color in childhood, adolescence, young adulthood, and adulthood.

   Definitely   *Likely*   *Not very likely*   *Unlikely*

   1   2   3   4

6. I have done or plan to do academic course work, fieldwork, and research on culturally diverse clients and groups.

   Definitely   *Likely*   *Not very likely*   *Unlikely*

   1   2   3   4

7. I have or plan to have professional employment experiences with culturally diverse clients and programs.

   Definitely   *Likely*   *Not very likely*   *Unlikely*

   1   2   3   4

8. I have assessed or plan to assess my academic and professional work experiences with cultural diversity and culturally diverse clients.

   Definitely   *Likely*   *Not very likely*   *Unlikely*

   1   2   3   4

KNOWLEDGE ACQUISITION

9. I understand the following terms: *ethnic minority, multiculturalism, diversity, people of color.*

   Definitely   *Likely*   *Not very likely*   *Unlikely*

   1   2   3   4

10. I have a knowledge of demographic profiles of some culturally diverse populations.

    Definitely   *Likely*   *Not very likely*   *Unlikely*

    1   2   3   4

11. I have developed a critical thinking perspective on cultural diversity.

    Definitely   *Likely*   *Not very likely*   *Unlikely*

    1   2   3   4

12. I understand the history of oppression and of multicultural social groups.

    Definitely   *Likely*   *Not very likely*   *Unlikely*

    1   2   3   4

13. I know about the strengths of men, women, and children of color.

Definitely	*Likely*	*Not very likely*	*Unlikely*
1	2	3	4

14. I know about culturally diverse values.

Definitely	*Likely*	*Not very likely*	*Unlikely*
1	2	3	4

15. I know how to apply systems theory and psychosocial theory to multicultural social work.

Definitely	*Likely*	*Not very likely*	*Unlikely*
1	2	3	4

16. I have knowledge of theories on ethnicity, culture, minority identity, and social class.

Definitely	*Likely*	*Not very likely*	*Unlikely*
1	2	3	4

17. I know how to draw on a range of social science theory from cross-cultural psychology, multicultural counseling and therapy, and cultural anthropology.

Definitely	*Likely*	*Not very likely*	*Unlikely*
1	2	3	4

SKILL DEVELOPMENT

18. I understand how to overcome the resistance and lower the communication barriers of a multicultural client.

Definitely	*Likely*	*Not very likely*	*Unlikely*
1	2	3	4

19. I know how to obtain personal and family background information and determine the extent of his or her ethnic/community sense of identity.

Definitely	*Likely*	*Not very likely*	*Unlikely*
1	2	3	4

20. I understand the concepts of ethnic community and practice relationship protocols with a multicultural client.

Definitely	*Likely*	*Not very likely*	*Unlikely*
1	2	3	4

21. I use professional self-disclosure with a multicultural client.

Definitely	*Likely*	*Not very likely*	*Unlikely*
1	2	3	4

22. I have a positive and open communication style and use open-ended listening responses.

Definitely	*Likely*	*Not very likely*	*Unlikely*
1	2	3	4

23. I know how to obtain problem information, facilitate problem area disclosure, and promote problem understanding.

Definitely	*Likely*	*Not very likely*	*Unlikely*
1	2	3	4

24. I view a problem as an unsatisfied want or an unfulfilled need.

Definitely	*Likely*	*Not very likely*	*Unlikely*
1	2	3	4

25. I know how to explain problems on micro, meso, and macro levels.

Definitely	*Likely*	*Not very likely*	*Unlikely*
1	2	3	4

26. I know how to explain problem themes (racism, prejudice, discrimination) and expressions (oppression, powerlessness, stereotyping, acculturation, and exploitation).

Definitely	*Likely*	*Not very likely*	*Unlikely*
1	2	3	4

27. I know how to find out problem details.

Definitely	*Likely*	*Not very likely*	*Unlikely*
1	2	3	4

28. I know how to assess socioenvironmental stressors, psychoindividual reactions, and cultural strengths.

Definitely	*Likely*	*Not very likely*	*Unlikely*
1	2	3	4

29. I know how to assess the biological, psychological, social, cultural, and spiritual dimensions of a multicultural client.

Definitely	*Likely*	*Not very likely*	*Unlikely*
1	2	3	4

30. I know how to establish joint goals and agreements with the client that are culturally acceptable.

Definitely	*Likely*	*Not very likely*	*Unlikely*
1	2	3	4

31. I know how to formulate micro, meso, and macro intervention strategies that address the cultural and special needs of the client.

Definitely	*Likely*	*Not very likely*	*Unlikely*
1	2	3	4

32. I know how to initiate termination in a way that links the client to an ethnic community resource, reviews significant progress and growth, evaluates goal outcomes, and establishes a follow-up strategy.

Definitely	*Likely*	*Not very likely*	*Unlikely*
1	2	3	4

33. I know how to design a service delivery and agency linkage and culturally effective social service programs in ethnic communities.

Definitely	*Likely*	*Not very likely*	*Unlikely*
1	2	3	4

34. I have been involved in services that have been accessible to the ethnic community.

Definitely	*Likely*	*Not very likely*	*Unlikely*
1	2	3	4

35. I have participated in delivering pragmatic and positive services that meet the tangible needs of the ethnic community.

Definitely	*Likely*	*Not very likely*	*Unlikely*
1	2	3	4

36. I have observed the effectiveness of bilingual/bicultural workers who reflect the ethnic composition of the clientele.

Definitely	*Likely*	*Not very likely*	*Unlikely*
1	2	3	4

37. I have participated in community outreach education and prevention that establish visible services, culturally sensitive programs, and credible staff.

Definitely	*Likely*	*Not very likely*	*Unlikely*
1	2	3	4

38. I have been involved in a service linkage network to related social agencies that ensures rapid referral and program collaboration.

    Definitely   *Likely*   *Not very likely*   *Unlikely*
        1   2   3   4

39. I have participated as a staff member in fostering a conducive agency setting with a friendly and helpful atmosphere.

    Definitely   *Likely*   *Not very likely*   *Unlikely*
        1   2   3   4

40. I am involved or plan to be involved with cultural skill development research in areas related to cultural empathy, clinical alliance, goal-obtaining styles, achieving styles, practice skills, and outcome research.

    Definitely   *Likely*   *Not very likely*   *Unlikely*
        1   2   3   4

INDUCTIVE LEARNING

41. I have participated or plan to participate in a study discussion group with culturally diverse social work educators, practitioners, students, and clients on cultural competency issues, emerging cultural trends, and future directions for multicultural social work.

    Definitely   *Likely*   *Not very likely*   *Unlikely*
        1   2   3   4

42. I have found or am seeking new journal articles and textbook material about cultural competency and culturally diverse practice.

    Definitely   *Likely*   *Not very likely*   *Unlikely*
        1   2   3   4

43. I have conducted or plan to conduct inductive research on cultural competency and culturally diverse practice, using survey, oral history, and/or participatory observation research methods.

    Definitely   *Likely*   *Not very likely*   *Unlikely*
        1   2   3   4

44. I have participated or will participate in the writing of articles and texts on cultural competency arid culturally diverse practice.

    Definitely   *Likely*   *Not very likely*   *Unlikely*
        1   2   3   4

What are your questions and views on cultural competency and cultural competencies?

_____

_____

_____

_____

_____

_____

_____

_____

What are your reactions to this self-assessment instrument?

_____

_____

_____

_____

_____

_____

_____

Please count up your scores on the 44 self-assessment items and rate your level of cultural competency. Circle the appropriate level and write your raw score in one of the following levels:

Level 1: Definitely (scores 43–95)

Level 2: Likely (scores 96–128)

Level 3: Not Very Likely (scores 129–171)

Level 4: Unlikely (scores 172 and over)

Thank you for your cooperation on this self-assessment instrument. You have made a significant contribution to our research on social work cultural competency.

SUMMARY

This chapter has presented the case for cultural competency for social work students. We have underscored the infancy of this emerging area. We have defined the crucial concepts, analyzed trends influencing cultural competency, posed questions about cultural competency/competencies, and shared a number of beliefs about this new theme.

Central to this book is the Social Work Cultural Competencies Self-Assessment instrument. The self-assessment instrument is a unique feature of this text that aids the social work student in the measurement of competencies at the beginning and the end of the semester.

In the subsequent chapters of this book, the cultural competency framework is presented along with detailed explanations of various aspects of awareness, knowledge, skills, and learning. I hope that social workers use this approach in working with multicultural clients.

REFERENCES

California Social Work Education Center at the University of California at Berkeley. (1996, June). *Revised competencies*. Berkeley, CA: Author.

Council on Social Work Education, Commission on Accreditation. (1994). *Handbook of accreditation standards and procedures* (4th ed.). Alexandria, VA: Council on Social Work Education.

Devore, W., & Schlesinger, E. G. (1981). *Ethnic-sensitive social work practice*. St. Louis: C. V. Mosby.

Draguns, J. G. (1996). Humanly universal and culturally distinctive: Charting the course of cultural counseling. In P. B. Pedersen, J. G. Draguns, W. J. Lonner, & J. F. Trible (Eds.), *Counseling across cultures* (pp. 1–20). Thousand Oaks, CA: Sage Publications.

Galan, F. J. (1992). Experiential focusing with Mexican-American males with bicultural identity problems. In K. Corcoran (Ed.), *Structuring change: Effective practice for common client problems* (pp. 234–254). Chicago: Lyceum Books.

Gordon, M. M. (1978). *Human nature, class, and ethnicity*. New York: Oxford University Press.

Green, J. W., & associates. (1982). *Cultural awareness in the human services*. Englewood Cliffs, NJ: Prentice-Hall.

Hepworth, D. H., Rooney, R. H., & Larsen, J. A. (1997). Direct social work practice: Theory and skills. Pacific Grove, CA: Brooks/Cole.

Higginbotham, H. N., West, S., & Forsyth, D. (1988). *Psychotherapy and behavior change: Social, cultural and methodological perspectives*. New York: Pergamon Press.

Hodge, J. L., Struckmann, D. K., & Trost, L. D. (1975). *Cultural bases of racism and group oppression*. Berkeley, CA: Two Riders Press.

LaFromboise, T., Coleman, H. L. K., & Gerton, J. (1993). Psychological impact of biculturalism: Evidence and theory. *Psychological Bulletin, 114*, 395–412.

Leigh, J. W. (1998). *Communicating for cultural competence*. Boston: Allyn & Bacon.

Lum, D. (1996). Social work practice and people of color: A process-stage approach (3rd ed.). Pacific Grove, CA: Brooks/Cole.

Lum, D., & Lu, Y. E. (1997, March). Developing cultural competency within a culturally sensitive environment. Paper presented to the Council on Social Work Education annual program meeting, Chicago.

Manoleas, P. (1994). An outcome approach to assessing the cultural competence of MSW students. *Journal of Multicultural Social Work, 3*, 43–57.

Miley, K. K., O'Melia, M., & DuBois, B. I., (1998). Generalist social work practice: An empowering approach. Boston: Allyn and Bacon.

Pantoja, A., & Perry, W. (1976). Social work in a culturally pluralistic society: An alternative paradigm. In M. Sotomayor (Ed.), *Cross-cultural perspectives in social work practice and education* (pp. 79–94). Houston: University of Houston, Graduate School of Social Work.

Pinderhughes, E. (1989). *Understanding race, ethnicity, and power: The key to efficacy in clinical practice.* New York: Free Press.

Ponterotto, J. G., Casas, J. M., Suzuki, L. A., & Alexander, C. M. (Eds.). (1995). *Handbook of multicultural counseling.* Thousand Oaks, CA: Sage Publications.

Pope-Davis, D. B., & Dings, J. G. (1995). The assessment of multicultural counseling competencies. In J. G. Ponterotto, J. M. Casas, L. A. Suzuki, & C. M. Alexander (Eds.), *Handbook of multicultural counseling* (pp. 287–311). Thousand Oaks, CA: Sage Publications.

Ridley, C. R., & Lingle, D. W. (1996). Cultural empathy in multicultural counseling: A multidimensional process model. In P. B. Pedersen, J. G. Draguns, W. J. Lonner, & J. E. Trimble (Eds.), *Counseling across cultures* (pp. 21–46). Thousand Oaks, CA: Sage Publications.

Sue, D. W., Arredondo, P., & McDavis, R. J. (1995). Multicultural counseling competencies and standards: A call to the profession, Appendix III. In J. G. Ponterotto, J. M. Casas, L. A. Suzuki, and C. M. Alexander (Eds.), *Handbook of multicultural counseling* (pp. 624–640). Thousand Oaks, CA: Sage Publications.

Sue, D. W., Ivey, A. E., & Pedersen, P. B. (Eds.). (1996). *A theory of multicultural counseling and therapy.* Pacific Grove, CA: Brooks/Cole.

CHAPTER TWO

A Framework for Cultural Competency

This chapter explains what a framework is and covers the cultural competencies framework of the Association for Multicultural Counseling and Development. It then outlines the social work cultural competencies framework.

A framework for cultural competency serves as a point of reference and a guideline for social workers who are developing competencies in working with ethnic groups in practice settings and service delivery structures. This framework is designed to orient social workers toward cultural self-awareness, knowledge acquisition, skill development, and inductive learning. It identifies specific concerns in each of these four areas. It also provides the social worker with a degree of flexibility to explore related themes unique to the cultivation of cultural competency.

In searching for an existing framework for cultural competency, I discovered a multicultural counseling model developed by Sue, Arredondo, and McDavis (1992). As mentioned in Chapter 1, to promote cultural competency and multiculturalism in the fields of clinical and counseling psychology, the Association for Multicultural Counseling and Development (AMCD) devised a framework of cultural competencies. The AMCD framework is discussed later in this chapter.

This chapter defines the characteristics of a framework and chronicles the activities of the AMCD during the decade of the 1990s to foster cultural competency. It is a fascinating history of the joint effort of many academicians and practitioners and an inspirational story for social workers who want a blueprint for developing cultural competency. Finally, this chapter presents my culturally competent practice (CCP) model for social workers.

DEFINITION AND CHARACTERISTICS OF A FRAMEWORK

A framework is a structure that serves to hold the parts of a system together. For example, in the construction of a house, the framework establishes the room layout and the roofline and holds together the various components of the house. Likewise, the frame of an automobile is the basic structure that determines the essence of the car. A good course outline is also a framework, holding together a set of ideas and/or facts. An effective instructor generally teaches from a theoretical framework, and a good textbook is usually built around a framework.

The term *framework* is derived from three Latin root words, which illuminate its meaning: (1) *framen*, which means a structure, frame, or problem; (2) *frami*, which connotes profit or benefit; and (3) *frama*, which denotes "to further." These root words describe a structure that provides a benefit or furthers some aim. A framework gives shape, establishes an operational perimeter, identifies procedural principles, and provides flexible application.

A framework for cultural competency has these basic characteristics:

- The framework has a systems theory foundation, which links and integrates categories. Evaluative Standard 1 of the Council on Social Work Education's *Handbook of Accreditation Standards and Procedures* identifies mission and goal inputs, program and curriculum throughputs, and program and curriculum outputs in a systems interaction. A major component of curriculum outputs are outcome measurements.
- The framework is a helpful point of reference in social work cultural competency discussions.
- The framework sets an operational perimeter, identifies characteristics of cultural competency, and offers procedural principles for social workers to follow.
- The framework teaches assumptions, principles, and skills, and provides a roadmap for social work practice.
- The framework supports the development of social work outcome measures relating to cultural competency.
- The framework brings together a number of themes (for example, cultural awareness, culture, ethnicity) and components of social work practice (such as process stages, generalist and advanced levels). There is an opportunity to create new terminology from basic concepts.
- The framework advances the state of the art of culturally competent practice by evaluating the existing multicultural counseling competencies model and proposing a social work cultural competencies orientation.

With these framework characteristics in mind, we turn to the cultural competencies model of the AMCD. An understanding of this existing framework is essential to formulating a social work counterpart.

THE AMCD'S FRAMEWORK FOR CULTURAL COMPETENCIES IN COUNSELING

In April 1991 the AMCD approved a document that emphasized the need and the rationale for a multicultural perspective in counseling. It was a momentous step toward the recognition of multicultural counseling and psychology by this group of counseling psychologists who were committed to a multicultural perspective in their doctoral education and training internships, professional standards and practices, and research and publication. The Professional Standards Committee of the American Association for Counseling and Development proposed 31 multicultural counseling competencies to its parent body and recommended the adoption of these competencies in its accreditation criteria. The *Journal of Counseling and Development* published the report in order to disseminate the proposal widely to the psychology profession (Sue, Arredondo, & McDavis, 1992).

Prior to this report, a 1977 curriculum survey of graduate psychology education programs found that fewer than 1% of the respondents reported instructional requirements for the study of racial and ethnic groups (McFadden & Wilson, 1977). However, by the early nineties 89% of counseling psychology programs offered a multiculturally focused course (Hills & Strozier, 1992). A major concern about these courses was the lack of a strong conceptual framework that linked specific competencies and the sociopolitical ramifications of counseling, particularly oppression, discrimination, and racism (Ponterotto & Casas, 1991). Therefore, part of the solution was seen to involve the adoption of specific multicultural standards and competencies in order to train a "culturally competent counselor" (Sue, Arredondo, & McDavis, 1992).

What is a culturally competent counselor? Sue and Sue (1990) identify three characteristics:

1. A culturally skilled counselor is one who is actively in the process of becoming *aware of his or her own values*, biases, preconceived notions, personal limitations, assumptions about human behavior, and so forth.
2. A culturally skilled counselor is one who actively attempts to understand *the world view of his or her culturally different client* without negative judgments.
3. A culturally skilled counselor is one who is in the process of actively developing and practicing appropriate, relevant, and sensitive *interventions strategies and skills* in working with his or her culturally different clients.

Sue, Arredondo, and McDavis (1992) juxtapose these three characteristics of the culturally competent counselor with three dimensions of cultural competency:

1. *Beliefs and attitudes* about racial and ethnic minorities that facilitate effective cross-cultural counseling, plus a positive orientation toward multiculturalism.
2. *Knowledge* and understanding of his or her own world view, cultural groups, and sociopolitical influences.
3. *Intervention* techniques and *strategy skills* in working with minority groups. These three characteristics of the culturally competent counselor and three dimensions of cultural competency form a cross-cultural counseling competency conceptual framework (Sue, Arredondo, & McDavis, 1992). This developed into AMCD's three-characteristics, three-dimensional matrix of cultural competencies (Sue, Arredondo, & McDavis, 1995). In sum, multicultural counseling competencies center on understanding the different experiences of members of various cultural groups, barriers to communication across cultures that exist as a result of these differences,

and abilities that make a counselor culturally skilled (Pope-Davis & Dings, 1995).

Now we'll take a more detailed look at the AMCD framework. We'll look at how each of the three dimensions applies to each of the three characteristics.

Culturally competency worker characteristics are an awareness of personal assumptions about human behavior, values, biases, preconceived notions, and personal limitations; understanding of the culturally different client without negative judgments; and development and practicing appropriate, relevant, and sensitive intervention strategies and skills in working with culturally different clients.

Cultural competency dimensions consist of beliefs and attitudes about racism and ethnic people, biases and stereotypes, and positive orientation toward multiculturalism; knowledge and understanding of one's world view, specific cultural groups, and sociopolitical influences; and skills related to individual and institutional intervention techniques and strategies with cultural groups.

Counselor awareness of own assumptions, values, and biases. *Beliefs and attitudes* pertaining to this awareness are sensitivity to one's own cultural heritage; valuing and respecting differences; recognizing the influence of cultural background and experiences, attitudes, values, and biases on psychological processes; recognizing the limits of competencies and expertise; and acknowledging the differences between the worker and the client pertaining to race, ethnicity, culture, and beliefs. Concerning *knowledge*, one must know about racial and cultural heritage and its effect on definitions of normality-abnormality and on the helping process; the effects of oppression, racism, discrimination, and stereotyping; one's own racist attitudes, beliefs, and feelings; and communication-style differences and their effect on the helping predicament. Among *skills* are those learned in educational, consultative, and training experiences to enrich understanding and effectiveness in working with culturally different populations; the ability to understand oneself as a racial and cultural being; and the ability to seek a nonracist identity.

Understanding the world view of the culturally different client. *Beliefs and attitudes* are an awareness of negative emotional reactions toward other racial and ethnic groups that might be detrimental to the client in the helping process; a willingness to be nonjudgmental; and an awareness of stereotypes and preconceived notions about racial and ethnic groups. *Knowledge* entails specific information about particular culturally different groups, especially life experiences, cultural heritage, and historical background; knowledge about the effect of race, culture, and ethnicity on personality formation, vocational choices, manifestation of psychological disorders, help-seeking behavior, and the appropriateness or inappropriateness of particular approaches; and knowledge about sociopolitical influences on the life of racial and ethnic minorities. *Skills* are knowing how to familiarize oneself with research and findings on mental health and mental disorders of ethnic and racial groups; and skills learned in involvement with ethnic individuals in community events, social and political functions, celebrations and neighborhood groups beyond academic or clinical helping.

Developing appropriate intervention strategies and techniques. *Beliefs and attitudes* center on respecting client religious and/or spiritual beliefs and values about physical and mental functioning; respecting indigenous helping practices and community help-giving networks; and valuing bilingualism. *Knowledge* focuses on recognizing the elements of culturally sensitive counseling; becoming aware of institutional barriers preventing clients from using services; becoming familiar with bias-free and culturally/linguistically attuned instruments, procedures, and findings; recognizing family and community structures, hierarchies, values, and beliefs; and becoming aware of social and community discriminatory practices affecting the psychological welfare of the population being served. *Skills* involve learning a variety of verbal and nonverbal helping responses; knowing how to cope with problems stemming from racism; consulting with traditional healers or religious and spiritual leaders and practitioners; interacting in the client's language or seeking a translator with cultural knowledge and appropriate professional background or a knowledgeable and competent bilingual worker; learning to be aware of the cultural limitations of traditional assessment and testing instruments; becoming cognizant of sociopolitical contexts for evaluations and interventions and of oppression, sexism, and racism; and educating clients about goals, expectations, legal rights, and the worker's orientation.

The AMCD's cultural competencies model delineates a set of cultural competency criteria for the helping professions. In the next section, we turn to an alternative model of cultural competencies for the social work profession.

SOCIAL WORK CULTURAL COMPETENCIES: GENERALIST AND ADVANCED

Cultural competencies are a set of culturally congruent beliefs, attitudes, and policies that make cross-cultural social work possible. Cultural competencies exist as points along a continuum, ranging from cultural destructiveness, cultural incapacity, cultural blindness, and precompetence to cultural competence and finally, cultural proficiency (Cross et al., 1989). Cultural competency includes acceptance of and respect for cultural differences, analysis of one's own cultural identity and biases, awareness of the dynamics of difference in ethnic clients, and recognition of the need for additional knowledge, research, and resources to work with clients (Lu, Lim, & Mezzich, 1995). The Association for Multicultural Counseling and Development is the first professional group to adopt and operationalize multicultural counseling competencies standards (Arredondo et al., 1996).

From a social work perspective, the term *cultural competency* denotes the ability to understand the dimensions of culture and cultural practice and apply them to the client and the cultural/social environment. This ability is developed in the classroom and in the field experience of the social worker in culturally diverse practice. To facilitate this learning, it would be helpful to have an agreement among multicultural social work educators and practitioners regarding a set of practice-oriented criteria for social work cultural competencies.

At present, the volume of literature devoted to culturally diverse or multicultural social work practice is growing at a steady rate (Congress, 1997; Devore & Schlesinger, 1996; Green, 1995; Lum, 1996). The Council on Social Work Education's Curriculum Policy Statement mandates curriculum content on ethnic and racial groups, although its requirement of field experience in working with people of color needs to be strengthened.

The social work cultural competencies framework I propose here addresses generalist and advanced levels in each of the cultural competencies areas. The generalist level describes the professional foundation of social work practice. According to the 1992 Curriculum Policy Statement of the Council on Social Work Education, there are five generalist practice characteristics:

1. An emphasis on professional relationships characterized by mutuality, collaboration, and respect for the client system.
2. A focus on practice assessment that examines client strengths and problems in the interactions among individuals and between people and their environments.
3. Knowledge, values, and skills to enhance the well-being of people and to help ameliorate the environmental conditions that affect people adversely.
4. The skills of defining issues, collecting and assessing data, planning and contracting, identifying alternative interventions, selecting and implementing appropriate courses of action, using appropriate research-based knowledge and technological advances, and termination.
5. Approaches and skills for practice with clients from different social, cultural, racial, religious, spiritual, and class backgrounds and with systems of all sizes. The generalist level of cultural competencies should be taught in foundation multicultural social work courses.

Likewise, there is an advanced level of cultural competencies that coincides with the standards of the advanced level of social work practice. This level consists of the following:

1. Advanced practice skills and knowledge, in accord with a conceptual framework that shapes the breadth and depth of knowledge and practice skills to be acquired.
2. Content areas that are designed to prepare students for advanced practice.

Both the generalist and advanced levels are familiar in social work education and distinguish this cultural competencies model for social work.

The social work cultural competencies model involves four areas, as mentioned in Chapter 1: (1) personal and professional awareness of ethnic persons and events that have been part of the upbringing and education of the worker; (2) knowledge acquisition related to culturally diverse practice; (3) skill development related to working with the culturally diverse client; and (4) inductive learning, which forms a continuum of heuristic information on culturally diverse persons, events, and places. Table 2.1 provides an overview of the social work cultural competencies framework.

Cultural Awareness

The first cultural competency area is cultural awareness. For culturally diverse social work, it is crucial to develop an awareness of ethnicity and racism and its impact on professional attitude, perception, and behavior.

Generalist Level. The following paragraphs describe competencies related to cultural awareness at the generalist level.

The social worker is aware of life experiences as a person related to a culture (for example, family heritage, household and community events, beliefs, and practices). Everyone has a set of unique life experiences related to family, community, beliefs, and practices that are embedded in culture. However, many persons in America have blended ethnic backgrounds as a result of intermarriage over many generations and are unable to point to a predominant ethnic and cultural heritage. They see themselves simply as Americans. But, on closer examination, the experiences of these people may reflect regional and sectional culture (southern culture, New England culture, midwestern culture, California culture) or residual traces of recognizable Irish, German, or English cultural behavior patterns. It is important for the social worker to talk about recognizable cultural life experiences. It is the beginning of cultural awareness for the social worker and prepares the worker for future discussion of cultural recognition with clients.

The social worker has contact with individuals, families, and groups of other cultures and ethnicities. As a person of culture, everyone knows another person, family, or group who is like and unlike him or her. As the social worker widens the range of contact, patterns emerge regarding cultural groups and communities. In some cities and rural areas, ethnic communities are still intact as functioning groups. Newly arrived cultural and ethnic groups have thriving neighborhoods. Some small ethnic communities are homogeneous and have minimal contact with individuals or families of different cultural and ethnic backgrounds. It is important to talk about the degree of contact a person has with other persons of distinct and blended cultures and ethnicities. Contact is established through school, work, sports activities, clubs, church, festivals, and other events. Contact could be sporadic or constant, superficial or intimate; short-lived or for a lifetime.

The social worker is aware of positive and negative experiences with persons and events of other cultures and ethnicities. Contact causes a set of positive and/or negative experiences to occur in the life and mind of a person. A positive or negative experience either dispels or confirms a stereotype. A positive experience with an individual of another culture or ethnicity may dispel a previous negative stereotype about this group. A negative experience may confirm an already held negative stereotype. Based on a series of such experiences, our stereotypes about other groups are deeply rooted in our psyches. Positive and negative experiences with persons and events of other cultures and ethnicities should be discussed, shared, and examined. A cultural awareness session is an opportunity to investigate stereotypes and beliefs based on our unique experiences and biases.

The social worker evaluates the cognitive, affective, and behavioral components of his or her racism, prejudice, and discrimination. Racism, prejudice, and discrimination

TABLE 2.1 *Social Work Cultural Competencies, Generalist and Advanced*

Cultural Awareness	Knowledge Acquisition
Generalist level:	*Generalist level:*
• Awareness of own life experiences related to culture • Contact with other cultures and ethnicities • Awareness of positive and negative experiences with other cultures and ethnicities • Awareness of own racism prejudice and discrimination	• Understanding of terms related to cultural diversity • Knowledge of demographics of culturally diverse populations • Development of a critical thinking perspective on cultural diversity • Understanding of the history of oppression and of social groups • Knowledge of the strengths of people of color • Knowledge of culturally diverse values
Advanced level:	*Advanced level:*
• Assessment of involvement with people of color throughout various life stages • Completion of course work, fieldwork, and research focused on cultural diversity • Participation in employment experiences with culturally diverse clients and programs • Adademic and employment evaluation on the progress toward attaining focused cultural awareness of academic material and professional career experiences with cultural diversity	• Application of systems and psychosocial theory to practice with clients of color • Knowledge of theories on ethnicity, culture, minority identity, and social class • Mastery of social science theory

are related to the cognitive, affective, and behavioral dimensions of an individual. Racism is the cognitive belief in the superiority of one group over another. Prejudice is negative feelings toward a group or its individual members. Discrimination is an unfavorable behavioral response or reaction to members of an ethnic or racial group. Racism, prejudice, and discrimination are universal; we are the oppressed recipients and the oppressive agents. The social worker must become aware of his or her own racism, prejudice, and discrimination. Uncovering and dealing with these inherent tendencies helps the worker be effective with a client of color.

Advanced Level. The following paragraphs describe competencies related to cultural awareness at the advanced level.

The social worker assesses his/her involvement with people of color in childhood, adolescence, young adulthood, and adulthood. It is important to take a longitudinal view of one's involvement with people of color in the various developmental stages of life. Childhood and adolescence represent the formative years of living and learning when incidents of racism, prejudice, and discrimination have a lasting effect upon the mind. Further contacts with people of color in young adulthood and

TABLE 2.1 *(continued)*

Skill Development	Inductive Learning
Generalist level:	*Generalist level:*
• Understanding of how to overcome client resistance • Knowledge of how to obtain client background • Understanding of the concept of ethnic community • Use of self-disclosure • Use of a positive and open communication style • Problem identification • View of the problem in terms of wants or needs • View of the problem in terms of levels • Explanation of problem themes • Excavation of problem details • Assessment of stressors and strengths • Assessment of all client dimensions • Establishment of culturally acceptable goals • Formulation of multilevel intervention strategies • Termination	• Participation in continuing discussions of multicultural social work practice • Gathering new information on cultural competency and culturally diverse practice *Advanced level:* • Participation in inductive research on cultural competency and culturally diverse practice • Participation in writing articles and texts on cultural competency and culturally diverse practice
Advanced level:	
• Design of social service programs in ethnic communities • Understanding that services must be accessible • Understanding that services must be pragmatic and positive • Belief in the importance of recruiting bilingual/bicultural workers • Participation in community outreach programs • Establishment of linkages with other social agencies • Fostering a conducive agency setting • Involvement with cultural skill development research	

adulthood may confirm or change attitudes from earlier developmental periods. Conducting a self-study of involvement uncovers an understanding of how past and present perceptions, attitudes, and beliefs about people of color affect the worker-client relationship. The social worker internalizes positive and negative experiences with people of color based on a series of developmental encounters during various life stages.

The social worker does academic course work, fieldwork, and research on culturally diverse clients and groups. Social work education requires course work on diversity, which may include consideration of groups distinguished by race, ethnicity, culture, class, gender, sexual orientation, religion, physical or mental ability, age, and national origin. A social work student is expected to have taken a course on racial, ethnic, or cultural diversity. A field practicum or a research project involving people of color as clients or subjects may or may not be a part of social work education. This does not mean that a social work student must intern at an ethnic field placement or conduct research with a primary focus on an ethnic population. Though ideally a social work student has seen several clients of color in a field agency or interviewed culturally diverse human subjects in the course of conducting social work research, there is no guarantee that every social work student has been exposed to this range of experiences. To ensure cultural competency might mean that a social work program provides every student with a planned series of course work, fieldwork, and ethnic social research focusing on cultural diversity.

The social worker has professional employment experiences with culturally diverse clients and programs. A social work career takes a person through a meaningful set of program and client experiences in the social service sector. Along the way it is crucial to have employment experiences with a wide range of culturally diverse clients and to be responsible for program services that impact this population. Career employment experiences with culturally diverse clients and programs will help the social worker to grow—in his or her general competency, as an effective professional; in his or her specific competency, as a culturally sensitive person.

The social worker evaluates academic material and professional experiences related to cultural awareness and cultural diversity. The beginning social worker relies initially on the body of academic knowledge and field experience on cultural diversity gleaned in school. Increasingly, the social worker reads new books and studies reports on racial, ethnic, and cultural factors that affect programs and services of his or her agency. Culturally diverse clients may be sources of new insights for the social worker. Interaction with ethnic colleagues and collaborative ethnic service agencies may broaden the understanding and perspective of the worker. Ideally, the social worker grows in his or her career through such contacts with cultural diversity and culturally diverse clients.

Knowledge Acquisition

Knowledge acquisition involves the acquisition of a body of information that organizes material about a topic into sets of facts that plausibly explain phenomena. Social work has been sensitive to the need for a theoretical foundation ever since the Flexner Report at the beginning of the 20th century criticized that social work was not a profession since it had no theory base.

Generalist Level. The following paragraphs describe competencies related to knowledge acquisition at the generalist level.

The social worker understands the following terms: ethnic minority, multiculturalism, diversity, people of color. The social worker understands and can explain a number of basic terms that are essential to culturally diverse social work. *Ethnic minority* denotes a numerically smaller or politically powerless group in relation to a larger, controlling, and dominating majority and was used during the civil rights struggle for political, economic, legal, and social opportunities for African, Latino, Asian, and Native Americans. *Multiculturalism* recognizes the pluralistic nature of cultures and societies and has been associated with academic and political movements. The term has been used in a positive sense to denote the collective movement of people who are committed to cultural reality and in a negative sense by detractors who associate the term with being politically correct. *Diversity* emphasizes the dissimilarity between numerous groups in society that have distinguishing characteristics. There is diversity in this country in terms of ethnicity, culture, gender, sexual orientation, age, religion, and related areas. *People of color* is a collective term that refers to the major groups of African, Latino, Asian, and Native Americans who have been distinguished from the dominant society by color.

The social worker has a knowledge of demographic profiles of culturally diverse populations. The 1990 U. S. Census reflects a major influx of immigrants, refugees, and aliens into the United States, mainly from Asia, Central America, and Eastern Europe. Accordingly, it is important to study shifting area population trends to determine how new ethnic groups have changed the face of the local community. What are the emerging social problems that have resulted from this influx? Have communities changed as a result? Have there been adverse or positive reactions to the socioeconomic situation of a locale? What new social service programs are needed to respond to these changes? These questions are crucial to the discussion of changing cultural profiles.

The social worker has developed a critical thinking perspective on cultural diversity. Kurfiss (1989) defines critical thinking as "the process of figuring out what to believe or not about a situation, phenomenon, problem or controversy for which no single definitive answer or solution exists. The term implies a diligent, open-minded search for understanding, rather than for discovery of a necessary conclusion" (p. 42). Critical thinking is an assessment of the nature of a problem or issue and an open-ended search for understanding of the cause-and-effect relationship. It is a mindset that is applied to a number of different situations.

Alter and Egan (1997) identify five social work critical thinking skills: (1) the ability to understand social work theories, (2) the ability to divide a theory into its components (assumptions, concepts, propositions, hypotheses), (3) the ability to assess the practice implications of a theory, (4) the ability to develop and apply criteria for evaluating a theory, and (5) the ability to identify common errors in reasoning. These skills are developed later in this book.

The social worker understands the history of oppression and of multicultural social groups. People of color share a common history of oppression, although there is variation in the histories of multicultural social groups. Native, African, Latino, and Asian Americans attest to a history of domination by the European-American majority society. Oppression occurs when one segment of the population systematically prevents another segment from obtaining access to resources or denies a fair and equal playing field. Native Americans were victims of genocide and were forced to relinquish their lands, their children, and their freedom of movement on reservations. African Americans were victims of slavery and have fought racism, prejudice, and discrimination in employment, housing, and related forms of segregation. Latino Americans have been the victims of political, social, and economic discrimination and have been the sources of cheap labor. Asian Americans were historically used as cheap labor, have been underrepresented in their political and legal rights, and have been the objects of hostility from the dominant society.

The social worker has knowledge of the strengths of men, women, and children of color. Previously in psychiatry, psychology, and somewhat in social work, there has been an emphasis on the pathology of people of color. A focus on psychological and socioeconomic disorders conveys a sense of the deviance of members of ethnic groups. The trend in education has shifted toward a focus on the cultural survival and familial strengths of gender and age groups. Building on this trend moves social work education toward a perspective that empowers men, women, and children of color.

The social worker has knowledge about culturally diverse values. Multicultural values revolve around collective structures such as family, spirituality, and group identity. These values are the source of group solidarity, cultural networks, and hierarchical authority. People of color have internal and external values that are a part of one's own being and existence as a cultural and ethnic person. Cultural consciousness, personality, attitudes, emotions, and perceptions are internal processes that are manifested in the external behavior of people of color who persist in the struggle for dignity and equality.

Advanced Level. The following paragraphs describe competencies related to knowledge acquisition at the advanced level.

The social worker applies systems theory and psychosocial theory to multicultural social work. Systems theory orients the client and the worker to a field of interrelated systems. In a cultural context, systems such as nuclear and extended family, clan/tribe/family associations, and ethnic/religious affiliations and bonding are interdependent and thus rely on each other. The social worker is able to understand interactions in terms of systems analysis and structuring and to devise new ways to formulate emerging arrangements.

Psychosocial theory views the individual, family, and/or group in the context of its interchange with the social environment of organizations, community, and region or nation. The social force field of the environment impacts the psychological persona of people in various arrangements. The social worker is able to analyze the dynamics of this exchange and explain them to the client.

The social worker has knowledge of theories on ethnicity, culture, minority identity, and social class. Theories on ethnicity deal with the racial heritage that is passed on from generation to generation. Theories of culture focus on the way of life of a particular group and encompass language, norms of behavior, values, religion, beliefs, customs, practices, food, music, and the arts. Theories on minority identity address an individual's or group's status in the dominant society and how it affects the response of and interaction with members of the whole society. Theories on social class involve social, economic, and political arrangements that affect power and social status.

The social worker draws on a range of social science theory from cross-cultural psychology, multicultural counseling and therapy, and cultural anthropology. Cross-cultural psychology has focused on East-West comparisons of group characteristics and has spread to other parts of the world. Multicultural counseling and therapy has been termed a fourth force in the field of counseling psychology in view of the fact that it has its own standards, theory base, and academic visibility. Cultural anthropology has been the forerunner of cultural studies and has sought to understand various cultures by interviewing members of a particular culture.

Skill Development

Skill development, which occurs when the worker applies what he or she knows to the helping situation, is based on cultural awareness and knowledge acquisition. Skills are developed in the course of working with a client from a set of practice principles.

Generalist Level. The following paragraphs describe competencies related to skill development at the generalist level.

The social worker understands how to overcome the resistance and lower the communication barriers of a multicultural client. At the outset of the helping relationship, it is important to minimize resistance and to maximize motivation (the mini-maxi principle). Overcoming resistance involves the willingness of the worker to reveal background and to build structure in the relationship with the client, to be a good person who is worthy of trust, and to be a part of the client's life situation. At the same time, lowering communication barriers is initiated by polite conversation, inquiry about the cultural story of the client, and decreasing language, stereotype, and stress barriers.

The social worker obtains personal and family background information from a multicultural client and determines the extent of his or her ethnic/community sense of identity. The worker should discover the personal and family background of the client to understand the person and to build a psychosocial profile. It is important to determine whether the client relates to his or her ethnic community. Being a part of an ethnic community means that the client has a degree of support from significant others such as family and community members. Being isolated from one's ethnic community may have an adverse effect on the client.

The social worker understands the concept of ethnic community and practices relationship protocols with a multicultural client. The social worker should understand the demographics of the ethnic community served by the agency. An ethnic community has a unique history and set of problems and needs that influence the life of a person who is part of the community. It is crucial for the worker to study these facts. Relationship protocols involve the expression of respect toward the client and/or the client's family. Parents, grandparents, and related significant others should be consulted about the problem situation. Rather than telling the client what to do, it is important to ask the client about his or her perspectives.

The social worker uses professional self disclosure with a multicultural client. The worker takes the initiative in building a relationship with the client by disclosing an area of interest they have in common. The purpose of professional self-disclosure is to humanize and deprofessionalize the helping relationship and to model the sharing of meaningful information. This relaxes the client and encourages him or her to disclose vital personal problem material in return.

The social worker develops a positive and open communication style and uses open-ended listening responses. The communication style of the worker is important in eliciting responses from the client. Many years ago when I was a young doctoral graduate in my first community mental health center job, I encountered a professor of psychiatry who conducted teaching interview sessions before large numbers of mental health professionals. Whenever it was his turn to preside over grand rounds (a session where various patients are examined before a teaching/learning audience in a hospital setting), I could anticipate his line of questioning. Indeed, the professor of psychiatry was schooled by a famous classical psychiatrist who taught his students to conduct extensive probing. In the interview process the poor client/patient was asked question upon question based on his or her answers. This single line of probing responses underscored to me as a young clinician the need for the worker to vary his or her responses by asking open-ended questions that offered an opportunity for the client to take the worker through a number of locked mental doors. At the same time, the worker's follow-up responses to open-ended questions should involve reflecting, summary, and directive expressions.

The social worker obtains problem information, facilitates problem area disclosure, and promotes problem understanding. Problem identification entails gathering the essential facts of the person and the social environment surrounding the problem by facilitating a positive process so that the client willingly discloses the problem area. The result is that both the client and the worker understand the problem from their different perspectives. Succeeding in uncovering the problem in a concise and careful way takes skill on the part of the worker, who has laid the groundwork since the initial contact.

The social worker views a problem as an unsatisfied want or an unfulfilled need. Reid (1978) described a problem as an unsatisfied want or an unfulfilled need. This perspective gets behind the pathology of a problem by understanding that a problem has a positive aspect. That is, a problem exists because of a lack of satisfaction (unsatisfied want) or a fulfillment (unfulfilled need). If the worker can help the client to reframe the problem around this perspective, the client can be redirected in a *positive* direction, toward ways in which to achieve need satisfaction and fulfillment.

The social worker classifies problems on micro, meso, and macro levels. From the social work practice vantage point, problems are multidimensional. The micro (individual, family, and small group), meso (community and organization), and macro (complex organization, geographical population) levels of a problem persist and interact with each other. For example, problems resulting from welfare reform involve a macro-level federal law that mandates the restructuring of welfare and employment, meso-level state and county mandates to implement the law, and micro-level impacts affecting single women, dependent children, and legal immigrants.

The social worker explains problem themes of racism, prejudice, and discrimination, and their expressions. Part of problem identification is uncovering the dynamics of racism, prejudice, and discrimination that may be present in the problems of the multicultural client. It is important to rule these themes in or out. Racism is a cognitive belief about superiority and inferiority, dominance and subordination learned from parents, neighborhood, and community. Prejudice is the negative attitude or emotional result of racism, while discrimination is the behavioral expression of racism and prejudice through a negative action taken against a person of color. Problems may be infected with racism, prejudice, and discrimination.

The social worker finds our problem details. Multicultural problems encompass a wide spectrum, ranging from psychosocial dysfunction during transitional adjustment for immigrants to persons who have indirect ways of expressing problems such as storytelling. The worker must be patient and assess the situation, often piecing together aspects of who is involved, when and where the problem occurs, and what the major issues are.

The social worker assesses socioenvironmental stressors, psychoindividual reactions, and cultural strengths. Psychosocial assessment takes into account both the socioenvironmental stressors and the psychological reaction to these stressors experienced by the client. The client generally has coping skills to process environmental stress and conflict. However, these resources may temporarily fail and the client may experience psychosomatic reactions that are symptomatic of internalized stress. The worker should also assess cultural strengths, internal and external resources for change.

The social worker assesses the biological, psychological, social, cultural and spiritual dimensions of a multicultural client. Social work practice normatively speaks about biopsychosocial assessment. However, from a multicultural viewpoint, assessment must address the cultural and spiritual aspects along with the physical, psychological, and social dimensions. A person is mind, body, and spirit in an environmental system. As such, a full assessment of the assets of the person considers the interaction and exchange between and among the biological/physical, psychological/mental, social/environmental, cultural/ethnic, and spiritual/religious aspects of the person.

The social worker establishes joint goals and agreements with the client that are culturally acceptable. Contracting with the client around mutually agreeable and culturally sensitive goals is the initial intervention step. In a cultural context, the agreement may be verbal rather than written, since in many cultures verbal agreements are binding. Goals provide an opportunity to structure the course of the change strategy.

The social worker formulates micro, meso, and macro intervention strategies that address the cultural and special needs of the client. Multicultural clients operate in interdependent spheres involving the individual as part of the family; the family and extended family as part of an association, clan, or tribe; and the group as part of a neighborhood, community, or organization. As a result, micro, meso, and macro intervention strategies should be devised to address these multiple levels. Individual and group empowerment, family and network casework, and use of church and community social services are examples of these three levels of intervention.

The social worker initiates termination in a way that links the client to an ethnic community resource, reviews significant progress and growth, evaluates goal outcomes, and establishes a follow-up strategy. Termination is the end of a beginning: new linkages to a sense of identity and helping persons in the ethnic community, recital of past progress, evaluation of goals that have been achieved, and follow-up on emerging problems are part of a continuing pattern.

Advanced Level. The following paragraphs describe competencies related to skill development at the advanced level.

The social worker designs a service delivery and agency linkage and culturally effective social service programs in ethnic communities. Service delivery design involves identifying workable program principles for agencies that wish to adopt and implement culturally sound programs for multicultural clients. Organizing a service program structure provides a vehicle for an agency to deliver a unit of service to a client in an effective manner.

The social worker understands that services must be accessible to the ethnic community. Location is basic to service delivery. An agency program must be located near the target population. It should be within walking distance or near main transportation routes, in community storefronts, recreation centers, and churches. Locating programs should be a joint decision between the agency and community leaders.

The social worker understands the importance of pragmatic and positive services that meet the tangible needs of the ethnic community. Pragmatic and positive services mean useful and stigma-free services arising from a survey of community needs. Avoid a mental illness connotation. Promote family education and child care and parenting themes. Ask the community for a list of its needs.

The social worker believes that it is important to recruit bilingual/bicultural workers who reflect the ethnic composition of the clientele. The staffing pattern of an agency program should reflect the ethnic, gender, and age composition of its constituencies. Staff should be able to speak another language in rudimentary and fluent levels and should know another culture. In this sense the entire staff has some bilingual and bicultural skills and knowledge.

The social worker should advocate for community outreach education and prevention with visible services, culturally sensitive programs, and credible staff. The ethnic community should be exposed to the staff of an agency through extensive community outreach programs that reach the home, the church, the school, and related community institutions. Community outreach builds the visibility, credibility, and integrity of the program and staff, and is an effective way to build referrals to the agency.

The social worker establishes linkages with related social agencies, which ensures rapid referral and program collaboration. It is important to build working relationships with colleagues in other social agencies who can refer cases. When there is an emergency same-day referral, collaborative colleagues can help each other.

The social worker fosters a conducive agency setting with a friendly and helpful atmosphere. The agency setting establishes a tone for the worker-client interaction. The most important person in the office is the receptionist, since that person is the first program contact for the client. A friendly, helpful, and bilingual person is a necessary ingredient. The decor of the office, staff tempo, and morale should convey a sense of nurture and caring.

The social worker is involved in cultural skill development research to gain new insights on new principles. The importance of relationship protocols and skills such as professional self-disclosure were recognized more than 15 years ago when I began to write a social work practice text on people of color (Lum, 1986, 1996). New skills are needed to keep up with ways of working with people of color. Culturally diverse social work practice needs to foster an empirical basis for confirming skills that are appropriate and effective for culturally sensitive practice with clients of color.

Inductive Learning

Inductive learning is concerned with teaching social work students and social workers creative ways to continue developing new skills and insights relating to multicultural social work so that new contributions are made to this field. Graduation from a social work program commences the acquisition of one's own knowledge and skill based on professional work experience, study, and reflection.

Generalist Level. The following paragraphs describe competencies related to inductive learning at the generalist level.

The social worker has dialogues with culturally diverse social work educators, practitioners, students, and clients on cultural competency issues, emerging cultural trends, and future directions for multicultural social work. Gathering a multicultural professional study and discussion group offers a way of fostering new knowledge and insight into the growing field of multicultural social work. Sharing client helping experiences, readings from texts, agency workshops and university courses, and program research findings are important ways to piece together new data.

The social worker finds new information about cultural competency and culturally diverse practice. Education is a constant quest for learning from books, courses, clients, colleagues, and current events. Formal education should merge into informal individual education. The social worker should be constantly reading on his or her own, reflecting and recording the thoughts and observations of clients, and thoughtfully interpreting these ideas on paper.

Advanced Level. The following paragraphs describe competencies related to inductive learning at the advanced level. The social worker conducts inductive research on cultural competency and culturally diverse practice, using survey, oral history, and/or participatory observation research

Even the social worker with a case overload in a busy and demanding agency should make time for research. The relevance and effectiveness of a social service agency is dependent on new inductive research about clients, communities, and social problems, which should direct the winds of change over an organization. Good inductive research makes no assumptions. Rather, it asks open-ended questions about a subject area and records the findings without bias. Survey, oral history, and participatory observation research are examples of inductive research that is inquiring, open-ended, and expansive.

The social worker participates in the writing of articles and texts on cultural competency and culturally diverse practice. The final act of social work cultural competency is to make a written contribution to this field of culturally diverse practice. Many social workers have written articles based on graduate school and social service agency research studies on cultural competency and culturally diverse practice. Several have contributed chapters to social work multicultural practice books. There is a need for many more published articles and books to deepen the knowledge of the field.

SUMMARY

This chapter has laid out two frameworks that address cultural competency and competencies from two related perspectives: multicultural counseling and psychology and culturally diverse social work practice. The culturally competent social work model addresses cultural awareness, knowledge acquisition, skill development, and inductive learning as essential components with generalist and advanced levels. I hope that social workers will understand and use cultural competency and competencies in their practice perspective. In the succeeding chapters of this book, the four areas of social work cultural competency are explained in detail with useful teaching and learning exercises.

REFERENCES

Alter, C., & Egan, M. (1997). Logic modeling: A tool for teaching practice evaluation. *Journal of Social Work Education, 33* (1), 75–84.

Arredondo, P., Topper, R., Brown, S., Jones, J., Locke, D. C., Sanchez, J., & Stadler, H. (1996). *Operationalization of the multicultural counseling competencies.* Washington, DC: Association for Multicultural Counseling and Development.

Congress, E. P. (Ed.). (1997). *Multicultural perspectives in working with families.* New York: Springer.

Cross, T. L., Bazron, B. J., Dennis, K. W., & Isaacs, M. R. (1989). *Towards a culturally competent system of care.* Washington, DC: CASSP Technical Assistance Center.

Devore, W., & Schlesinger, E. G. (1996). *Ethnic-sensitive social work practice.* New York: Allyn & Bacon.

Green, J. W. (1995). *Cultural awareness in the human services: A multi-ethnic approach.* Boston: Allyn & Bacon.

Hills, H. I., & Strozier, A. L. (1992). Multicultural training in APA approved counseling psychology programs: A survey. *Professional Psychology: Research and Practice, 23,* 43–51.

Kurfiss, J. G. (1989). Helping faculty foster students' critical thinking in the disciplines. In A. F. Lucas (Ed.), *New directions for teaching and learning* (no. 37). San Francisco: Jossey-Bass.

Lu, F. G., Lim, R. F., & Mezzich, J. E. (1995). Issues in the assessment and diagnosis of culturally diverse individuals. In J. Oldham & M. Riba (Eds.), *Review of psychiatry, 14,* 477–510. Washington, DC: American Psychiatric Association Press.

Lum, D. (1986). *Social work practice and people of color: A process-stage approach.* Monterey, CA: Brooks/Cole.

Lum, D. (1996). *Social work practice and people of color: A process-stage approach* (3rd ed.). Pacific Grove, CA: Brooks/Cole.

McFadden, J., & Wilson, T. (1977). Non-white academic training with counselor education rehabilitation counseling and student personnel programs. Unpublished research.

Ponterotto, J., & Casas, M. (1991). *Handbook of racial/ethnic minority counseling research.* Springfield, IL: Charles C Thomas.

Pope-Davis, D. B., & Dings, J. G. (1995). The assessment of multicultural counseling competencies. In J. G. Ponterotto, J. M. Casas, L.A. Suzuki, & C. M. Alexander (Eds.), *Handbook of multicultural counseling* (pp. 287–311). Thousand Oaks, CA: Sage Publications.

Reid, W. J. (1978). *The task-centered system.* New York: Columbia University Press.

Sue, D. W., Arredondo, P., & McDavis, R. J. (1992). Multicultural counseling competencies and standards: A call to the profession. *Journal of Counseling and Development, 70,* 477–486.

Sue, D. W., Arredondo, P., & McDavis, R. J. (1995). Multicultural counseling competencies and standards: A call to the profession, Appendix III. In J. G. Ponterotto, J. M. Casas, L.A. Suzuki, & C. M. Alexander (Eds.), *Handbook of multicultural counseling* (pp. 624–640). Thousand Oaks, CA: Sage Publications.

Sue, D. W., & Sue, D. (1990). *Counseling the culturally different: Theory and practice.* New York: Wiley.

CHAPTER THREE

Cultural Awareness

This chapter will help you develop cultural competencies in the area of cultural awareness.

Generalist level:

- Awareness of own life experiences related to culture
- Contact with other cultures and ethnicities
- Awareness of positive and negative experiences with other cultures and ethnicities
- Awareness of own racism, prejudice, and discrimination

Advanced level:

- Assessment of involvement with people of color throughout various life stages
- Completion of course work, fieldwork, and research focused on cultural diversity
- Participation in employment experiences with culturally diverse clients and programs
- Evaluation of academic material and professional experiences related to cultural awareness and cultural diversity

The road to cultural competency begins with an understanding of your own personal and professional cultural awareness. From the personal perspective, a search for cultural self-awareness involves cultural group experiences and contacts with people of other ethnicities. In turn, personal cultural awareness has a direct effect on how you as a social work professional will interact with a multicultural client. Social workers bring a set of cognitive, attitudinal, and behavioral responses to the helping situation and must be aware of how these dynamics affect the relationship.

The purpose of this chapter is to lay out the first cultural competency area, cultural awareness, from both personal and professional perspectives. We define *cultural awareness* in a contextual setting. Next, we explore the fragmentary nature of European-American cultural identity and the need for a cultural search, rediscovery, and formulation on the part of white Americans. Then we explain the philosophical assumptions that underlie a cultural awareness perspective. We also focus on the individual, family, group, and community dimensions of personal cultural awareness. These entities shape who we are and how we see ourselves. As a result we learn cognitive, affective, and behavioral responses. Finally, the chapter identifies principles of professional cultural awareness that should be practiced in the worker-client helping relationship.

Reynolds (1995, p. 320) points out that "cultural self-awareness is a vital first step toward cultural sensitivity." In turn, beliefs and values are best explored through introspection and reflective self-evaluation in an environment of trust and openness. The classroom is an effective laboratory to explore these thoughts and feelings in a nonthreatening manner.

DEFINITION OF CULTURAL AWARENESS

The term *cultural awareness* has several levels of meaning for our discussion. Awareness deals with conscious attention and knowledge through the mind and the senses. In other words, a person's awareness has both cognitive and sensory dimensions. Culture involves the transmission of beliefs, values, traditions, customs, and practices from one generation to the next. Cultural awareness involves the self in a cultural context. Hardy and Laszloffy (1995) describe cultural awareness as the learning of cultural background, issues, and relationships in a contextual sense. The emphasis on cultural context is important to our understanding of cultural awareness.

In Competency Study 3.1, Kadushin and Kadushin (1997) remind us that good cross-cultural interviewing involves cultural awareness on the part of the worker.

COMPETENCY STUDY 3.1

Cultural Awareness in an Interview

The available research, however indefinite, suggests that workers can conduct a productive interview despite ethnic, racial, age, and sexual preference differences between interviewer and interviewee if interviewers observe some cardinal principles of good interviewing.

Interviewers must

- be conscious of cultural factors that may intrude on the interview,
- acknowledge any stereotypical ideas they hold regarding the group the client represents,
- apply such stereotypes flexibly with a conscious effort to modify or discard the generalization if it appears inappropriate for the particular interview,
- take the responsibility to learn about the culture of the interviewee so as to better understand any culturally derived behaviors the interviewee might manifest, and
- respond to interviewees with respect, empathy, and acceptance, whatever their differences. Effective cross-cultural interviewing combines an acknowledgment of cultural differences with the general principles of good interviewing applicable to all groups of interviewees. (pp. 343, 344)

Sanday (1976) categorizes individuals as relating to cultural contexts in one of four different ways that affect cultural awareness and involvement:

- *Mainstream* individuals have assimilated the values of the dominant society and attempt to emulate these values in their behavior. In this country the

Arnericanization of persons involves individualism, freedom of expression, casual and fashionable dress, youthful appearance, patriotism, and merging into the predominant thinking and behavior.

• *Bicultural* individuals move in two distinct cultural worlds: the mainstream, dominant culture of work and society and their culture of origin, which may have traces of old world traditions, beliefs, and practices. They have a dual commitment to survive and maintain themselves in both spheres, which have meaning and purpose for them.

• The *culturally different* have been exposed to the mainstream culture but have chosen to affiliate and focus their activities in a culturally different and distinct structure. They have made a conscious choice to remain in their cultural and ethnic enclave. They become self-contained residents of Chinatown, Little Italy, Little Havana, or Little Saigon, where they are able to function in an autonomous ethnic setting where language, customs, food, and business exchanges occur.

• The *culturally marginal* have detached themselves from an identified cultural and ethnic identity and live their lives apart from distinct groups. They may be persons who were raised away from their ethnic group and now feel neither a part of that group nor a member of their adopted group. Indian children who were removed and placed in white foster care may now feel a part of neither the Indian tribe nor the white culture. Due to limited acceptance and lack of a sense of belonging to either party, they are marginal people caught outside their ethnicity and the dominant society. The same may be true of the person who rejects his or her own ethnic group, marries and seeks to identify with another racial group, alters physical appearance for assimilation purposes, and realizes that there is limited acceptance in both the original and the alternative ethnic group.

These categories underscore the importance of cultural context when considering the degree of cultural awareness of an individual. What is your own sense of cultural awareness as a person strongly, moderately, or slightly related to a cultural context? How has your individual, family, neighborhood, and community context affected your cultural self-awareness and your awareness of other people's cultures? How would you classify yourself according to Sanday: mainstream, bicultural, culturally different, or culturally marginal? How would Sanday's categories help you to understand a multicultural client?

Cultural context or knowledge of the cultural environment is a critical determinant of how one evolves as a cultural being. Personal relationships with family, neighbors, primary peers, and local community groups, events, and experiences occur in a cultural context. In turn, these relationships have a profound impact on a person's memories, beliefs, attitudes, and actions.

THE WHITE AMERICAN DILEMMA

Giordano and McGoldrick (1996) start their discussion of the white American dilemma with the comment of a colleague who said: "Come on, White ethnics

The Hernandez Family: A Case Study

Mr. Platt is the social worker who has been assigned to the Hernandez family. The family includes a father and a mother who were born in Mexico and have immigrated to California, and three children, one of whom has a school learning and behavior problem. Mr. Platt has sought to become culturally aware of his own ethnic background and those of ethnic clients. In his social work education, Mr. Platt received undergraduate and graduate degrees in social work and took several ethnic studies and multicultural practice courses. In one class he wrote a paper explaining his ethnic background and cultural beliefs and practices.

His first-year MSW field placement was in an East Los Angeles social service center that served Spanish-speaking clients. He did a research paper on the family structure of Latinos.

On a personal level, Mr. Platt has endeavored to integrate the cultural dynamics of the dominant society and his own ethnic culture with his knowledge of Latinos. He still is learning about the similarities and differences among these three cultural orientations as he strives to integrate culture into his life.

TASK RECOMMENDATIONS

The following questions form the basis for a discussion of cultural awareness from the social worker's perspective:

- How can Mr. Platt increase his personal sense of cultural awareness so that he can be effective with the Hernandez family?
- How can Mr. Platt become aware of the Hernandez family's culture?
- How can a person who is from the mainstream society become culturally self-aware and aware of the cultural beliefs and practices of others?

today don't have ethnic issues; they're totally American" (p. 427). Giordano and McGoldrick point out some interesting facts about European Americans:

- They are the majority population. They form 80% of the U.S. population and involve 53 categories. The largest groups are German Americans (58 million), English ancestry (41 million), and Irish Americans (39 million). This is because U.S. immigration policy favored Western and Central Europeans until the 1965 McCarran Immigration Act, which opened immigration from countries in Asia and Central and South America.
- They are multigenerational in the history of the United States. Most families from European American groups have been in the United States for three or more generations. However, an American descendant of the Jamestown colony of 1608 would be 20 generations removed from Europe. In the nearly 400 years since the first colony, most traces of European culture and ethnicity have been reduced to residual fragments. Cultural awareness of European roots has simply faded over time.
- Anglo Protestant culture, religion, and values have been dominant due to the presence of Western European settlers in the United States. The founding fa-

thers of this country represented the white English-American privileged class of the time. The first Irish Catholic president of the United States was John F. Kennedy, who was elected in 1960. Until this point, there had been strong resistance to a non-Protestant in the White House. The English (Anglo-Saxon) brought with them their racism, prejudice, and discrimination. In England the Irish were termed "savages" by the British. This label was transferred to the American Indians in the New World. The Protestant work ethic influenced the dominant negative social attitude toward welfare recipients. The moral virtue of the society affected social attitudes toward gays and lesbians.

• European Americans display ambivalence about particular ethnic identity and achievement of success in the dominant society. Giordano and McGoldrick (1996) observe: "Ethnicity persists in the consciousness of European Americans, in their perceptions, preferences, and behavior, even while mass production and mass communication homogenize their outward appearances. Psychologically, European Americans are often ambivalent about their identities, and are constantly trying to balance the pull of their family histories and experiences with their individual desires to be accepted and successful in the larger society" (p. 439). It is difficult to build cultural awareness in European Americans who have become so blended into the American culture. Many simply respond: "I am an American" when asked to trace their ethnic and cultural background and distinctive traditions, values, and practices.

The white American dilemma is aptly described by Green (1995) when he states:

> White Americans often view the matter differently for … many of them have difficulty in thinking of themselves as 'ethnic.' Typically they resort to national labels when asked to describe themselves culturally, and their idiom of ethnic affiliation is more geographical. As the dominant group, whites hear the claims of shared substance … made by Latinos, Asian Americans, and others whose ethnicity they can easily see, but they do not find anything like that in themselves. That is because for them ethnicity is perceived only in the surface features…. From the point of view of whites, that is a convenient perspective to have, especially in a political sense. It locates ethnicity exclusively in others and excuses them from having to consider their own participation in the management and enforcement of separateness. (p. 21)

Going beyond the dilemma of ethnic disengagement and lack of identification, we must consider the need for European Americans to bring cultural awareness to social work practice. Learning to discover one's own cultural awareness, to raise it to a conscious level, and to incorporate it into one's life and professional helping are worthwhile goals.

Green (1995) offers a number of practical ways to reduce the white American dilemma from a social work perspective:

- Adopting a systematic learning style and developing a supportive agency environment that recognizes culturally distinctive modes of behavior with appropriate responses.

CULTURAL COMPETENCY IN ACTION

The Hernandez Family: A Case Study

Gaining cultural competency means developing a sense of cultural self-awareness. The white American dilemma is a reality facing many social workers who are from families of European-American origin. It may be difficult to articulate an ethnic or cultural identity. It is natural to respond with a national origin ("I am an American") or a geographic label ("I am a midwesterner"). Can we transcend this dilemma, discover our cultural awareness, and incorporate it into our lives?

Mr. Platt seems to have made efforts along these lines. In his social work education, he looked for ways to learn about his culture and other ethnic groups, and sought out agency experiences with multicultural clients. He has been willing to take a diverse caseload and to reflect on various cultural behavior traits, including his own and his clients'.

TASK RECOMMENDATIONS

- Think about the white American dilemma regarding yourself and discuss this theme in class. Do you agree with the comment: "Come on, White ethnics today don't have ethnic issues; they're totally American"?
- Are we socially segregated from people who do not look, act, or think like us?
- Have we sealed ourselves off in selected homogeneous social groupings from other people who are ethnically different from us?
- Are we part of a diverse community where we have a variety of friends and acquaintances who represent a cross-section of ethnic groups?
- Is there a white American dilemma or is this a false dichotomy that is an unnecessary concern?

- Acknowledging the cultural characteristics of client communities, the realities of power and systematic inequality, and the need for staff and administration commitment to follow through on training initiatives in order for cultural awareness to penetrate the social work profession.
- Participating in discovery of the beliefs and thinking of the client, comparing these to the life and experiences of the worker, and trying to understand the meaning of differences between the two.

In sum, willingness to learn about self and others and to bridge the gap between worker and client is key to reducing the dilemma.

PHILOSOPHICAL ASSUMPTIONS ABOUT CULTURAL AWARENESS

Philosophical assumptions about cultural awareness are important to discuss if one believes that the training emphasis in social work cultural competency education depends on cultural orientation. Everyone has a culture; the culturally competent social worker must become aware of it and the cultures of others. Kadushin and Kadushin (1997) discuss cultural competency in terms of cultural self-awareness and cultural awareness of others. In Competency Study 3.2 they explain the importance of this dual awareness (cultural self and cultural other).

Cultural Self-Awareness and Other-Awareness

COMPETENCY STUDY 3.2

Competence in multicultural interviewing is different from interviewing competence in general. General interviewing competence is a necessary but insufficient basis for effective multicultural interviewing.

The best interviewer, then, has cultural sensitivity and general competence in interviewing.

What does the culturally sensitive interviewer need to know and do to maximize the possibility of conducting a successful cross-cultural interview? What characteristics identify the culturally sensitive interviewer?

White interviewers need to recognize that they too have a culture—have been taught that certain ways of doing things are right and proper, to think in a certain way, perceive the world in a certain way, for example, as a white Christian middle-income female. Just as everyone else has an accent and we don't, we fail to recognize that we are products of our culture. We are like fishes who, never having experienced anything but water, are unaware of the water. White people generally tend not to clearly identify themselves as being racially white. They do not see themselves as a people of color, having a sense of racial identity and a distinct culture. Culturally sensitive interviewers are consciously aware of their culture and are explicitly knowledgeable of the stereotypes associated with it.

Culturally sensitive interviewers are aware of the stereotypes they hold in regard to others and test them flexibly against the reality of the individual client with a readiness and willingness to modify or discard the stereotype in the attempt to understand the individual. (p. 345)

Competency Study 3.2 raises some philosophical issues concerning how one regards one's self as a cultural being and how one views the client as the other cultural being in the helping relationship. Carter and Qureshi (1995) have developed a typology of multicultural philosophical assumptions that offers five perspectives about cultural knowledge and self-awareness: universal, ubiquitous, traditional, race-based, and pan-national. These alternative orientations illuminate our discussion of worker cultural awareness. While there are philosophical similarities and differences between and among all five, our task is to explain each viewpoint and to apply them to our discussion of training social workers in cultural awareness.

The universal approach. The universal or etic (culture-common) approach to culture believes that all people are the same, as human beings with greater intragroup (within group) differences than intergroup (between group) differences. There is a humanistic vision of all people living in harmony with minimal group differences. Primarily all people are seen as human beings and secondarily their experience and identity are derived from ethnicity, race, and gender. People have many common characteristics and yet are unique as individuals.

From a training standpoint, special populations are understood from a unifying perspective that uses the analogy of a salad bowl: separate groups tossed together in a unified whole. Cultural differences are minimized and said to result from socialization of a particular group. From a social work perspective, there are common cultural traits that transcend particular ethnic groups and are true of all cultures, such as family and values of freedom and acceptance. There are universal cultural competencies that apply to clients in general and to multicultural clients in particular. The principles of relationship protocol (communication of respect to the client, particularly the head of a household) and professional self-disclosure (the worker's sharing a common experience as a bridge and point of reference) can be applied to all clients, regardless of ethnicity and culture.

The ubiquitous approach. The term *ubiquitous* means omnipresent or being present everywhere at the same time. The particular emphasis of the ubiquitous approach is cultural difference. Being different is common across special populations according to ethnic, gender, or disabled status. Ethnic groups are placed in different status levels by superordinate cultural patterns as other races are subordinated to one's own racial group. There are cultural differences that must be acknowledged, and this results in a focus on multiple group differences.

From a training perspective, students must be aware of their own culture and others as well as the stereotypes and prejudice associated with differences. Social work students and practitioners must be aware of cultural and ethnic differences between European, African, Latino, Asian, and Native Americans. Culture-specific elements (such as unique ethnic group characteristics) must be taught to students.

The traditional approach. The traditional approach holds that culture is the context in which differences find their unique expressions. Carter and Qureshi (1995) explain:

> Culture provides and limits the range of possible experiences. An individual's cultural (identity) development is, for the most part, a function of how the individual interprets his or her world according to the possibilities and limitations set forth by his or her culture. Thus, one interacts with external factors in a strictly adaptive manner. (p. 248)

Shared background is the basis of culture. That is, one's identity is related to world view, which influences upbringing and life experiences. A person's cultural membership responds to the surrounding environment of different races, ethnic groups, and social arrangements.

In terms of training, the student must be exposed to another culture and increase cultural knowledge through a series of learning contacts. One must develop rapport with the culturally different. Ethnic and cultural prejudice are seen as erroneous individual beliefs. Discussion of sociopolitical power dynamics is minimized, and the consequences of racism and intergroup sociopolitical power dynamics are deemphasized.

The race-based approach. Race is the locus of culture in the United States. People are classified according to race and grouped by skin color, language, and physical features. The race-based approach highlights the issues of American races and racist practices and looks at interactive culture from sociopolitical history and intergroup power perspectives. Membership in a racial group is seen as the primary experience and the ultimate measure of social exclusion and inclusion. Race is considered to be a visible issue between whites and other racial groups that determines individual psychosocial development.

Racial boundaries have occurred and are still in place across America. One's place in society, where one lives, what one is allowed to learn and later earn, and one's access to social services are part of the social and psychological boundaries established by history, tradition, and law. Early white America's interactions with Indians and Africans formed the basis for educational, social, political, moral, religious, and economic systems organized along color lines. Racism and racial boundaries are invisibly and visibly understood and are in place in this country. Racial identity, attitudes, and status must be seen in parallel attitudes, thoughts, feelings, and behaviors between ethnic minority racial groups and the dominant white racial group.

From a training perspective, students must scrutinize their own racial identity development, racism, and the psychological intercultural effect of their own race and that of the client. The racial identity level of the worker and the client affects the helping relationship. One must face racism, power differentials, white ethnocentrism, and feelings of superiority. These racial dynamics are often painful to explore and much easier to ignore. Carter and Qureshi (1995) aptly state: "… all people who are White identified seem to have no interest in working toward developing consciousness of the inequities inherent in the status quo, or in taking any action to effect any kind of social or psychological change" (p. 254). They suggest a number of areas that should be investigated during training: the trainee's racial identity; social, cultural, and institutional racism; and the linkage of sociopolitical and historical dynamics to current events. At the same time, the race-based approach requires a painful, discomforting, and soul-searching journey of self-exploration and understanding. Facing one's own racism and oppression lead to a greater awareness of the racial and ethnic dynamics between worker and client.

The pan-national approach. The pan-national approach holds that racial group membership determines culture in a geographic global sense. Developed by non-Europeans as an alternative to European and American culture, pan-Afrocentrism is an example of this model. It emphasizes Afrocentric psychology in terms of African self-consciousness, spirituality, and social theory. It views colonialism and slavery as a distortion of African self-consciousness and supports the black struggle for survival and liberation. Because of the violence of colonialism and slavery, non-European people of color have been alienated from themselves and their cultures, while whites have developed a culture based on violence. Oppressed people are alienated from a worldwide sociopolitical context.

From a training standpoint, a pan-national approach rejects Eurocentric social work and advocates knowledge of ethnic history and shared racial and cul-

The Hernandez Family: A Case Study

Which philosophy of cultural awareness orients you in your work with multicultural clients? Mr. Platt, the social worker, could relate to the Hernandez family in a number of ways, based on different philosophies about cultural awareness with varying emphases. As you recall, Mr. and Mrs. Hernandez are a legal immigrant couple who understand Spanish and speak some English. Mr. Hernandez is a gardener who works long hours, while Mrs. Hernandez stays home and cares for the three elementary school-age children. She works part time when the children are in school or when her husband returns from his work.

Discuss an emphasis based on the Carter-Qureshi typology that would be appropriate for Mr. Platt as he relates to the Hernandez family.

- The universal approach emphasizes the primary humanity and commonality of people and the secondary experience and identity of ethnicity, race, and gender.
- The ubiquitous approach recognizes cultural differences between worker and client in a multiple society and culture-specific factors (such as unique group characteristics) that must be kept in mind.

- The traditional approach appreciates that culture is the context where the expression of cultural uniqueness and differences takes place.
- The race-based approach recognizes the reality of racism and racial barriers between people as something that must be recognized and worked through in the relationship between the social worker and the client.
- The pan-national approach embraces an indigenous non-Eurocentric view of ethnic history, culture, and behavior and may reject traditional social work problem analysis and intervention strategies.

TASK RECOMMENDATIONS

- Which approach or combinations would be effective with the Hernandez family in order to establish cultural competency?
- If in your opinion none of the five approaches fit this family, what perspective on cultural knowledge and awareness would you offer as an alternative?

tural characteristics and experiences. Ethnic self-consciousness, personality and culture, and the psychology of liberation are areas for cultural learning.

The universal, ubiquitous, traditional, race-based, and pan-national approaches emphasize different facets of training in the development of cultural awareness. The universal approach suggests that universal characteristics are common cultural links between worker and client as persons, while the ubiquitous approach points out that cultural differences must be understood and mastered if the worker is to be effective with multicultural clients. The traditional approach asserts that the worker must acquire traditional cultural knowledge about ethnic groups and draw on this body of knowledge in working with people of color. The race-based approach forces the worker to confront his or her own racism and racial identity in order to understand the racial dynamics of the helping relationship. Finally, the pan-national approach underscores the need to uncover indigenous ethnic beliefs and practices and to incorporate them into the worker's helping repertoire.

EXPERIENCES OF FAMILY CULTURAL SELF-AWARENESS

Green (1995) points out that each individual exists in a cultural matrix and not as a unique entity, stating that "both clients and professional helpers swim in their own cultural pond, and neither has much experience outside of it" (p. 164). If the worker and the client each are a part of a different cultural pond, there will be experiential differences between them. Thus a primary task of building cultural competency is to assist the worker in exploring his or her cultural pond and becoming aware of the client's cultural pond.

Individual and family experiences are central to an understanding of one's cultural pond. The discovery of family of origin uncovers family heritage or cultural history. Past family events influence present family attitudes and cultural life experiences. Beliefs and practices from parents and grandparents have a major effect on an individual. The family is the individual's primary group, representing the familiar, the intimate, the positive, the similar, the in-group. Family life experiences and practices shape the worker's beliefs, attitudes, behavior, and view of life and the surrounding world.

McGoldrick and Giordano (1996) point out that each ethnic culture has its own unique set of experiences. In Competency Study 3.3, they draw distinctions among different cultures in terms of how verbal communication is used.

How Different Cultures Use Words

COMPETENCY STUDY 3.3

- In Jewish culture, articulating one's experience may be as important as the experience itself, for important historical reasons. Jews have long valued cognitive clarity. Clarifying and sharing ideas and perceptions helps them find meaning in life. Given the anti-Semitic societies in which Jews have lived for so long, with their rights and experiences so often obliterated, one can understand that they have come to place so much importance on analyzing, understanding, and acknowledging what has happened.
- In Anglo culture, words are used primarily to accomplish one's goals. They are valued mainly for their utilitarian value. As the son says about his brother's death in the movie *Ordinary People*: "What's the point of talking about it? It doesn't change anything."
- In Chinese culture, families may communicate many important issues through food rather than through words. They generally do not accept the dominant American idea of "laying your cards on the table."
- Italians often use words primarily for drama, to convey the emotional intensity of an experience.

- The Irish, perhaps the world's greatest poets, use words to buffer experience—using poetry or humor to somehow make reality more tolerable, not to tell the truth, but perhaps to cover it up or embellish it. The Irish have raised poetry, mystification, double meanings, humorous indirection, and ambiguity to an art form in part, perhaps, because their history of oppression led them to realize that telling the truth could be dangerous.
- In Sioux Indian culture, talking is actually proscribed in certain family relationships. A woman who has never exchanged a single word with her father-in-law may experience deep intimacy with him, a relationship that is almost inconceivable in our pragmatic world. The reduced emphasis on verbal expression seems to free Native American families for other kinds of experience of each other, of nature, and of the spiritual realm. (p. 11)

Family and culture fulfill our needs. They are the source of our self-perception and world view. From our family we view, interpret, and respond to the outside world. The family provides protection, comfort, and care throughout our life span, particularly during times of transition and major change. We derive strength for coping and survival from our family, who become our natural support system. In brief, family and culture help the individual become a fully functioning person.

McGoldrick and Giordano (1996) stress that it is crucial for the worker to understand his or her own ethnic identity. Cultural awareness lessens negative reactions to ethnic characteristics of clients and judgmental attitudes about group values. As McGoldrick and Giordano observe, "When people are secure in their identity, they act with greater flexibility and openness to those of other cultural backgrounds. . . . if people receive negative or distorted images of their ethnic group, they often develop a sense of inferiority, even self-hate, that can lead to aggressive behavior and discrimination toward outsiders" (p. 9). Exploring and affirming the cultural identity of the social work student and practitioner enable culturally sensitive relationships with clients.

CULTURAL OTHER-AWARENESS

It is important to explore personal contacts with individuals and groups of other cultures and ethnicities in order to determine the breadth and depth of one's experience with people of color. Human service workers cannot mask their feelings toward multicultural clients. Green (1995) observes: "As most social workers know, countertransference is projection onto the client of the therapist's feelings and experiences from previous relationships. These feelings may have resulted from prior frustrations or from a lifelong pattern of dislike of certain people. In the service encounter, they become part of the dynamics of the event and may be difficult to mask or control" (p. 169). Thus, it is mandatory to revisit the range of previous contact experiences—both positive and negative—in order to become aware of feelings toward culturally different others. Cultural aware-

---

CULTURAL COMPETENCY IN ACTION

The Hernandez Family: A Case Study

Cultural awareness includes appreciation of family cultural life experiences. How can Mr. Platt, the social worker, learn about this area of the Hernandez family? Green (1995) mentions that every individual exists in a cultural matrix (a place of origin) and swims in his or her own cultural pond. Individual and family experiences—past, present, and future—influence our attitudes and life perspectives. Family and culture fulfill our needs. Positive or negative ethnic and cultural identity experiences have an effect on how we feel about ourselves and how we treat others.

TASK RECOMMENDATIONS

- Describe the cultural matrix and cultural ponds of the following people: Mr. and Mrs. Hernandez, the Hernandez children (Ricardo, Isabella, and Eduardo), and Mr. Platt, the social worker.
- How would you bring these cultural ponds together? Would you attempt to swim in any of these ponds? Would you combine these ponds so that everyone could "jump in" and have a good time swimming together?
- How would you describe your cultural matrix and cultural pond?

---

ness provides a perspective on the worker's contacts outside his or her own cultural and ethnic group, an evaluation of relationships and experiences, and an understanding of individual reactions and biases.

There are a number of ways to approach the subject of previous contacts with people of color. One could recall one's life span development and focus on specific incidents where there was significant contact with a person of color. Childhood incidents are often formative building blocks that shape later beliefs and attitudes about, and behavioral responses to, people of color. Did you have meaningful contact with European, African, Latino, Asian, or Native American individuals and families in your childhood years? Did you live in a homogeneous white neighborhood or a heterogeneous, diverse neighborhood? Who were your neighborhood and school friends? Did you attend an integrated school system? Do you recall positive and/or negative incidents involving you and a person of color that made a lasting impression on your life? These are significant questions to ask from a life development perspective.

Based on past and present contact with people of color, it is crucial to ask about the degree of tolerance and/or acceptance of cultural differences that you have felt. Tolerance is the degree of acceptance of views, beliefs, and practices that differ from one's own. It also denotes the degree of freedom one has from internalized bigotry or prejudice. Finally, it includes the willingness to allow, permit, and respect the divergent beliefs and practices of others. In sum, tolerance is the willingness to accept another person and to allow him or her to be what he or she wants to be, as long as the individual does not harm someone else.

Tools for Student Learning 3.1 provides an opportunity to explore in a discussion format your own cultural life experiences and contacts outside your own cultural and ethnic group. You should answer the questions before attending class and then spend at least thirty minutes in a small group laboratory discussing your answers and those of others. These self-help and self-discovery groups are vehicles for you to help each other with these areas of living.

TOOLS FOR STUDENT LEARNING 3.1

Family Cultural Life Experiences and Contacts Outside One's Own Cultural/Ethnic Group

This is a self-assessment of your family cultural life experiences and your significant contacts with members of other cultural and ethnic groups in your neighborhood and community. You are asked to provide the following information and to bring it to class for group discussion.

1. My ethnic family background is: (circle those that apply)

   a. European origin

1. Amish	7. Hungarian	13. combination of the following:
2. English	8. Irish	
3. Dutch	9. Italian	
4. French Canadian	10. Portuguese	
5. German	11. Scandinavian	
6. Greek	12. other	

   b. Slavic

1. Polish	4. Czech
2. Slovak	5. other
3. Russian	6. combination of the following:

   c. Jewish

1. American	4. European
2. Soviet	5. other
3. Israeli	6. combination of the following:

   d. American Indian

1. Tribe	2. other

   3. combination of the following:

e. African origin

    1. African American   5. Nigerian

    2. Jamaican   6. other

    3. Haitian   7. combination of the following:

    4. African-American Muslim

f. Latino

    1. Cuban   5. Central American

    2. Mexican   6. other

    3. Puerto Rican   7. combination of the following:

    4. Brazilian

g. Asian American

    1. Chinese   6. Indonesian

    2. Japanese   7. Pilipino

    3. Korean   8. other

    4. Vietnamese   9. combination of the following:

    5. Cambodian

h. Asian Indian

    1. Hindu   4. other

    2. Christian   5. combination of the following:

    3. Muslim

i. Middle Eastern

    1. Arab   4. Armenian

    2. Iranian   5. other

    3. Lebanese   6. combination of the following:

2. My level of acculturation is: (circle one)

    a. very Americanized   d. traditional culture of origin

    b. somewhat Americanized   e. other (please explain)

    c. bicultural

3. My regional culture (circle one) does / does not influence me.
If it does, my regional culture is: (circle one)

    a. southern   f. New England

   b. midwestern   g. New York

   c. eastern   h. California

   d. northern   i. Texas

   e. western   j. other (please explain)

4. The keeper of culture in my family is: (circle one)

   a. my mother   f. my grandmother

   b. my father   g. my grandfather

   c. my mother and father   h. my grandmother and grandfather

   d. my sister   i. other (please explain)

   e. my brother   j. no one

5. My family observes the following cultural practices: (check relevant ones)

   a. ethnic holidays   f. ethnic birthday traditions

   b. ethnic religious worship   g. ethnic funeral traditions

   c. ethnic and cultural food   h. other (please explain)

   d. ethnic conversational language   i. none (please explain)

   e. ethnic marriage traditions

6. My best friends in my neighborhood were: (check one)

   a. the same race   c. other (please explain)

   b. different races (please specify)

7. My best friends in school were: (check one)

   a. the same race   c. other (please explain)

   b. different races (please specify)

8. My closest friends are: (check one)

   a. the same race   c. other (please explain)

   b. different races (please specify)

9. I have married or will probably marry: (check one)

   a. a person of my specific ethnic subgroup   d. uncertain

   b. a person of my general ethnic background   e. other (please explain)
      (for example, European-European, Latino-Latino)

   c. a person of another race

10. My levels of contact with individuals, families, and groups outside my own cultural and ethnic group in the following settings are: (check relevant ones)

Level of Contact	Setting			
	Neighborhood	School	Social Activities	Work
minimal				
moderate				
frequent				

11. My experiences with persons of other cultures and ethnicities have been: (circle relevant ones)

    positive   negative   mixed

    a. Describe a positive experience: _____

    _____

    _____

    _____

    b. Describe a negative experience: _____

    _____

    _____

    _____

    c. Describe a mixed experience: _____

    _____

    _____

    _____

12. I have a number of stereotypes about the following groups: (circle relevant ones)

    a. European Americans   d. Asian Americans

    b. African Americans   e. Native Americans

    c. Latino Americans

    Give an example of a group stereotype that you have: _____

    _____

    _____

    _____

    _____

13. People have a stereotype about me due to: (circle relevant ones)

a. my ethnic background   e. my career choice   i. other (explain)

b. my gender   f. my income

c. my appearance   g. my place of residence

d. my student status   h. the make of my car

14. I (circle one) would / would not like to increase my cultural awareness.
If so, I am interested in the following areas: (check relevant ones)

a. studying my ethnic/cultural family roots

b. visiting my country of origin

c. learning my ethnic language

d. learning about other ethnic and cultural history, beliefs, and interaction patterns

e. working with multicultural clients in social service agencies

f. learning a multicultural language

g. working in my country of origin

h. working in a Third World country

i. other (please explain)

RACISM, PREJUDICE, AND DISCRIMINATION

Racism, prejudice, and discrimination are universal characteristics of all people. They are not exclusively owned by whites. European, African, Latino, Asian, and Native Americans experience racism, prejudice, and discrimination as victims and also victimize others as agents of racial oppression. As a person of color and a university professor, I have often observed students and faculty of color in controversy. They exclaim in frustration and anguish, "I am a victim of racism!" when related factors of ability and performance are clearly in question. This is not to discount that racism and racial bias are still alive today.

A newspaper article entitled "School District Shuffles Bosses: Board Changes Job of 25 Administrators" (1997) reported the reaction of a Latino middle-range administrator whose school district job was changed: "I believe I have been targeted for demotion because of my race and my support of the previous board." Later in the news story, the school district superintendent reported that overall, the reassignments or demotions would affect 18 minority educators and 14 whites, and that 52% of the district's management posts and 60% of the principals were ethnic minority members. Like most school organizations, the school district was top-heavy with administrators and required major overhauling and trimming of personnel. It seems to me that some charged that racism and racial discrimination were the reasons for the bureaucratic downsizing.

There are overt and covert expressions of racism, prejudice, and discrimination. Racism is an ideological belief that it is right for one social or ethnic group to dominate another. Generally, white European Americans have assumed the racist role, while people of color have been subjugated in the history of American racism. People of color accuse whites, who are the majority population, of racism. In turn, whites subtly make people of color feel unwelcome and uncomfortable when they walk by and do not acknowledge the presence of a person of color. This is an example of intergroup racism. There is also intragroup racism based on social class, language fluency, skin color, and educational attainment. Light-skinned African Americans from wealthy, established families who are alumni of prestigious black private colleges, Mandarin-speaking Taiwanese-born Chinese-American professionals from upper-class families, Cuban-born, light-skinned, wealthy families living in the Miami area, and other similar groups are examples of elites who assume a superior role in their ethnic groups. They make social class distinctions within their ethnic groups that border on racism, prejudice, and discrimination.

The issue of racism raises some interesting questions, such as:

- Are white European Americans, who form the majority of the population of the United States, racists in light of the history of ethnic oppression in this country? Is racism a white American problem?
- Are there racists and is there racism in all cultures and societal groups? Is racism a universal reality?
- Has the charge of racism been used as a diversion, or an excuse to deflect the pressing issues confronting a person or society? Some would argue that this was the case in O. J. Simpson's trial, Clarence Thomas's confirmation hearings before the Senate Judiciary Committee, and Governor Pete Wilson's campaign for Proposition 189 on illegal immigrants, which focused attention away from the state of the California economy during Wilson's first term in office.

You may wish to discuss these controversial issues as you confront racism in American society.

Prejudice is an attitudinal response that expresses racist beliefs in an unfavorable feeling—such as hatred, anger, or hostility—toward an excluded group or individual members. Discrimination is an unfavorable behavioral response directed at members of an excluded ethnic or racial group. It is a visible or a subtle action that denies equal opportunity in society.

How does a person confront racism, prejudice, and discrimination and seek to change these realities in individuals, groups, and society? Pope (1993) offers a helpful step-by-step procedural model that copes with these issues, the multicultural change intervention matrix (MCIM). The MCIM addresses systemic planned change, multicultural organization development, and multicultural interventions and activities. The matrix has two dimensions: target of change (individual, group, institution) and type of change (first-order change, second-order change). At the individual target level of changing racism, the first-order change involves awareness, knowledge, and information about one's own racism. The second-order change at the individual level is education to restructure thinking about racism. This involves the examination of racist belief and thought systems, interactive or experiential new learning, and consciousness raising about where racism came from and how we need to transcend racism.

At the group level, the first-order change is a change in the composition of the group so that members of unrepresented groups are added. Change in the group composition forces the issue of how people relate to each other and dispels stereotypes about people of color. It also reverses the majority-minority numbers. More diversity in group composition results in more diverse thoughts, feelings, and behaviors that move away from racism, prejudice, and discrimination. The second-order change at the group level involves restructuring a program based on an examination of existing group composition, values, philosophy, purposes, and goals, and the infusion of a program with a new mission, goals, and members. For example, the introduction of multicultural staff recruitment, cultural knowledge about dealing with multicultural clients, and loaning personnel for community service in underserved areas might be new directions for a business organization that is committed to making a contribution to diversity.

At the institutional level, the first-order change involves a program intervention that addresses the problem of racism and offers a change effort that undergirds the institutional values and structure. Examples are an ombudsman or advocate for multicultural staff and clients, a staff position devoted to multicultural activities and affairs, or a university chair in social ethnic or multicultural social work studies. The second-order change examines institutional values, goals, and evaluation, and links them to multicultural values and efforts. Multicultural content and effort pervade the entire institutional system, which is transformed toward a multicultural emphasis and moves away from a racist viewpoint. Major initiatives and institutional decision making proceed from this commitment.

The MCIM is a useful paradigm for addressing racism at the individual, group, and institutional levels. It suggests six first-order and second-order steps toward change that are fluid and dynamic. It begins with individual awareness of racism and moves toward institutional system change. Along the way it plots out a course of action to cope with racism in an innovative way.

Tools for Student Learning 3.2 offers some discussion questions about racism, prejudice, and discrimination. It considers the past and present status of a person who has been influenced by racism and how to move such a person beyond this stage of belief, attitude, and behavior. Coping with and facing racism, prejudice, and discrimination in our own lives and the life of our nation is an essential part of developing cultural awareness.

TOOLS FOR STUDENT LEARNING 3.2

Discussion Questions on Racism, Prejudice, and Discrimination

1. Describe racism, prejudice, and discrimination based on your experiences in your own words.

_____

_____

_____

2. Who teaches a person to be a racist, to show prejudice, and to discriminate against another person?

_____

_____

_____

3. Do you know a racist? Is everyone in the world a racist?

_____

_____

_____

4. Is there anyone in your family who is a racist? Are you a racist?

_____

_____

_____

5. How can you cope with racism? Can a racist person change?

_____

_____

_____

6. Can racism be eliminated in this country? What positive steps can be taken toward transcending racism?

_____

_____

_____

7. What are your present thoughts about racism, prejudice, and discrimination?

_____

_____

_____

MULTICULTURAL INVOLVEMENT OVER THE LIFE SPAN

All of us have a unique story about our multicultural involvement at different stages of our life. That is, throughout our life what has been the extent of our contact with people of color? Most Americans are a part of the predominant

European-American culture that forms the majority society. Many Americans are of English, Irish, French, and German ancestry. Most Americans have singular contacts with various people of color. Neighborhoods are still segregated communities, while multicultural contact is prevalent at school and in the work place. But even in these settings, people are selective in their choice of school friends and work colleagues.

My life story begins with the Second World War, the year that England and France declared war on Nazi Germany over the invasion of Poland. I was born on September 23, 1938, in Hamilton, Ohio (population 60,000). Situated in southwestern Ohio between Cincinnati and Dayton on the Miami River, the city was a small industrial center for two quality paper manufacturing companies, Champion Paper and Beckett Paper, and an internationally known safe company, Mosler Safes. My parents were both from Honolulu, Hawaii. My father was a 1923 graduate in chemistry from the University of Chicago and the only one of seven children to graduate from college. He settled with my mother in Hamilton in the late 1920s to learn the paper-making business. He was the chief chemist of the Beckett Paper Company. His dream was to return to China to help the new Republic of China under Dr. Sun Yat-Sen, its first president, with a paper factory. Unfortunately the Sino-Japanese War in the early 1930s ended his vision.

During the 1940s and 1950s, Hamilton, Ohio, was a Republican, conservative, and segregated town. The Miami River divided the city into the west and east sides. The west side was all white; in fact, we were the sole minority family on that side of town. The east side consisted of the downtown, residences of low-income white families, and an isolated, segregated section by the river for African Americans who were called Negroes, colored people, or "the colors" in those days. This area contained a public housing project called Bamboo Harris.

My elementary and junior high schoolmates were all white. I was the only minority child in my schools. I grew up during World War II and the postwar era. I remember going to the Saturday afternoon movies (two cowboy Western features, cartoons, and a thriller serial for a dime) and being threatened by older children during intermission. They were going to beat me up because they thought that I was "a Jap." I remember telling them: "I am Chinese—one of your allies."

My mother attended the local United Presbyterian church and took her children to Sunday school. It was an all-white church and the members readily accepted us. Her social life centered around a few church women friends. Many years later my father remarked that he was never invited to his friends' homes, because he was Chinese.

During my childhood and early adolescence, I experienced racial slurs and stares. As a child I was invited to neighborhood birthday parties, but as I attended junior high, invitations to private parties and dates with white girls ceased. About that time my older sister, a beautiful teenager, was seriously involved with a white boyfriend and my parents decided that it was time to move back to Honolulu, Hawaii.

It was a difficult transition. My father did not have a job and was in his middle fifties. He struggled financially for several years until he finally got a position as a safety engineer with the State of Hawaii. Moving from a small all-white culture to a large island multicultural environment took years of adjustment for me. I was a banana: yellow on the outside but white on the inside. Island teenage boys were mean to this Oriental "haole" (white foreigner). Most of my junior high and high school classmates were Japanese, Chinese, and Pilipino, with some white, Hawaiian, and Portuguese. There were no blacks in my high school in Hawaii. Most of my teachers during high school and university were white. We lived in a predominantly Asian neighborhood and I attended a Chinese Protestant church where I became accepted and active in the youth group. I never lost my mainland English accent, but I adopted the island culture and lifestyle. My dates were mainly Asians, although there were no serious romantic relationships in my adolescence. I never learned to speak Chinese, although this was my ethnic background. I knew little Chinese cultural history and few of the beliefs and practices. I was an American Chinese rather than a Chinese American.

I left for graduate school in Southern California at two institutions in Pasadena and Claremont. My classmates and professors were predominantly white, with few Asian and some black students. I attended several Chinese churches to maintain my ethnic contact and lived in dorms on campus. Several Chinese students would get together on occasion for dinner and conversation and served as a support system.

My first romantic relationship was with a Chinese girl in her late teens, but her father did not like me and ended the relationship. However, several years later I met a Chinese woman at church who had come to Los Angeles to teach elementary school. She became my wife after a year and a half of courtship. Years earlier, my mother had taken me aside and said, "I want you to marry a nice Chinese girl." Those words had become a part of my unconscious. Although I dated many ethnic women, I remembered my mother's words and obeyed her wishes. I was able to pass on my ethnic heritage and culture and my family name to the next generation. We have two sons and two daughters.

As a young married couple, we spent five years in Honolulu. We attended a Japanese church, built close relationships with three Asian couples, and maintained contact with them over the years. We lived in a small apartment complex surrounded by young adult Asian singles and married couples.

I returned to graduate school in Cleveland, Ohio. My doctoral graduate class consisted of eight whites, two Jewish, one African American, and me. I was able to complete classes in a calendar year and wrote my doctoral dissertation during my second year. We lived in one suburban community (Euclid, Ohio) in a large apartment complex that was predominantly white. My wife attended a large state university in Cleveland. Her education classes were composed of white and black students who sat in their separate groups. As an Asian she was baffled about where to sit and sat next to a young black woman who became her friend. After the first year, my wife worked in several elementary schools in a school district outside Cleveland, where she was the only minority teacher. During a beginning-of-the-year open house, several parents criticized my wife about being Asian and not being able to speak English correctly. They were forbidden to trespass on the school campus during the year by the principal, who stood up for her along with several teacher friends. This is the only racial incident that I can remember from our two years in the greater Cleveland area. I was treated very well by my university professors and classmates. Our oldest daughter was born in Taiwan and adopted by us during our last year in Cleveland.

Our 24 years in Sacramento have been filled with my teaching and writing at California State University, Sacramento. There have been racial tensions on our faculty and at the university and community levels. However, one third of the social work faculty are persons of color. I have had an opportunity to grow and develop multicultural theory and practice in social work. We live in south Sacramento in an area called Greenhaven, which has been a wonderful place to raise four children. We live in a predominantly white and Asian community on a double cul-de-sac and have friendly neighbors. Our children's friends are multiracial and predominantly Asian. Our two oldest are away in Los Angeles and Fresno, while the two youngest are living at home and going to community college. My wife works at an elementary school as a first-grade teacher.

I share these experiences knowing that my life journey as a Chinese American has been limited by living situations, life choices, and educational and career experiences. As each of us shares his or her life background, it will help us understand where we are coming from and where we have to go in our journey with people on this earth.

It is important to share aspects of your life journey with others who will appreciate and understand you. Tools for Student Learning 3.3 will help you explore your childhood adolescence, young adulthood, and adult years in relationship to contact with people of color. Please fill out this exercise and bring it to class for sharing.

TOOLS FOR STUDENT LEARNING 3.3

Multicultural Involvement Over the Life Span

This questionnaire surveys your involvement with people of color in childhood, adolescence, young adulthood, and adulthood. You are asked to provide the following information and to share it in class discussion.

1. I was born in: (name of city, population) _____

2. My ethnic group is: (circle one)

   a. European American   d. Asian American

   b. African American   e. Native American

   c. Latino American   f. other (please explain)

3. My childhood years were spent in: (name of city or cities)

_____

_____

4. When I was a child, my neighborhood was predominantly: (circle one)

    a. European American   d. Asian American

    b. African American   e. Native American

    c. Latino American   f. multiracial (list ethnic groups)

5. When I was a child my contact with people of different ethnic groups was as indicated. (circle one in each category)

    a. African Americans: rare / somewhat frequent / frequent

    b. Mexican Americans: rare / somewhat frequent / frequent

    c. Puerto Rican Americans: rare / somewhat frequent / frequent

    d. Cuban Americans: rare / somewhat frequent / frequent

    e. Chinese Americans: rare / somewhat frequent / frequent

    f. Japanese Americans: rare / somewhat frequent / frequent

    g. Korean Americans: rare / somewhat frequent / frequent

    h. Vietnamese Americans: rare / somewhat frequent / frequent

    i. Native Americans: rare / somewhat frequent / frequent

6. When I was a child, my impressions about people of different ethnic groups were as indicated. (circle one in each category)

    a. African Americans: favorable / somewhat favorable / unfavorable

    b. Latino Americans: favorable / somewhat favorable / unfavorable

    c. Asian Americans: favorable / somewhat favorable / unfavorable

    d. Native Americans: favorable / somewhat favorable / unfavorable

7. As a child, I formulated my impressions about people of color from: (circle relevant ones)

    a. my parents' attitudes   d. my peer group

    b. my experiences with ethnic individuals   e. other (please explain)

    c. neighbors' attitudes

8. My adolescent years were spent in: (name of city or cities)

---

9. When I was a teenager, my neighborhood was predominantly: (circle one)

    a. European American   d. Asian American

    b. African American   e. Native American

    c. Latino American   f. multiracial (list ethnic groups)

10. When I was a teenager, my close friends were predominantly: (circle one)

    a. whites

    b. African Americans

    c. Latino Americans

    d. Asian Americans

    e. Native Americans

    f. multiracial (list ethnic groups)

12. As a teenager, I dated predominantly: (circle one)

    a. whites

    b. African Americans

    c. Latino Americans

    d. Asian Americans

    e. Native Americans

    f. multiracial (list ethnic groups)

11. When I was a teenager, my impressions from childhood about people of different ethnic groups changed (or not) as indicated. (circle one in each category)

    a. African Americans:

       remained the same / changed more favorably / changed less favorably

    b. Latino Americans:

       remained the same / changed more favorably / changed less favorably

    c. Asian Americans:

       remained the same / changed more favorably / changed less favorably

    d. Native Americans:

       remained the same / changed more favorably / changed less favorably

    Explain the reasons for your change in impressions about specific ethnic groups.

    _____

    _____

    _____

    _____

13. As a young adult, I lived in: (name of city or cities)

    _____

    _____

14. I went to the following colleges and universities:

    _____

    _____

15. My undergraduate college major was: _____

16. My college degrees are: (circle relevant ones)

    baccalaureate   master   doctorate

17. When I was a young adult, my close friends were predominantly: (circle one)

    a. whites

    b. African Americans

    c. Latino Americans

    d. Asian Americans

    c. Native Americans

    f. multiracial (list ethnic groups)

18. When I was a young adult, my serious romantic relationships were predominantly with: (circle one)

    a. whites

    b. African Americans

    c. Latino Americans

    d. Asian Americans

    e. Native Americans

    f. multiracial (list ethnic groups)

19. When I was a young adult, my first full-time job after graduation from college was with an organization whose employees were predominantly: (circle one)

    a. whites

    b. African Americans

    c. Latino Americans

    d. Asian Americans

    e. Native Americans

    f. multiracial (list ethnic groups)

20. As an adult, I have lived in: (name of city or cities)

    I now am living in: (name of city)

21. As an adult, I married or am living with a partner whose ethnic background is: (circle one)

    a. the same as mine

    b. different from mine (please explain)

    _____

    _____

22. As an adult, I live in a neighborhood that is predominantly: (circle one)

    a. white

    b. African American

    c. Latino American

    d. Asian American

    e. Native American

    f. multiracial (list ethnic groups)

23. My present employer is: (name of the company) _____

24. My fellow employees are predominantly: (circle one)

    a. white

    b. African American

    c. Latino American

    d. Asian American

    e. Native American

    f. multiracial (list ethnic groups)

25. Throughout my life, the degree of contact and involvement with people of color that I have had has been: (circle one)

    a. minimal   b. somewhat frequent   c. frequent   d. other
                                                       (please explain)

_____

_____

_____

CULTURALLY DIVERSE SOCIAL WORK EDUCATION

The 1992 Curriculum Policy Statement of the Council on Social Work Education (Council on Social Work Education, 1992) has two categories that require course content on people of color. This policy statement mandates uniform standards and themes for social work education in cultural diversity.

The first category is diversity, which addresses differences and similarities in the experiences, needs, and beliefs of people distinguished by race, ethnicity, culture, class, gender, sexual orientation, religion, physical or mental ability, age, and national origin. In this category the policy statement specifies that practitioners who serve diverse groups must use differential assessment and intervention skills.

The second category is populations-at-risk, which may include those distinguished by age, ethnicity, culture, class, religion, and physical or mental ability, depending on the mission of a particular social work program. Theoretical and practice content about the patterns, dynamics, and consequences of discrimination, economic deprivation, and oppression for populations-at-risk must be present in social work education.

Along with these two curriculum content areas is Evaluative Standard 3: Nondiscrimination, addresses cultural diversity in social work education. This standard specifies that the social work program must be conducted without discrimination based on race, color, gender, age, creed, ethnic or national origin, disability, political orientation, or sexual orientation. It must make specific and continuous efforts to ensure equity in faculty and staff recruitment, work load, retention, promotion, tenure, assignment, and remuneration. It must also ensure equity to administrative personnel and support staff as well as to students through recruitment, admission, retention, and financial aid policies and procedures. The social work program must indicate to faculty, administrative and support personnel, and students how the institution's, the program's, and federal and state policies on nondiscrimination are carried out. These groups must be informed about institutional and program policies, procedures, and mechanisms regarding grievance and appeal procedures, nondiscrimination, and sexual harassment.

These three criteria should guide undergraduate and graduate social work education in academic course work, fieldwork experiences, and research projects on culturally diverse clients and groups. Social work education requires course content on cultural and ethnic diversity, differential assessment and intervention techniques for major ethnic groups, oppression and discrimination, and related themes. In social work programs, there is at least one required course in this area and integration of cultural and ethnic themes throughout the curriculum in other courses.

Fieldwork experiences and research projects on cultural and ethnic diversity may or may not be present in social work education programs. It is important to require work with culturally diverse clients as part of the fieldwork experience. While social work educators would probably agree with the importance of such experiences, it may be only by chance that a social work student has multicultural client cases in the field practicum. It is vital to require and to incorporate into the learning agreement these types of clients for student field learning.

Still rare are research papers, projects, and theses on cultural and ethnic diversity. It is important to conduct survey research on timely questions regarding culturally diverse groups and issues. Many ethnic students select topics related to their ethnic groups. However, it is crucial for research instructors and advisers to teach ethnographic interviewing, oral history research, and related methodology to all students. Exposure to these research methods and sample research studies gives students a taste of multicultural research interests.

The mission of the Council on Social Work Education is to assist social work undergraduate and graduate programs with self-appraisal and self-improvement of existing programs and evaluation of new programs. The effects of the Council's educational goals and standards are felt by baccalaureate and graduate member schools, university and college candidates that seek entrance into the accreditation process, agencies that participate in field practicum instruction of social work students and that employ graduates of social work programs, professional membership associations engaged in the formulation of standards for practice, representatives of higher education who are affected by social work accreditation standards and procedures, related professional disciplines, social work students, and the general public desiring an understanding of social work education.

Clear and strong standards are needed requiring curriculum content on cultural diversity, people of color, and historical oppression and discrimination. These requirements send a message to social work faculty and students that it is essential to master cultural competency in classroom courses, fieldwork, and research efforts. In turn, these efforts produce social work graduates who are more competent to deal with multicultural clients than previous generations of social work professionals. In the end there is significant improvement in professional social work education and the promotion of prepared graduates to meet the changing demands of professional practice.

The Hernandez Family: A Case Study

Culturally diverse social work education is necessary if social work students are to develop cultural competency and cultural awareness. The Hernandez family represents a microcosm of the many multicultural client families that social workers see in their student practicums and professional careers. Mr. Platt is an alumnus of undergraduate and graduate social work programs. He has taken courses on human diversity and populations-at-risk that cover people of color, women, and gays and lesbians; discrimination, economic deprivation, and oppression; and differential assessment and intervention skills with diverse groups. One of his field placements was in an ethnic/cultural setting where he conducted research for his project paper. He is working for a Family Service Association agency and has multicultural clients in his caseload.

TASK RECOMMENDATIONS

• What are some steps that Mr. Platt can take to enhance his cultural knowledge, skills, and experiences?

• How can this generation of social work students and practitioners become more competent to deal with multicultural clients than previous generations?

CULTURALLY DIVERSE SOCIAL WORK PRACTICE

Culturally diverse social work practice involves working with clients from a perspective of cultural awareness. Green (1995) has set forth a help-seeking behavior model that enhances cultural awareness from the client's perspective. Green is a cultural anthropologist who has applied ethnographic interviewing principles to social work practice.

The Green model consists of four major components:

• The individual's definition and understanding of an experience as a problem. Green discusses this principle in terms of perspective taking; that is, the willingness and ability of the practitioner to elicit the client's understanding of his or her needs. The procedure is primarily to gather information about the client's willingness to communicate and to give feedback that the client's position has been heard by the worker.

• The client's semantic evaluation of a problem. Language is the medium of cultural knowledge about an individual and an ethnic group. It is crucial to know and understand the meaning of cultural and ethnic words, what Green describes as "cover terms" or special categories of ideas, objects, concepts, or relationships that are familiar and part of the client's cultural experience. These cover terms have cultural significance and psychological reality to the client. Green also uses "ethnographic descriptors" to explain the meaning of cover terms and suggests the importance of a cultural guide who serves as a teaching resource to explain the subtleties and complexities of a particular community and to interpret cover terms to the worker.

- Indigenous strategies of problem intervention. Here Green is seeking appropriate sources of help that are a part of the client's culture. Rather than imposing external social work intervention modalities, Green is concerned about ethnic community resources, family and extended family support, indigenous advice giving from respected community authority figures, religious resources, and use of meditation and exercise.
- Culturally-based criteria of problem resolution. Green suggests a focus on how people generally solve their problems in their own communities and what are reasonable outcomes to those efforts from their perspectives. The worker should be knowledgeable about the recent history and daily experiences of the client's ethnic community. The worker should also be aware of the cultural variations that may exist in a particular community and how different clients may respond to specific therapeutic techniques.

An essential part of the cultural awareness practice model centers on ethnographic interviewing. Thornton and Garrett (1995) believe that ethnography is a crucial bridge to multicultural practice. In Competency Study 3.4 they explain how to incorporate ethnography into practice.

Cultural Awareness and Ethnographic Practice

COMPETENCY STUDY 3.4

Social workers who work cross-culturally must know not only how to conduct an ethnographic study, but also how to apply this knowledge in practice. Becoming familiar with a culture is not enough, just as listening alone is not enough to help clients solve the problems. Social workers should learn about clients both as individuals and as members of their culture or ethnic community, they should investigate the relevance of culture to the clients' lives, and then they should build on this knowledge and incorporate it into the helping process. Although social workers need to "start where the client is," they also need to help clients move beyond that starting point. Goal development must be based on clients' perceptions of needs (Goldstein, 1983). As obvious as this sounds, the meaning of clients' problems may depend upon the culture in which they are based. Cultural practices that appear problematic or dysfunctional to outsiders may be acceptable or normal when viewed within the context of the culture (Bourguignon, 1979). Therefore, the problems, goals, and outcomes determined by clients may differ from those chosen by workers.

Preconceived solutions are inappropriate in cross-cultural social work. Services tend to be ineffective when they are incongruent with clients' expectations and cultural backgrounds (Leigh & Green, 1989). Social workers who use ethnographic interviewing have established themselves as learners in their client's culture. Clients are viewed as experts on their lives and cultures, workers as experts on the problem-solving process. The two become collaborators, working together to find ways to meet client needs in an effective and culturally acceptable way. (pp. 70–71)

Green's model underscores the importance of cultivating and applying cultural awareness to the helping relationship. Rather than superimposing a foreign social work practice intervention, the worker starts with the client's cultural understanding of the problem, moves toward examining the meaning of semantic concepts surrounding the culture and the problem, and then seeks indigenous intervention strategies and problem resolution from the ethnic community perspective. This cultural awareness procedure arises from the recognition that the client's culture is primary and holds the key to solving the problem itself.

CULTURALLY DIVERSE PROFESSIONAL EMPLOYMENT EXPERIENCES

Graduation from an undergraduate or a graduate social work program is the commencement of learning in professional agency settings. A typical social work graduate has several tools: knowledge, skills, fieldwork experiences, and research expertise in a specific area. However, the question becomes: How can social work graduates who become social workers sustain their knowledge, clinical and community practice skills, and research interest in cultural diversity? In brief, how can social work professionals remain culturally competent?

Social work education should plant in the minds and hearts of social work graduates a commitment to cultural diversity as a field of interest and maintenance of cultural competency as a professional goal. There are a number of ways you can ensure that you continue to grow in cultural competency throughout your career as a social work professional:

- Have a culturally diverse caseload and use this as an opportunity to learn new information about the various ethnic groups that is not in the literature.
- Have your multicultural clients, as your teachers, help you understand them in transcultural (across cultures) and cross-cultural (between cultures) dimensions.
- Learn about your agency's multicultural clients from senior staff who have had numerous contacts and experiences in the agency setting.
- Establish short-term research projects with social work student interns about characteristics of and issues related to multicultural clients, families, groups, and communities.
- Take cultural diversity workshops sponsored by public and private agencies and universities in your area.
- Keep up with current books and journal articles on cultural diversity (for example, Guilford Press, Sage Publications, and Brooks/Cole Publishing Company each have a series of books on multiculturalism; the *Journal of Multicultural Social Work*, the *Journal of Social Work*, and the *Journal of Social Work Education* feature articles on multicultural topics).

CULTURAL COMPETENCY IN ACTION

The Hernandez Family: A Case Study

Cultural awareness is an integral part of cultural competency. Mr. Platt, the social worker, found that Mr. Hernandez has two jobs and has been away from the family due to long working hours. He usually helps his son, Ricardo, with his homework but has not been able to do so because of work. As a result, Ricardo's school work has suffered and he has become disruptive in the classroom.

TASK RECOMMENDATIONS

The Green help-seeking behavior model is applicable to the Hernandez family. Describe how you would apply the following principles to the Hernandez case:

- The individual's definition and understanding of an experience as a problem. The worker elicits the client's understanding of needs. Would you ask Mr. Hernandez, Mrs. Hernandez, or their son, Ricardo, to define the problem?
- The client's semantic evaluation of a problem. Particular cultural and ethnic language describes the problem in specific detail. A cultural guide is suggested to interpret the client description of the problem to the worker. Would you enlist a resource person from Mr. Hernandez's community who is fluent in Spanish and English to come and explain the problem in both languages?
- Indigenous strategies of problem intervention. Cultural sources of help include ethnic community resources, family and extended family support, indigenous advice giving, religious resources, and meditation and exercise. Which strategies would you use for intervention?
- Cultural problem resolution. This focus is on how people in their own communities solve their problems. Problems confronting the Hernandez family are the absence of Mr. Hernandez due to his working at two jobs, Ricardo's school problems, and relatives immigrating from Mexico. Is it advantageous for the social worker to ask Mr. and Mrs. Hemandez how persons in their ethnic community would solve similar problems?

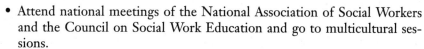

- Attend national meetings of the National Association of Social Workers and the Council on Social Work Education and go to multicultural sessions.
- Keep up periodic correspondence with former professors from your alma mater who have a commitment to culturally diverse social work practice.
- Return to graduate school after working in the social work field and specialize in multicultural studies and social work (a specialty available at schools such as the University of Michigan's School of Social Work; the University of California at Berkeley's School of Social Welfare; the University of California at Los Angeles's Department of Social Welfare; and the University of Washington's School of Social Work).

These are some ways to foster and cultivate cultural competency on a continuing basis throughout your social work career.

SUMMARY

This chapter has defined cultural awareness from the personal and professional perspectives. It has encouraged you to assess your own cultural background and identity as well as your contacts with groups and individuals of other cultures and ethnicities. It has urged you to confront your own racism, prejudice, and discrimination, challenging you to explore and resolve this aspect of your beliefs, attitudes, and behavioral responses. It has emphasized the importance of cultivating essential knowledge and skills in social work education and employment experiences. Ideally, you will not be hindered by past negative events and persons and can work competently with multicultural clients in the present. As a result, clients will feel affirmed and can work on the pressing problems facing them.

REFERENCES

Bourguignon, E. (1979). *Psychological anthropology*. New York; Holt, Rinehart, & Winston.

Carter, R. T., & Qureshi, A. (1995). A typology of philosophical assumptions in multicultural counseling and training. In J. G. Ponterotto, J. M Casas, L. A. Suzuki, & C. M. Alexander (Eds.), *Handbook of multicultural counseling* (pp. 239–262). Thousand Oaks, CA: Sage Publications.

Council on Social Work Education, Commission on Accreditation. (1992). *Handbook of accreditation standards and procedures* (4th ed.). Alexandria, VA: Council on Social Work Education.

Giordano, J., & McGoldrick, M. (1996). European families: An overview. In M. MeGoldrick, J. Giordano, & J. K. Pearce (Eds.), *Ethnicity and family therapy* (pp. 427–441). New York: Guilford Press.

Goldstein, H. (1983). Starting where the client is. *Social Casework, 64*, 267–275.

Green, J. W. (1995). *Cultural awareness in the human services: A multi-ethnic approach*. Boston: Allyn & Bacon.

Hardy, K. V., & Laszloffy, T. A. (1995). The cultural genogram: Key to training culturally competent family therapists. *Journal of Marital and Family Therapy, 21*, 227–237.

Kadushin, A., & Kadushin, G. (1997). *The social work interview: A guide for human service professionals*. New York: Columbia University Press.

Leigh, J., & Green, J. (1989). Teaching ethnographic methods to social service workers. *Practicing Anthropology, 11*, 8–10.

McGoldrick, M., & Giordano, J. (1996). Overview: Ethnicity and family therapy. In M. McGoldrick, J. Giordano, & J. K. Pearce (Eds.), *Ethnicity and family therapy* (pp. 1–27). New York: Guilford Press.

Pope, R. L. (1993). An analysis of multiracial change efforts in student affairs (Doctoral dissertation, University of Massachusetts at Amherst, 1982). *Dissertation Abstracts International, 53–10*, 3457A.

Reynolds, A. L. (1995). Challenges and strategies for teaching multicultural counseling courses. In J. G. Ponterotto, J. M. Casas, L. A. Suzuki, & C. M. Alexander (Eds.), *Handbook of multicultural counseling* (pp. 312–330). Thousand Oaks, CA: Sage Publications.

Sanday, P.R. (1976). *Anthropology and the public interest*. New York: Academic Press.

School district shuffles bosses: Board changes job of 25 administrators. (1997, May 13). *Sacramento Bee*, pp. B1, B4.

Thornton, S., & Garrett, K. J. (1995). Ethnography as a bridge to multicultural practice. *Journal of Social Work Education, 31*, 67–74.

CHAPTER FOUR

Knowledge Acquisition

This chapter will help you develop cultural competencies in the area of knowledge acquisition.

Generalist level:

- Understanding of terms related to cultural diversity
- Knowledge of demographics of culturally diverse populations
- Development of a critical thinking perspective on cultural diversity
- Understanding of the history of oppression and of social groups
- Knowledge of the strengths of people of color
- Knowledge of culturally diverse values

Advanced level:

- Application of systems and psychosocial theory to practice with clients of color
- Knowledge of theories on ethnicity, culture, minority identity, and social class
- Mastery of social science theory

Cultural competency rests on a foundation of knowledge—information, facts, theories, and principles that facilitate culturally diverse social work. The social work student needs to master a body of knowledge and become familiar with certain basic issues and theories. Theories may consist of single propositions or of a series of general principles that provide a systemic explanation.

This chapter surveys the range of knowledge related to culturally diverse social work that is essential to cultural competency. It begins with basic concepts that must be clearly understood. It also covers demographic trends that contribute to ethnic group profiles. Next it focuses on critical thinking as a means of analyzing knowledge. It explores the effect of the history of group oppression on how knowledge about cultural diversity is formulated. It addresses gender issues, particularly multicultural feminist themes, and examines values that influence how the client and the social worker formulate and interpret social problems, make choices, and implement behavioral change.

On an advanced level, cultural competency is enhanced by knowledge of systems and psychosocial theory, as well as theories about ethnicity, culture, minority status, and social class. Finally, the chapter presents social science theory and its application to social work practice with culturally diverse clients.

TERMINOLOGY RELATED TO CULTURAL DIVERSITY

A beginning step toward the mastery of cultural competency knowledge is the understanding of basic terms. Among them are *ethnicity*, *minority*, *culture*, *multiculturalism*, and *diversity*. These terms form the basis for understanding concepts and theories.

Ethnicity is identity based on ancestry, nationality, and/or race. The ethnic group shares a heritage that is passed on from generation to generation. Past, present, and future family or group membership is defined by ethnic identity, as is face, hair, and skin color. McGoldrick and Giordano (1996) state:

> Ethnicity refers to a common ancestry through which individuals have evolved shared values and customs. It is deeply tied to the family, through which it is transmitted. A group's sense of commonality is transmitted over generations by the family and reinforced by the surrounding community. Ethnicity is a powerful influence in determining identity. A sense of belonging and of historical continuity are basic psychological needs. We may ignore our ethnicity or deny it by changing our names and rejecting our families and social backgrounds, but we do so to the detriment of our well-being. (p. 1)

Minority underscores the status of people of color in the United States. It depicts a group that has been discriminated against or subjected to unequal treatment. It highlights the group's inferior and powerless status. It was widely used during the civil rights period of the sixties as the term of preference for ethnic groups. However, it has fallen into disrepute (DeLaCancela, Jenkins, & Chin, 1993) because of the global reality of populations and the oppressive connotations of the term. Yet current texts on ethnicity and culture (Green, 1995; Iglehart & Becerra, 1995; Ponterotto, Casas, Suzuki, & Alexander, 1995) continue to use the term when describing minority status in this country.

Culture refers to the way of life of a society and life patterns related to conduct, beliefs, traditions, values, language, art, skills, and social/interpersonal relationships. It is used in such terms as *cultural pluralism, bicultural conflict, bicultural integration, cultural duality, acculturation, enculturation, transcultural,* and *cross-cultural.* Matsumoto (1996) defines culture as "the set of attitudes, values, beliefs, and behavior shared by a group of people, but different for each individual, communicated from one generation to the next" (p. 16). Matsumoto further distinguishes individual and shared cultures. In the former, each person individually understands and interprets the influence of culture. In the latter, culture is an experience shared among members from a psychological perspective. Matsumoto (1996) explains:

> It is the sharing of ideas, attitudes, values, beliefs—the contents of the minds of each and every individual who lives in that culture. Moreover, not only are these ideas in the minds of people, but they also exist as a social consciousness above and beyond each and every individual. The behaviors that are shared are indeed observable and are often seen in rituals or common, automatic behavior patterns that arise because of shared cultural values and norms for behavior. (pp. 16, 17)

This dual understanding of individual and shared cultures has implications for cultural competency. The culturally competent worker must understand the client's individual culture and ascertain whether there is similarity or difference between the client's individual culture and the corporate shared meaning of group culture. Furthermore, Lum (1996) has written about five cultural perspectives that emphasize the interactive nature of culture: transcultural, cross-cultural, paracultural, metacultural, and pancultural.

A related term, *multiculturalism*, reflects the nature of American society. It focuses on the coexistence of many cultures as recognized parts of society. Multiculturalism has been described as an educational and political movement that has been associated with the politically correct position of affirmative action, which has lost favor with conservative politicians. In its narrow sense, multiculturalism focuses exclusively on racial and ethnic issues (Helms, 1994). In its broadest sense, multiculturalism includes gender, socioeconomic status, sexual/affectional orientation, and national origin (Pedersen, 1988).

Diversity encompasses differences in and among societal groups based on race and/or ethnicity, gender, age, physical/mental abilities, sexual orientation, size, and other distinguishing characteristics. The diversification of the United States (Sue, Arredondo, & McDavis, 1992) refers to the changing complexion of society due to immigration and birth rates among racial and ethnic populations. Lum (1996) uses the term *culturally diverse social work practice* in recognition of the current multicultural and diversity emphases.

Schriver (1995, p. 114) coins the phrase *diversity in diversity* to underscore the development of members of minority groups. Schriver recognizes the wide variation among African, Asian, and Native American family groups. For example, African American families range from single-parent, female-headed families to nuclear, two-parent families to large, extended, multigenerational families. Among Native Americans there are 200 different languages and 438 tribes. Moreover, Asian Americans vary depending on history, traditions, language, and generational differences. Chinese and Japanese people are termed Asian Americans, but the history of these two nations includes military conflict against each other in the 1930s and 1940s. Diversity is an interesting concept with broad dimensions.

In summary, the culturally competent student must understand and master basic terminology. Concepts have a life of their own and lead to the formulation of theory. This is a basic building block of cultural competency knowledge.

THE DEMOGRAPHICS OF CULTURAL DIVERSITY

In survey research, *demographics* is understood to mean the distribution of a sample population. The word *demography* comes from *demos* (the people) and *graphia* (writing), which describes the process of writing about the people under study. In a social work context, the demography of the client population is the basis for program planning and evaluation.

The demographic profile of people of color in the United States is constantly changing due to significant growth in this population in the last 30 years. Leigh (1998) reports:

> In 1995, Asians composed 3.3 percent of the population. In 2030, Asians will be 6.6 percent of the population; in 2050, Asians will be 8.2 percent of the population. Hispanics composed 10.2 percent of the population in 1995. In 2030, Hispanics will make up 18.9 percent of the population; by 2050, that figure will be 24.5 percent. In 1995, blacks composed 12.2 percent of the population. In 2030, blacks will compose 13.1 percent of the population; by 2050, that figure will be 13.6 percent of the population. (p. 2)

Atkinson, Morten, and Sue (1993) report that by the year 2000 more than one third of the U. S. population will be racial and ethnic minorities, with the proportion at 45% in the public schools. By the year 2010, racial and ethnic minorities will be a numerical majority (52%), while white Americans will constitute 48% of the population. Changing population trends are due to two factors: current immigration patterns and differential birth rates among the majority and minority populations. Immigration rates indicate high increases in the Asian (34%) and Latino (34%) populations in the United States. Large numbers of Southeast Asians have immigrated since the 1965 McCarran Immigration Act. Latinos will reach 55 million by the year 2000 and will constitute the largest population group by the year 2025.

Furthermore, Sue, Arredondo, and McDavis (1992) report that along with a growing aging population, both white and ethnic minority Americans have declining birth rates (1.7 children per mother for whites, 2.4 children per mother for African Americans, 2.9 children per mother for Mexican Americans, 3.4 children per mother for Vietnamese, 4.6 children per mother for Latinos, 7.4 children per mother for Cambodians, and 11.9 children per mother for Hmong). Approximately 75% of the entering labor force are racial and ethnic minorities and women. Interestingly, the majority of the work force paying into social security and pension plans for baby boomer retirees will be racial and ethnic minorities. From a business industry perspective, ethnic minorities constitute a marketplace equal to the GNP (gross national product) of Canada and constitute a diverse work force at the same time. Public educational institutions are directly affected by the increase in numbers of ethnic minority students, many of whom are foreign-born and come from homes where English is not spoken as the primary language.

In Competency Study 4.1, Gutierrez and Nagda (1996) give us a 50-year projection of demographic trends that will shape knowledge.

New Millennium Demographics

COMPETENCY STUDY 4.1

The growing ethnic diversity of the coming millennium will present many challenges to our profession. It is projected that within the next 50 years immigration and fertility patterns will lead to an increasingly multiracial, multicultural, and multiethnic society (Gutierrez, 1992). At the same time, conditions of economic inequality and economic stratification by gender and race have not abated (Dressel, 1994; Simon, 1994). Because both women and people of color continue to experience economic and social disadvantage, these demographic projections have led to concerns that the United States could become a nation of poor children and youth of color and older European Americans, with neither group being capable of producing the economic resources necessary for supporting existing social services or other social goods (Ozawa, 1986; Sarri, 1986; Williams, 1990). These trends in the substance and structure of our society challenge our profession to evaluate how it can best address these demographic shifts (Gutierrez, 1992).

These demographic trends have implications for health care, housing, education, employment, social services, and related human service areas. Such data are the raw material for social welfare planning, programs, and administration of services. Moreover, demographic knowledge is a strong pointer to new and significant findings. It increases our understanding of new immigrant adjustment patterns, customs, family structure, and related data, which furthers our cultural competency.

CRITICAL THINKING ABOUT CULTURAL DIVERSITY

Critical thinking is a learning process that can help anyone

- to formulate, analyze, and assess a problem, question, or issue;
- to segment an argument or assertion into its components (points of view, major concepts and ideas, theories and underlying assumptions, reasoning, interpretations, and implications and consequences) (Paul, 1992, p. 11);
- to differentiate theories about culturally diverse social work practice issues; and
- to build theories of cultural diversity as sources of new knowledge.

Critical thinking is relevant to culturally diverse social work practice. Mumm and Kerstling (1997) have presented a list of five interrelated skills that promote critical thinking for social workers: (1) the ability to understand social work theories; (2) the ability to divide a theory into its components (assumptions, concepts, propositions, hypotheses); (3) the ability to assess the practice implications of a theory; (4) the ability to develop and apply criteria for evaluating a theory; and (5) the ability to identify common errors in reasoning.

These authors propose a number of critical thinking ways to evaluate theories:

- Historical perspective, or a discussion of how and why a theory developed in a historical context.
- Assumptions, or a discussion about the explicit and implicit premises of a theory concerning the client, human nature, the role of the social worker and the client, and the change process.
- Logical flaws, or a discussion about the logic, contradictions among theories, fit with the mission of social work, and errors in reasoning.
- Usefulness in practice, or a discussion about the application of a theory to one's own practice.
- Strengths and weaknesses of a theory and a comparison of theories and their potential benefit to specific problems, clients, or settings.
- Practice dilemmas, or a discussion of how theories apply to specific problems, clients, or settings.

New theories regarding ethnic-sensitive social work practice (Devore & Schlesinger, 1996), cultural awareness in the human services (Green, 1995), and social work practice with people of color (Lum, 1996) emerged in the eighties and are still in development, as described in Competency Study 4.2. We can apply critical thinking skills to these theories.

COMPETENCY STUDY 4.2

Applying Critical Thinking to Three Theories of Culturally Diverse Social Work Practice

Devore and Schlesinger (1996), in their theory of ethnic-sensitive social work practice, use a number of theoretical building blocks: the case method in teaching and learning; ethnic stratification, ethnic conflict theory, and social class, which are subsumed under the concept of ethnic reality; and a seven-layer model of understanding involving values, knowledge and skills, self-awareness, the client, and the social worker. The concepts of ethnicity, social class, and layers of understanding are the major theoretical underpinnings that could be discussed in a critical thinking context.

Among the critical thinking questions that could be posed about Devore and Schlesinger's assumptions are the following:

- What are the major components and emphases of the ethnic reality involving ethnicity and social class issues?
- Are ethnicity and social class important elements in understanding the background and behavioral dynamics of clients?
- Explain and interrelate the seven layers of understanding as the foundation for ethnic-sensitive practice.
- Do the seven layers of understanding illumine the client's situation from a generalist practice, direct practice, macro practice, and applications to refugees and new immigrants, families, public sector and health care settings?

Green (1995) builds his multi-ethnic cultural awareness practice approach by integrating cultural anthropology with social work practice. Ethnicity is a primary theme, expressed as ethnic group relationships, ethnic community, and ethnic competence. The help-seeking behavior model is based on an inductive ethnographic interviewing approach. The major components are the client's definition and understanding of an experience as a problem, the client's semantic evaluation of a problem, indigenous strategies of problem intervention, and culturally based criteria for problem resolution. Cross-cultural social work consists of cross-cultural learning and ethnic competence, which involve entering an unfamiliar community, key respondents as cultural guides, and participant observation. Language, working with a translator, and ethnographic interviewing are involved in the process.

Green's approach evokes a number of critical thinking questions:

- Is the cultural anthropology concept of ethnography compatible with multi-ethnic cross-cultural social work?
- Green's help-seeking behavior model is based on ethnographic interviewing principles that focus on the client's definition and understanding of the problem, semantic evaluation of the problem, indigenous strategies, and culturally based problem resolution. Does this approach offer a specific way to focus culturally diverse social work practice or is it too narrow a perspective?

Lum's (1996) theory of social work practice with people of color advocates culturally diverse social work. The underpinnings of this approach center on the meaning of culture. Lum has devised five perspectives on culture: transcultural, cross-cultural, paracultural, metacultural, and pancultural. Culture is the basis for understanding the client from various ethnic groups.

The culturally diverse approach deals with emic (culture-specific) and etic (culture-common) dimensions of culture. Close analysis of his text finds that themes such as family, religion, and identity are common to these groups, while at the same time, culture-specific distinctions are made about each separate group. These culture-common and culture-specific themes are consistent throughout his system.

This theory tries to infuse culturally diverse meaning into clinical and community terms such as *resistance, communication barriers, service delivery*, and *micro-meso-macro intervention*. It also introduces new concepts that have multicultural meaning such as relationship protocols, professional self-disclosure, communication style, socioenvironmental impacts, psychoindividual reactions, and cultural and spiritual assessment. These themes are applied in a process-stage approach where the social worker and the client engage in contact, problem identification, assessment, intervention, and termination.

There are three major paradigms: a framework for culturally diverse social work practice, a multicultural problem typology, and an intervention levels and strategies model.

Among the critical thinking questions that could be raised concerning Lum are:

- Is the cultural diversity orientation a reflection of current culture and diversity emphases?
- Are etic (culture-common) and emic (culture-specific) distinctions necessary when discussing people of color as an etic entity and separate and distinct emic groups such as African, Latino, Asian, or Native Americans?
- Is the infusion-of-new-meaning approach to classic practice terminology helpful or a distortion of the intent of these concepts?
- Is the introduction of new and distinctive multicultural concepts a validation that culturally diverse social work is able to stand as a specialized field of practice?

You are encouraged to apply critical thinking questions to increase your cultural competency. Critical thinking must recognize that ethnic-sensitive social work practice, cultural awareness in the human services, and culturally diverse social work practice are still in the process of development. Nevertheless, you should apply critical thinking to these approaches.

UNDERSTANDING THE HISTORY OF OPPRESSION AND OF OPPRESSED GROUPS

History is a great teacher of past achievements, mistakes, and failures, as well as lessons for the present and the future. It is a chronological narrative of a series of events that reflect cause and effect or circular repetition. We should not be sentenced to repeat the mistakes of the past but strive to overcome present and future challenges with a historical perspective, by asking critical questions about people, events, and happenings in order to gain an accurate picture of the circumstances. In short, history is a record of the past that has implications for the present and future.

The history of African, Latino, Asian, and Native Americans reaches into the oldest existing civilizations in the world. The history of these groups in the United States represents only a four-hundred-year fraction of their cultural past.

The theme of oppression features prominently in the American experience with ethnic minority groups. Oppression occurs when one segment of the population keeps another segment from obtaining social, economic, political, and related human rights through institutional practices and social stratification. The dynamics of oppression involve the oppressor, with presumed power and control, and the oppressed, who is powerless. The victimization of the oppressed by the oppressor or oppressive forces occurs in a social and political context.

Oppression began in the United States with the concept of Republicanism (Takaki, 1990), which advocated the virtuous self-control of the American population during colonial times. Morality, education, and virtue were the hallmarks of the white American male. Women were the bearers of children, the property of their husbands and the teachers of their male offspring. African-American

---

The Hernandez Family: A Case Study

Critical thinking is a major tool to uncover our practice approach to the Hernandez family. It is appropriate to critically analyze the rationale behind how the social worker deals with clients. Critical thinking helps us to question and justify what we do as social work practitioners. With critical thinking as a form of reflection, we have an opportunity to think about what we are doing before we engage the client in the social work helping process.

Among the critical thinking aspects of theory related to this case are:

- A historical perspective on social work theory. From a historical perspective, one could assert that the theory of historical oppression applies to the economic and social struggle of the Hernandez family. They represent the legal immigrant minority poor of this country.
- Client, worker, and change process assumptions of social work theory. From a client, worker, and change process perspective, critical thinking advocates the use of indigenous cultural change prac-

tices that arise from the Latino community rather than traditional middle-class social work interventions.

- Theory application to specific problems, clients, or settings. From a theory application perspective, it is important to develop a culturally diverse social work practice approach that uses cultural beliefs, behavior, and mutual assistance. The Hernandez family believes in helping members of the extended family who in turn aided them. The Latino community operates under mutual obligation through religious, employment, and educational resources.

TASK RECOMMENDATIONS

- Discuss the meaning of critical thinking and its application to the issues of the Hernandez family in a cultural competency context.
- Are the critical thinking issues (such as historical oppression, indigenous cultural practice, and mutual obligation and assistance) relevant to the Hernandez family?

---

slaves were inferior, while Native Americans were savage (a term used by the English to describe the Irish in their country before the settlement of the Americas).

The history in America of African, Latino, Asian, and Native Americans reveals a number of common themes:

- African, Latino, Asian, and Native Americans were exploited for their land and cheap labor and became subservient to white Americans from social, economic, and political perspectives.
- Treaties and laws were enacted that either removed these groups from land or barred them from immigration into the United States.
- African, Latino, Asian, and Native Americans lived in segregated, isolated communities—such as reservations, Harlem, or Chinatown—and were barred from equal education, employment, and housing opportunities.

The Hernandez Family: A Case Study

History is a source of knowledge as we strive to learn from the past. Ethnic minorities have historically been oppressed. Mr. and Mrs. Hernandez are a part of this history affecting poor Latinos.

Mr. and Mrs. Hernandez are legal immigrants from Mexico who live in the barrio. They speak little English and have relatives who recently migrated from Mexico like themselves. Mr. Hernandez is a hard-working gardener, while Mrs. Hernandez works part-time in a laundry. Thus, both are service workers. His-

torically, Latinos have been sources of cheap labor who were exploited in low-paying jobs. These dynamics of oppression are still seen in the Hernandez family.

TASK RECOMMENDATIONS

- Are historical remnants of oppression operating in the Hernandez family background?
- Can the Hernandez family be liberated from socioeconomic oppression?
- Can the Hernandez children have a better life than their parents?

- Ethnic minority groups used the legal court system in their struggle for civil rights and equal justice under the law.
- Poverty, family fragmentation, and social dysfunction are major symptoms of class stratification affecting the black underclass, reservation Indians, Mexican farm workers, and recent waves of Southeast Asian refugees.

Takaki (1990) offers a negative and a positive view of ethnic history in Competency Study 4.3.

COMPETENCY STUDY 4.3

Historical Fall and Rise

The final decade of the 20th century may draw some parallels: racial and class divisions are widening, new immigrants from Asia and Latin America are encountering a resurgence of xenophobia, the economy is in deep difficulty, and the age of global ascendancy for America—our national "frontier" in the world economy—is coming to an end. Measured against world production, the economy has begun to experience relative decline. The trade deficit has ballooned, and this nation, once the world's largest creditor, has suddenly found itself the world's largest debtor country. As a "great power," according to historian Paul Kennedy, the United States has begun to "fall."

Such tragic moments compel us to pause—to wonder where we are going as a multiracial America. They also urge us to imagine what kind of society we could have in the next century if we spent 60 cents of every dollar in taxes for social programs and the rebuilding of our inner cities rather than for Stealth bombers and MX missiles, if we reoriented our research and development from armaments to consumer goods for the international market and so revitalize America's economy, and if we "re-visioned" American's past and future in all of its racial and ethnic diversity. (pp. 292, 309–310)

A major task in the area of gaining knowledge for cultural competency is an investigative study and analysis of oppression on a group-by-group basis. The historical remnants of oppression are still a part of contemporary social history.

KNOWLEDGE ON GENDER AND CULTURAL DIVERSITY

Multicultural feminist theory is concerned with women of color (African, Latino, Asian, and Native Americans) in the United States. Major contributions to studies on women of color have been made in texts by Mirkin (1994) and Comas-Diaz and Greene (1994). Along with the development of texts on women of color, an alternative knowledge base (social constructionism) has emerged that relies on personal narratives of experiences of individual women of color and lays the basis for establishing some common themes (Holland, Gallant, and Colosetti, 1994; McNamee & Gergen, 1992; Radtke & Stam, 1994). Moreover, white feminist therapy has recognized that racial, ethnic, social class, and related issues need to be addressed along with gender opposition (Greene, 1994; Kliman, 1994; Kopacsi & Faulkner, 1988).

During the seventies and eighties, there was limited research on ethnically related gender differences and feminist issues in culturally diverse populations due to the domination of feminist therapy by white women writers. Gender oppression and therapeutic solutions to these issues dominated the scene at the expense of admitting the problem of ethnic/racial oppression and its resulting consequences in the lives of women of color. During the nineties there was a gradual dawning of awareness that racial, ethnic, and cultural factors were just as important as gender oppression for women. Moreover, women of color practitioners (Aguilar & Williams, 1993; Collins, 1990; Comas-Diaz & Greene, 1994; Greene, 1994; and Kliman, 1994) began to reflect and write on the unique problems and issues facing multiethnic and culturally diverse female clients. These contributions represented crucial components of the women of color mosaic that delineate particular helping approaches.

Regarding the etiology of a multicultural feminist perspective, Brown (1990) analyzed the limitations of existing feminist therapy and the need for multicultural theory building. On the one hand, feminist therapy and feminist therapy theory were developed by white women who excluded diversity issues, which were the concerns of women of color, poor or working-class women, and non–North American women. Past feminist therapy theory was based on a sociological description of the external reality and social context (that is, gender and societal oppression) and a phenomenological recollection of the lived and inner reality of women's life experiences. Both approaches describe the interactive relationships of internal and external realities of predominantly white working-class and middle-class women.

Brown, on the other hand, advocated the development of an alternative culturally diverse gender knowledge. There are four goals of multicultural feminist therapy theory:

- The creation of a multicultural, nonwhite and non-Western feminist data base reflecting the varieties of female experiences, connected with research questions and data gathering that are guided by a feminist consciousness.
- The deemphasis of gender oppression as the primary central issue for women of color, poor women, and women from non-Western cultures and the inclusion of multicultural female socialization experiences, which may vary according to ethnic and cultural factors.
- The search for how internal reality is shaped by diverse external experiences utilizing phenomenology (observable reported experiences) and introspection (personal sharing of an ethnic-cultural perspective in relationship to one's culture of origin and participation in the dominant society) as tools for theory development.
- The acknowledgment of cultural factors outside the control of particular group members that shape the internal experiences of individual women related to a particular ethnic group and become symbolic representations of how women accept culturally defined roles and yet transcend them to become liberated persons in their cultural society.

Yet Brown (1990) warns educators and practitioners concerned with cultural diversity:

> If we do not soon undertake the process of making feminist theory a multicultural theory, we may lose our chance and become yet another white, exclusionary system. Some therapists who are women of color and feminist in their theoretical perspectives have refused to take on an identification with feminist therapy in part because of its overly white bias, and in part because feminist political theory has seemed to deny to women of color the importance of their racial and cultural identities. (p. 17)

However, we believe that we must move beyond refusal and criticism of past feminist theory and forge ahead with the development of systematic multicultural knowledge that addresses understanding and helping women of color in their personal growth and life development.

At the same time, most feminist groups in the nineties recognize the need for a multicultural emphasis that addresses racism, social class inequality, and homophobia along with sexism. Renzetti and Curran (1995) state:

> If the movement is to remain strong and make up ground lost as a result of the conservative backlash of the 1980s, then the needs and experiences of diverse groups of women must not just be taken into account by the powers that be within feminism, they must reshape the focus and course of the movement itself. (p. 566)

As mainstream feminists incorporate multicultural concerns, there must be adequate literature on women of color.

Morris (1993) identifies five challenges facing women of color: societal oppressions, interacting oppression, family bonds and oppression of men of color, stereotypes and myths, and power differentials. Song (1995) has developed a helping process-stage approach that addresses women of color in particular and is equally applicable to women and men in general. The women-centered perspective focuses on five psychosocial stages (before the dawning, awakening, immersion, emergence, and woman-centered action) that reflect the multicultural woman's journey of awareness and growth and afford a treatment approach for multicultural women who are confronted with the issues of sexual harassment, spousal abuse, family violence, and related areas.

- The *before-the-dawning* stage reflects the acceptance of women of their traditional social roles imposed by the male-dominated culture. Physical, mental, and sexual abuse and related painful experiences are denied or carefully hidden. Women come to the conclusion that they are bound to lose, which sets up a psychology of defeatism and strengthens male domination and control.
- During the *awakening* stage, women begin to question their state of existence. They become increasingly aware that things are not right with the world, they experience a growing sense of anger, bitterness, restlessness, and dissatisfaction with the present situation, and they search for alternative ways of relating.
- The *immersion* stage is characterized by submergence of personal values, priorities, and beliefs, and searching for an emerging alternative value system. There is a conviction that change must come and that present assumptions and stereotypes about gender differentiation must be reconsidered.
- The *emergence* stage calls women to take responsibility and make choices about personal alternatives. Women view patriarchal relations rather than individual men as the primary target for change and acknowledge the importance of the class dimension of women's oppression.
- During the *woman-centered action* stage, women recognize their own personal needs and priorities and commit themselves to work for social change in ways appropriate for women as individuals. It is a liberation philosophy promoting the nurturance of the self as well as concern with collective well-being. It is concerned with ending domination, resisting oppression, and providing equality of opportunity for all women.

Integral to the woman-centered action stage, Lum (1995) has added four resource levels related to the individual woman, the family, the group, and the community. Under each resource level are four related themes of ethnic/gender identity, family interactions, social network, and cultural strengths. This women-centered perspective is committed to the liberation of women and men from class oppression, work alienation, and a corrupt male-dominated culture. There is a present need to listen to one another, to realize the need to transcend the present patriarchal system, and to forgive each other. At the same time, in several cultures, especially among traditional Latino women, there is a need for discretion as women redefine their place in the world of the family, extended family, and neighborhood systems. Rather than imposing a feminist agenda on the family, a multicultural woman may have to pace change in rhythm with how much she can risk losing the support of her traditional family and cultural systems.

In Competency Study 4.4, GlenMaye (1998) offers some practical ways that social workers can empower women.

COMPETENCY STUDY 4.4

Empowering Women

1. Practitioners must acknowledge and understand the role of oppression in the lives of women. This understanding will grow as practitioners themselves undergo the process of personal and political consciousness raising.
2. The empowerment of women requires an environment of safety, trust, and support in which women are encouraged to believe in themselves and their own reality and to find their voice to speak their truth. The presence of other women is integral to the creation of this environment.
3. Women must be given concrete opportunities to experience their own capability, strength, and worth. For instance, women who have experienced physical assault should be encouraged to find ways to experience bodily and emotional strength, and women who have experienced social indignities and assaults, such as homelessness, poverty, or racism, should be presented with opportunities to regain dignity and worth.
4. Though empowerment for women is fundamentally related to autonomy and self-determination, women must also work together to change themselves and society. Rather than work merely for individual solutions to individual problems, practitioners must find ways to bring women together and to work with women clients toward social change.
5. The many roles of the practitioner in empowerment practice include educator, supporter, advocate, activist, option clarifier, facilitator of concrete experiences of power, and model of lived empowerment. (pp. 49–50)

Nonsexist resocialization involves enacting liberating changes in family, education, religion, economy, and politics while preserving the best of traditional social values. To this end, we hope that gender barriers will be removed and that the potentials of women and men as respected and genuine persons will be realized in significant ways.

KNOWLEDGE OF CULTURALLY DIVERSE VALUES

Values are beliefs about preferred choices that govern conduct, life decisions, and related normative action by individuals, families, groups, and society. Social institutional values are broad in nature and protect and promote social well-being and the public good. Individual values are personal idiosyncratic choices

---

CULTURAL COMPETENCY IN ACTION

The Hernandez Family: A Case Study

Mrs. Hernandez is a quiet, unassuming Latina who cares for her family, goes to mass at a nearby Catholic church, and works part-time to supplement her husband's income. Mrs. Hernandez's pride is in her children and home. Later she attends an English as a second language class and gains a measure of success and independence in some English fluency. However, as a woman of color, there are several areas of growth for Mrs. Hernandez.

TASK RECOMMENDATIONS

Using the five psychosocial stages of Song's women-centered perspective, suggest a plan for Mrs. Hernandez that reflects a personal journey of awareness and growth and a realistic appraisal of changes in her family roles.

• Before-the-dawning stage (traditional social role for Mrs. Hernandez imposed on her by Latino cultural expectations).

• Awakening stage (questioning of Mrs. Hernandez's present existence and alternative ways of relating to her situation).

• Immersion stage (Mrs. Hernandez's search for an alternative value system and accompanying changes).

• Emergence stage (Mrs. Hernandez's assumption of responsibility and choices about personal and family alternatives).

• Woman-centered action stage (opportunity for social change and equal opportunity, self-nurturing, and collective well-being for Mrs. Hernandez).

In the midst of growth, Mrs. Hernandez is shaping her ethnic and gender identity, maintaining family interactions and social network, and experiencing cultural strengths. How can she emerge as a woman without alienating her family, culture, and community?

---

based on the orientation of the person and influential significant others such as peers, parents, and family members. Cultural values are rooted in ethnic, religious, and generational beliefs, traditions, and practices, which influence individual and social values. In strong traditional communities, cultural and religious values are the basis for how community members interact with each other.

Knowledge of culturally diverse values is part of cultural competency. The 1997 National Association of Social Workers Code of Ethics has several sections on cultural competence and social diversity:

1.05 (a) Social workers should understand culture and its function in human behavior and society, recognizing the strengths that exist in all cultures.

1.05 (b) Social workers should have a knowledge base of their clients' cultures and be able to demonstrate competence in the provision of services that are sensitive to clients' culture and to differences among people and cultural groups.

1.05 (c) Social workers should obtain education about and seek to understand the nature of social diversity and oppression with respect to race, ethnicity, national origin, sex, sexual orientation, age, marital status, political belief, religion and mental or physical development.

There is a range of culturally diverse values. However, five values are central to our discussion: family, respect, harmony, spirituality, and cooperation.

The multicultural *family* revolves around interdependent collective and/or hierarchical structures. The family is the basic transmitter of cultural values and traditions. It is the source of ethnic identity from biological, psychological, and social perspectives. In many ethnic families, the individual's sense of freedom and choice are subsumed under the good of the family as a whole. The individual family member is interdependent, not independent of or dependent on the family. The family may operate on a collective, extended basis with nuclear/extended family systems or similar social networks. The collective nature of the multicultural family fosters mutual support and may center around a hierarchical authority figure such as a parent, grandparent, or godfather.

Closely related to the value of family is the concept and practice of *respect*. The word *respect* comes from the root word *respicere*, which has a past tense meaning (to look back on) and a present tense understanding (to look at). The implied meaning is that one shows honor and regard for those who are held in high esteem in the past and the present. Many cultures express respect for ancestors. Latinos often name children in honor of past and present relatives, while Asians reverently remember their parents and grandparents in ancestor worship. Native Americans have undergone spiritual quests to communicate with the spirits of their ancestors, while African Americans have communed with their deceased love ones in quiet and prayerful conversations.

Respect is shown toward father and mother, older relatives and adults, and people in general. Polite manners, formal address, and deference of children to the wishes of parents are manifestations of respect in African and Latino American cultures. Respect for the personhood of people cornmunicates a sense of reverence for life, which is an important value for Asian and Native American traditional cultures.

Harmony is a sense of congruity and agreement in feelings, action, ideas, and interest within and between persons. *Harmony* comes from the Greek word *harmos*, which means a fitting or joining. For Native Americans, harmony is essential to maintain balance in the universe. Illness is the absence of harmony or an imbalance in the body or in relations to self, others, and the world. For Asian Americans, harmony or peace is important to maintain, rather than conflict or disharmony, in ethnic group relationships. Harmony is a part of individual and group continuity rather than alienation. As a result, many Asian Americans avoid confrontation and defer argumentation to maintain a higher order: interpersonal harmony.

Spirituality refers to a personal sense of meaning and purpose based on belief in a transcendent cosmic Being or Ultimate Truth. Spirituality may encompass a

---

CULTURAL COMPETENCY IN ACTION

The Hernandez Family: A Case Study

Cultural values are held beliefs that assist clients of color to function in their communities as they interact with family, friends, and neighbors. We identify the important values of family, respect, harmony, spirituality, and cooperation. As a social worker Mr. Platt has uncovered these values in the Hernandez family:

- Strong sense of family: hard-working father, caring mother, family as the center of life.
- Mutual respect: father's concern for the social and educational well-being of his son, division of labor in parental-sibling roles.
- Harmonious relationship: minimal conflict, ability to get along with each other, parental response to the concerns of Ricardo's teacher.

- Spiritual practice: mother goes to church, family goes to Catholic Social Service for follow-up referral.
- Cooperation: father and mother work with the social worker to resolve family problems.

TASK RECOMMENDATIONS

- Discuss the importance of such values as family, respect, harmony, spirituality, and cooperation and provide further examples in the Hernandez family.
- Describe practical ways in which the social worker can mirror these values in his relationship with this family.

---

sense of morality or a personal code of ethical behavior. African, Latino, and Asian Americans traditionally have practiced their spirituality in an institutional religious setting through ethnic churches. Native Americans have combined cultural and spiritual rituals of cleansing and healing through ceremonies presided over by a medicine man.

Cooperation is a value that brings ethnic families and groups together in a common sense of purpose. For African Americans, cooperation or pooling of resources is essential for survival in terms of housing, child care, and related necessities of life. For Latino Americans, cooperation involves helping extended-family members who are immigrant newcomers or working together on church and community projects. Japanese Americans have worked together to support legal, political, and social causes in the local Asian community through local churches and legal rights organizations such as the Japanese American Citizenship League. Among Native Americans, there is a sense of purpose when Indian people celebrate their cultures in pow-wows and sweat lodge ceremonies and run Indian gaming casinos for the good of the tribe.

There are many more values that are important to each ethnic group beyond these five values. Values reflect a range of cultural beliefs, practices, and behaviors that come from ethnic traditions. Culturally competent social workers must understand and respect these cultural values, which are essential to the well-being of people of color.

EMERGING THEORIES

Systems theory, psychosocial theory, role theory, family theory, and conflict theory can all be drawn upon in culturally diverse social work practice. At the micro level (problem-solving/task-centered, existential, crisis, empowerment) social work practice has embraced working with individuals, families, and small groups, and related individual-oriented theories. Lum (1996, Chapter 7) details these intervention strategies.

The emerging theory known as social constructionism has an inductive approach that asks open-ended questions about a person's life experiences. Pieper (1994) has moved research-oriented social work practice toward a naturalistic and qualitative compatibility with social constructionism.

Social Constructionism: Definition and Characteristics

Social constructionism is an emerging theory that emphasizes the situational interchanges between people, particularly the historical and cultural influences on how a person's world is constructed. The ways that a person describes his or her experiences and activities are important ingredients in constructing an understanding of an individual. The term *social constructionism* alludes to these aspects of social interaction among and between persons.

Norton (1993) introduces the social construction of meaning and ecology as an epistemology of social cognition. People use the ecology of their environment to construct meaning for themselves based on their experiences. Relationship stages are a part of a person's life development. Norton (1993) describes how children construct meaning as a part of their families.

> Children who are immersed in the environment of their families and neighborhoods begin to build on their perceptions about their world and gradually construct what is reality to them. The content of that construction is determined by their personalities in interaction with their social, physical, linguistic, historical, and cultural experiences determined primarily by their families. The children extract information from these experiences at all levels and organize it into schemas that are consistent with their personalities. These schemas help them make sense out of the environment. The process is both interdependent and circular, with the environment and the individual influencing each other. This construction of meaning largely determines the children's behavior. (p. 84)

The individual constructs a world view from life experiences throughout the life span.

Social construction theory has been applied to persons (Gergen & Davis, 1985) in the helping relationship. Therapy is seen as a process of social construction. The following principles are important in this process.

• Social construction encourages a therapeutic conversation or dialogue where the therapist and client undergo a mutual search for understanding and exploring problems. It involves a "talking with" rather than a "talking to" one another. There are new narratives, open spaces for conversation and "not-yet-said" stories (Anderson & Goolishian, 1992).

• In social construction, the therapist adopts a "not-knowing" position or takes on an open, inquiring stance of wanting to know about what has been said, being informed by the client, and joining a mutual exploration of the client's understanding and experience (Anderson & Goolishian, 1992).

• The personal narrative or the story about one's life describes individual problems that provide an opportunity to enter this person's world. Important in the narrative is the client's language and problem metaphors. Anderson and Goolishian (1992, p. 37) explain: "Telling one's story is a re-presentation of experience; it is constructing history in the present. The re-presentation reflects the teller's re-description and re-explanation of the experience in response to what is not known by the therapist. Each evolves together and influences the other, as well as the experience, and thus, the re-presentation of the experience." Epston, White, and Murray (1992, p. 97) state: "The 'story' or 'narrative' provides the dominant frame for live experience and for the organization and patterning of lived experience. Following this proposal, a story is a unit of meaning that provides a frame for lived experience. It is through these stories that lived experience is interpreted. We enter into stories; we are entered into stories by others; and we live our lives through these stories." This discourse with others is a co-construction of two persons and a framework for lived experience.

• The focus of helping is an interpersonal construction process and a context for problem-solving, evolution, and change. The emphasis is on the interpersonal and social dynamics and processes in the experience between the therapist and the client (Froggeri, 1992).

• Social construction has drawn on cultural assumptions and frameworks to express stories relevant to the individual (Sivan, 1986). The individual may use cultural themes and attributes from relatives and community leaders or interpret events and experiences based on cultural patterns. These cultural influences are housed in the mind of the individual who carries and uses them (Geertz, 1973; Parker & Shotter, 1990).

• The practitioner offers a client alternative themes to make sense of experiences and encourages self-observation, reflections, and developments. The client may reflect on patterns, explore alternatives, and understand experiences in a self-help approach that is a different response to the past. Both parties help to make sense out of daily experiences with others in relationship. This is the re-storying of life stories (Holland, Gallant, & Colosetti, 1994).

• Social work practice has emphasized the need to focus on client strengths and capacities and to develop meaning and direction to deal with the issues of daily living. This leads to empowerment or mastery of challenges. The client's own strengths, energy, and insights become resources for learning. Holland, Gallant, and Colosetti (1994, pp. 49–50) observe: "The constructivist approach to teaching social work practice emphasizes the student's strengths, rather than deficits, emphasizes exceptions or times when problems were not overwhelming, and builds upon those times when something the student tried did work effectively."

In Competency Study 4.5, Holmes (1992) discusses empowerment research and focuses on the story narrative and strengths perspective, which are related themes of social constructionism.

COMPETENCY STUDY 4.5

Life-Story Narratives

Empowerment research in social work attempts to identify sources and varieties of, and the means to extend, participatory competence. Romanyshyn (1982) argued that human psychological life is characterized not by fact but by story. Stories are autobiographical "I" narratives of personal meaning (Goldstein, 1986, p. 355). As Sacks (1987) expressed it, "We have, each of us, a life-story, an inner narrative—whose continuity, whose sense, *is* our lives" (p. 110). Life stories are vital to social work's understanding of how the individual perceives his or her life condition in relation to having or not having power to act. Ideally, the social work encounter and social work research help client groups understand their own strengths and potentials to alter or embellish definitions of life as lived. And as life is lived, we can assist client groups to redefine their experience of the world, to act within it from a position of greater human potential and power. (p. 164)

Application to Culturally Diverse Practice

Social construction theory facilitates several avenues to working with people of color. It highlights the importance of the cultural perspective of clients in terms of their world view and interactions with other people. Cultural beliefs, customs, and traditions learned from parents, family, and extended family are crucial connections to understanding how multicultural clients react and respond to normal problems of living and to crisis situations. Cognitive beliefs, affective feelings, and behavioral actions can be traced back to cultural learning from the family as it interacts with a friendly or hostile environment.

Social construction emphasizes the value of narratives or life experience stories, where the practitioner and the client talk with each other. In many cultures, information about the client and the problem situation is communicated indirectly through story. Indeed, the life of a client is a story of the past, present, and future that is unfolding. The story of a person of color contains ups and downs, joys and concerns, heartbreak and happiness.

As the story unfolds, the practitioner and client endeavor to bring meaning to what has happened in the client's life. It is particularly important to highlight the strengths rather than the pathology of the person. Building on the strengths enables a multicultural client to move forward and to make necessary changes based on affirmation of self and self-empowerment of culture and person. In these ways, social construction theory includes many emerging themes associated with culturally diverse social work practice.

The Hernandez Family: A Case Study

Social constructionism as a theory teaches that persons construct meaningful experiences and relationships from the environment. Among the principles relevant to the Hernandez case are:

- Therapeutic conversation: a mutual search for understanding and exploring problems, which is part of contact and problem identification; the emergence of new and yet-to-be told stories.
- Open, inquiring stance: no presuppositions or assumptions on the part of the worker; the client as the information giver.
- Personal narrative and story telling of life experiences: many cultures communicate thoughts, feelings, and actions through telling one's story; the content, expression, and personal style of story telling are as important as the story itself.
- Re-storying of life stories: the piecing together of various story segments into a coherent whole; the worker and the client cooperate in this process of

constructing the story into realistic connecting chapters.

- Client strengths and capacities: the ability to develop meaning, direction, and purpose; the will to persevere in the problems of daily living; the affirmation and empowerment of cultural self and family.

TASK RECOMMENDATIONS

- Describe how Mr. Platt could use the social construction approach with Mr. and Mrs. Hernandez and their children.
- Imagine the new stories, story telling, and personal narratives that might emerge from each member of the Hernandez family.
- Describe how Mr. Platt might help the family put their stories together in a coherent form so that the family understands past, present, and future segments.

THEORIES ON ETHNICITY, CULTURE, MINORITY STATUS, AND SOCIAL CLASS

Ethnicity, culture, minority status, and social class have been the focus of theories essential to culturally diverse practice. Devore and Schlesinger (1996) have emphasized ethnicity (ethnic reality) and social class (working, middle, and under classes) and have borrowed Gordon's (1973) term *ethclass* to describe the fusion between ethnicity and social class. Green (1995) has explained ethnicity in terms of its categorical and transactional features. The former relate to ethnicity as a combination of traits such as color, musical styles, foods, and sometimes poverty; the latter include relations across ethnic boundaries, ethnic distinctions, and individual management of ethnic identity. Iglehart and Becerra (1995) underscore the historical struggle of ethnic minorities who suffered discrimination, racial violence, and social/legal injustice as well as exclusion from the social work system. These themes are examined from social work practice and policy perspectives.

Ethnicity involves ancestry and racial origin, present membership in an ethnic family and community group, and future participation in generations of ethnic offspring. Ethnicity is a powerful unifying force that gives an individual a heritage and a sense of identity and belonging. From ethnicity flows a history of forebearers and country of origin, racial and language identity, family membership and participation, and social, economic, and religious ties to an ethnic community.

Culture is closely allied to ethnicity. However, it deals with prescribed ways of conduct, beliefs, values, traditions and customs, and related life patterns of a people or community group. Culture has a flexible range of applications. Cultural pluralism involves the coexistence and interrelations of various cultural communities with particular styles, customs, languages, and values. Bicultural conflict involves the tension and incongruities between the dominant culture and one's culture of origin in terms of values and behaviors. Traditional culture-of-origin parents and acculturated children who identify with the dominant culture are major players. Cultural duality contrasts the nurturing culture, which is part of the indigenous culture and provides psychological and social gratification and identity, and the sustaining culture, which provides the necessary goods and services for survival and is associated with the dominant culture.

Acculturation involves the adjustment and adaptation of the individual from the culture of origin to the dominant culture. Acculturation may or may not involve rejection of the culture of origin. Bicultural integration occurs where an individual evaluates aspects of both cultures and connects them in a functional way. Cultural barriers are societal and exist along a continuum from segregation (geographic, social, educational, and marital separation of races and socioeconomic classes) to assimilation (acceptance and adaptation into the dominant society, particularly in terms of social and marital inclusion).

Minority status relates to the inferior and unequal rank in power and access to resources of a subordinate and disadvantaged group in relation to the superiority in power and resources of the dominant majority. Racial myths and stereotypes, prejudice and discrimination are invented and practiced by the majority group. Legislation as well as civilian and military force are used to maintain the status quo. On the other hand, throughout the history of the United States, the courts and the legal system have been used to overturn unjust laws and practices on behalf of people of color, women, and gays and lesbians.

Shifts in population, political representation, and social policies and programs are occurring that have implications for minorities. People of color, specifically Latino Americans, are projected to be the numerical majority of the population in the 21st century. Political power, social policies, legislation, and programs have yet to shift in favor of the needs of ethnic minorities. With the white majority in control of political and economic power, it is doubtful that there can be major changes away from the status quo.

Social class is closely related to minority status because it addresses social stratification or the social hierarchical arrangement of persons based on economic, power, and status differences. People of color tend to be class-bound due to racial discrimination and socioeconomic constraints. Social class affects our perspective on life. Devore and Schlesinger (1996) observe:

> In the view of many, our perceptions of opportunities and constraints derive from class position, which affects family life, attitude toward sex, and extent of involvement in the world of politics and voluntary organizations. Our perceptions affect our views of the education our children receive, our marriages, and the other intimate relationships in which we are involved, as well as the importance we attach to what is happening in the world beyond our daily existence. (p. 61)

Social class distinctions reflect degrees of social inequality based on economic (wealth, income, consumption, occupation), social (influence, community power, group identification), and family status. These social boundaries reinforce the belief that ethnic groups are class-bound.

Minority status and social class reinforce negative determinism for people of color, who constantly struggle to transcend minority and class barriers and to move toward social equality and social justice. At the same time, ethnicity and culture are motivators and sources of strength for those who draw on their ethnic identity and cultural beliefs. Ethnicity, culture, minority status, and social class interact and are closely linked. The culturally competent worker must be aware of the dynamics of these four themes.

SOCIAL SCIENCE THEORY AND CULTURALLY DIVERSE SOCIAL WORK

Social work practice draws on a wide range of social theories because it serves a diverse target population with many needs. The culturally competent social worker is well read and broadly educated in the social sciences. The liberal arts approach to social work education prescribes background courses in psychology, sociology, anthropology, government, history, ethnic and women's studies, economics, and related areas. The continuous development of social science theory means translating it and applying it to the field of social work.

Social science theory is transmitted to and transformed by social work and filters through the social work education process to particular curriculum areas. Diversity and populations-at-risk are two content areas focused on in culturally diverse social work. Culturally competent faculty, program resources, and administrative leadership and commitment are necessary to translate social science theory into program realities for students of culturally diverse social work.

Cultural competency develops when faculty and program resources are committed to a multicultural approach. Ponterotto (1997) reports on a 22-item multicultural competency checklist survey of 66 program training directors regarding multicultural competency aspects of their programs (49 American Psychological Association accredited doctoral programs in counseling psychology and 17 non–APA-accredited programs). The accrediting body is the Council for Accreditation of Counseling and Related Educational Programs.

The survey was divided into six sections: (1) faculty, student, and staff minority representation; (2) multicultural curriculum content, teaching, and methods issues; (3) counseling field and supervision; (4) faculty and student research considerations; (5) student and faculty competency evaluation; and (6) physical environment of the program.

Of the 22 items, 10 items received affirmative responses from more than 60% of respondents. Under curriculum, 94% of the programs indicated that written and oral assessment methods were used to evaluate student performance and learning; 89% had a required multicultural counseling course; 89% used a diversity of teaching strategies and procedures; and 62% required or recommended one more multicultural course besides the required multicultural counseling course. Regarding research, 88% reported the use of quantitative and qualitative research methods in faculty and student research; 86% had at least a faculty member whose primary research interest was multicultural issues; 83% had clear faculty research productivity (journal publications and conference presentations) in multicultural issues; and 80% indicated faculty-student mentoring and coauthored work on multicultural issues, research, and dissertation topics. On student and faculty competency evaluation, 74% reported that multicultural issues were a part of student comprehensive examinations. Finally, on counseling practice and supervision, 73% indicated that multicultural issues were considered an important component of clinical supervision.

There were 7 items that received affirmative responses from fewer than 35% of respondents. Concerning minority representation, 33% stated that at least 30% of students were from racial/ethnic minorities; 29% of the programs had at least 30% of faculty members from racial/ethnic minorities; and 29% had 30% of support staff from racial/ethnic minorities. Regarding counseling practice and supervision, 20% had a faculty-student multicultural program leadership and support steering committee called a multicultural affairs committee. On student and faculty competency evaluation, 18% reported faculty teaching evaluations with items measuring the instructor's ability to integrate multicultural issues into the course and assessing faculty ability to make all students feel equally comfortable in class. Similarly, on physical environment, only 17% had a multicultural resource center where students could convene and use multicultural resources in a cultural diversity setting.

In a discussion of these findings, Ponterotto (1997) indicated strengths in multicultural research competency, infusion of cultural issues throughout the curriculum, student exposure to minority clients during the practicum, inclusion of multicultural issues on faculty and student evaluations, and the recruitment of more minority faculty members and students from an enlarged pool.

Along these lines, Ridley, Espelage, and Rubinstein (1997) have suggested a number of multicultural course topical areas: prejudice, racism, and power; psychological assessment and diagnosis; therapy process variables and outcome goals; intervention strategies; multicultural counseling research; racial identity development; ethical issues in multicultural counseling; and normative group information on the major racial/ethnic minority groups.

Multicultural counseling is in the process of setting up standards and program content for counseling psychology. Similar efforts in social work education have been structured since the late sixties. A modification of Ponterotto's multicultural competency checklist survey for social work education may reveal a similar pattern. Coverage of a body of knowledge about cultural diversity is an essential component of any social work program committed to cultural diversity in program structure, curriculum, and faculty-student representation.

Tools for Student Learning 4.1 measures your comprehension and retention of the essential emphases of this chapter. You should complete the test outside class and come prepared to review and discuss the items covered.

TOOLS FOR STUDENT LEARNING 4.1

Test of Knowledge Basic to Cultural Competency

This test covers the essential information included in Chapter 4. It is designed to measure the extent to which you have comprehended the various aspects of knowledge basic to cultural competency.

1. Define the following terms:

    a. *Knowledge* is _____

    _____

    b. *Theory* is _____

    _____

    c. *Ethnicity* is _____

    _____

    d. *Minority* is _____

    _____

    e. *Culture* is _____

    _____

    f. *Multiculturalism* is _____

    _____

    g. *Diversity* is _____

    _____

2. By the year 2000, what proportion of the U.S. population will be racial and ethnic minorities? (check one)

    ____ one fourth   ____ one third   ____ one half

3. By the year 2010, what percentage of the population will be racial and
   ethnic minorities in this country? (check one)

   ____ 51%   ____ 52%   ____ 55%   ____ 60%

4. Changing population trends affecting people of color are due to: (check
   appropriate ones)

   ____ immigration restrictions   ____ immigration patterns   ____ differential birthrates

   ____ overcounting minority groups ____ accurate census data   ____ family planning

5. What percentage of those entering the labor force are racial and ethnic
   minorities and women?

   ____ 50%   ____ 60%   ____ 70%   ____ 75%

6. *Critical thinking* is _____

   _____

   _____

   _____

7. Five interrelated skills that promote critical thinking for social workers,
   according to Mumm and Kerstling, are:

   a. _____

   b. _____

   c. _____

   d. _____

   e. _____

8. The three ethnic and cultural social work practice texts used to illustrate
   theory assumptions and pose critical thinking questions in this chapter
   are:

   a. _____

   b. _____

   c. _____

9. *Emic* means _____ while

   etic means _____

10. As a part of historical oppression, according to Takaki, Republicanism is

   _____

   _____

_____

_____

11. Three common themes of group history of oppression are:

    a. _____

    b. _____

    c. _____

12. According to Morris, the five multicultural feminist issues facing women of color are:

    a. _____

    b. _____

    c. _____

    d. _____

    e. _____

13 Song's five psychosocial stages of the women-centered perspective are:

    a. _____   b. _____

    c. _____   d. _____

    e. _____

14. A *value* is _____

    _____

15. Five multicultural values are:

    a. _____   b. _____   c. _____

    d. _____   e. _____

16. *Social constructionism* is _____

    _____

    _____

    _____

17. Culture, ethnicity, minority status, and social class are interrelated in the following ways:

    _____

    _____

    _____

18. On his multicultural competency checklist survey, Ponterotto found more than 60% agreement in the following areas: (check appropriate ones)

____ faculty, student, and staff minority representation

____ multicultural curriculum content, teaching, and methods issues

____ counseling field and supervision

____ faculty and student research considerations

____ student and faculty competency evaluation

____ physical environment of the program

19. On the same survey, Ponterotto found less than 35% agreement in the following areas: (check appropriate ones)

____ faculty, student, and staff minority representation

____ multicultural curriculum content, teaching, and methods issues

____ counseling field and supervision

____ faculty and student research considerations

____ student and faculty competency evaluation

____ physical environment of the program

Scoring: There are 50 items, and each item is worth 2 points.
   100–90 = excellent
   89–80 = good
   79–70 = fair
   69–60 = needs review
   59 and below = needs comprehension

SUMMARY

Knowledge about cultural diversity is a foundational component of cultural competency. This chapter has surveyed a wide range of cultural diversity knowledge for social work students and practitioners. Starting with basic terminology (*ethnicity, minority, culture, multiculturalism,* and *diversity*), it considered demographic trends, critical thinking, history of oppression, gender knowledge, values, the emerging theory of social constructionism, the themes of ethnicity, culture, minority status, and social class, and social science theory. These areas of knowledge are crucial to master in the development of cultural competency.

REFERENCES

Aguilar, M. A., & Williams, L. P. (1993). Factors contributing to the success and achievements of minority women. *Affilia 8* (4), 410–424.

Anderson, H., & Goolishian, H. (1992). The client is the expert: A not-knowing approach to therapy. In S. McNamee & K. J. Gergen (Eds.), *Therapy as social construction* (pp. 25–39). London: Sage Publications.

Atkinson, D., Morten, G., & Sue, D. W. (1993). *Counseling American minorities: A cross-cultural perspective.* Madison, WI: William C. Brown and Benchmark.

Brown, L. S. (1990). The meaning of a multicultural perspective for theory-building in feminist therapy. In L. S. Brown, & M. P. P. Root (Eds.), *Diversity and complexity in feminist therapy* (pp. 1–21). New York: Haworth Press.

Collins, P. H. (1990). *Black feminist thought.* Boston: Unwin Hyman.

Comas-Diaz, L., & Greene, B. (Eds.).(1994). *Women of color: Integrating ethnic and gender identities in psychotherapy.* New York: Guilford Press.

DeLaCancela, V., Jenkins, Y. M., & Chin, J. L. (1993). Diversity in psychotherapy: Examination of racial, ethnic, gender, and political issues. In J. L. Chin, V. DeLaCancela, & Y. M. Jenkins (Eds.), *Diversity in psychotherapy: The politics of race, ethnicity, and gender* (pp. 5–15). Westport, CT: Praeger.

Devore, W., & Schlesinger, E.G. (1996). *Ethnic-sensitive social work practice.* New York: Allyn & Bacon.

Dressel, P. L. (1994). . . . And we keep on building prisons: Racism, poverty and challenges to the welfare state. *Journal of Sociology and Social Welfare, 21,* 7–30.

Epston, D., White, M., & Murray, K. (1992). A proposal for a re-authoring therapy: Rose's revisioning of her life and a commentary. In S. McNamee & K. J. Gergen (Eds.), *Therapy as social construction* (pp. 96–115). London: Sage Publications.

Froggeri, L. (1992). Therapeutic process as the social construction of change. In S. McNamee & K. J. Gergen (Eds.), *Therapy as social construction* (pp. 40–53). London: Sage Publications.

Geertz, C. (1973). *The interpretation of cultures.* New York: Basic Books.

Gergen, K. J. (1985). The social constructionist movement in modern psychology. *American Psychologist, 40,* 266–275.

Gergen, K. J., & Davis, K. E. (1985). *The social construction of the person.* New York: Springer-Verlag.

GlenMaye, L. (1998). Empowerment of women. In L. M. Gutierrez, R. J. Parsons, & E. O. Cox (Eds.), *Empowerment in social work practice: A sourcebook* (pp. 29–51). Pacific Grove, CA: Brooks/Cole.

Goldstein, H. (1986). Toward the integration of theory and practice: A humanistic approach. *Social Work, 3,* 352–357.

Gordon, M. M. (1973). *Human nature, class, and ethnicity.* New York: Oxford University Press.

Green, J. W. (1995). *Cultural awareness in the human services: A multi-ethnic approach.* Boston: Allyn & Bacon.

Greene, B. (1994). Diversity and difference: Race and feminist psychotherapy. In M. P. Mirkin (Ed.), *Women in context: Toward a feminist reconstruction of psychotherapy* (pp. 333–351). New York: Guilford Press.

Gutierrez, L. (1992). Empowering clients in the twenty-first century: The role of human service organizations. In Y. Hasenfeld (Ed.), *Human service organizations as complex organizations* (pp. 320–338). Newbury Park, CA: Sage Publications.

Gutierrez, L., & Nagda, B. A. (1996). The multicultural imperative in human services organizations: Issues for the twenty-first century. In P. R. Raffoul & C. A. McNeece (Eds.), *Future issues for social work practice* (pp. 203–213). Boston: Allyn & Bacon.

Helms, J. E. (1994). How multiculturalism obscures racial factors in the therapy process. *Journal of Counseling Psychology, 41,* 162–165.

Holland, T. P., Gallant, J. P., & Colosetti, S. (1994). Assessment of teaching a constructivist approach to social work practice. *Arete, 18*, 45–60.

Holmes, G. E. (1992). Social work research and the empowerment paradigm. In D. Saleebey (Ed.), *The strengths perspective in social work practice* (pp. 158–168). White Plains, NY: Longman.

Iglehart, A. P., & Becerra, R. M. (1995). *Social services and the ethnic community.* Boston: Allyn & Bacon.

Kliman, J. (1994). The interweaving of gender, class, and race in family therapy. In M. P. Mirkin (Ed.), *Women in context: Toward a feminist reconstruction of psychotherapy* (pp. 25–47). New York: Guilford Press.

Kopacsi, R., & Faulkner, A. O. (1988). The papers that might be: The unity of white and black feminist. *Affilia, 3 (3)*, 33–50.

Leigh, J. W. (1998). *Communicating for cultural competence.* Boston: Allyn & Bacon.

Lum, D. (1995) *Woman-centered perspective framework.* Unpublished manuscript.

Lum, D. (1996). *Social work practice and people of color: A process-stage approach* (3rd ed.). Pacific Grove, CA: Brooks/Cole.

Matsumoto, D. (1996). *Culture and psychology.* Pacific Grove, CA: Brooks/Cole.

McGoldrick, M., & Giordano, J. (1996). Overview: Ethnicity and family therapy. In M. McGoldrick, J. Giordano, & J. K. Pearce (Eds.), *Ethnicity and family therapy* (pp. 1–27). New York: Guilford Press.

McNamee, S., & Gergen, K. J. (Eds.). (1992). *Therapy as social construction.* London: Sage Publications.

Mirkin, M. P. (Ed.). (1994). *Women in context: Toward a feminist reconstruction of psychotherapy.* New York: Guilford Press.

Morris, J. K. (1993). Interacting oppressions: Teaching social work content on women of color. *Journal of Social Work Education, 29*(1), 99–110.

Mumm, A. M., & Kerstling, R. C. (1997). Teaching critical thinking in social work practice courses. *Journal of Social Work Education, 33*, 75–84.

Norton, D. G. (1993). Diversity, early socialization, and temporal development: The dual perspective revisited. *Social Work, 38*(1), 82–90.

Ozawa, M. (1986). Nonwhites and the demographic imperative in social welfare spending. *Social Work, 31*, 440–445.

Parker, I., & Shotter, J. (Eds.). (1990). *Reconstructing social psychology.* London: Routledge.

Paul, R. (1992). Critical thinking: what, why, and how. *New Directions for Community Colleges, 77*, 3–24.

Pedersen, P. (1988). *Handbook for developing multicultural awareness.* Alexandria, VA: American Association of Counseling and Development.

Pieper, M. H. (1994). Science, not scientism: The robustness of naturalistic clinical research. In E. Sherman & W. J. Reid (Eds.), *Qualitative research in social work* (pp. 71–88). New York: Columbia University Press.

Ponterotto, J. G. (1997). Multicultural counseling training: A competency model and national survey. In D. B. Pope-Davis & H. L. K. Coleman (Eds.), *Multicultural counseling competencies: Assessment, education and training, and supervision* (pp. 11–130). Thousand Oaks, CA: Sage Publications.

Ponterotto, J. G., Casas, J. M., Suzuki, L. A., & Alexander, C. M. (Eds.). (1995). *Handbook of multicultural counseling.* Thousand Oaks, CA: Sage Publications.

Radtke, H. L., & Stam, H. J. (Eds.). (1994). *Power/gender: Social relations in theory and practice.* Thousand Oaks, CA: Sage Publications.

Renzetti, C. M., & Curran, D. J. (1995). *Women, men, and society.* Boston: Allyn & Bacon.

Ridley, C. R., Espelage, D. L., & Rubinstein, K. J. (1997). Course development in multicultural counseling. In D. B. Pope-Davis & H. L. K. Coleman (Eds.), *Multicultural counseling competencies: Assessment, education and training, and supervision* (pp. 131–158). Thousand Oaks, CA: Sage Publications.

Romanyshyn, R. D. (1982). *Psychological life: From science to metaphor.* Austin: University of Texas Press.

Sacks, O. (1987). *The man who mistook his wife for a hat and other clinical tales.* New York: Harper & Row.

Sarri, R. (1986). Organizational and policy practice in social work: Challenges for the future. *Urban and Social Change Review, 19,* 14–19.

Schriver, J. M. (1995). Human behavior and the social environment: Shifting paradigms in essential knowledge for social work practice. New York: Allyn & Bacon.

Simon, B. L. (1994). *The empowerment tradition in American social work.* New York: Columbia University Press.

Sivan, E. (1986). Motivation in social constructivist theory. *Educational Psychologist, 2,* 209–233.

Song, Y. I. (1995). *A women-centered perspective on Korean American women today.* Paper presented at the second joint symposium of Korean social worker educators in the United States and Korea, Soong-Sil University, Seoul, Korea.

Sue, D. W., Arredondo, P., & McDavis, R. J. (1992). Multicultural counseling competencies and standards: A call to the profession. *Journal of Counseling and Development, 70,* 477–486.

Takaki, R. (1990). *Iron cages: Race and culture in 19th-century America.* New York: Oxford University Press.

Williams, L. (1990). The challenge of education to social work: The case of minority children. *Social Work, 35,* 236–242.

CHAPTER FIVE

Skill Development

DOMAN LUM AND YUHWA EVA LU

This chapter will help you develop skills for culturally competent social work practice.

Generalist level:

- Understanding of how to overcome client resistance
- Knowledge of how to obtain client background
- Understanding of the concept of ethnic community
- Use of self-disclosure
- Use of a positive and open communication style
- Problem identification
- View of the problem in terms of want or need
- View of the problem in terms of levels
- Explanation of problem themes
- Excavation of problem details
- Assessment of stressors and strengths
- Assessment of all client dimensions
- Establishment of culturally acceptable goals
- Formulation of multilevel intervention strategies
- Termination

Advanced level:

- Design of social service programs in ethnic communities
- Understanding that services must be accessible
- Understanding that services must be pragmatic and positive
- Belief in the importance of recruiting bilingual/bicultural workers
- Participation in community outreach programs
- Establishment of linkages with other social agencies
- Fostering a conducive agency setting
- Involvement with cultural skill development research

Skill development is the creation of a repertoire of behaviors for the social worker to use in the helping situation. Skills represent the practical application of cultural awareness and knowledge. The word *skill* comes from the root word *skel*, which means the ability to separate or discern. In the helping sense, skills are practical tools for working with the client that have been discerned from knowledge of cultural diversity. Helms and Richardson (1997, p. 75) define skills as "the capacity to use awareness and knowledge to interact effectively with clients and colleagues regardless of their racial classification or cultural origins." Skills are applied at the interface between the social worker and the multicultural client.

Ridley, Espelage, and Rubinstein (1997, p. 140) speak about "culturally responsive skills," which reflect cultural sensitivity. A wide range of skills are identified: the ability to work with multiple roles and identities and multiple layers of environmental oppression (Comas-Diaz, 1994; Reynolds & Pope, 1991); advocacy and assertiveness training for women; identification of community resources for lesbian, gay, and bisexual clients (Fassinger & Richie, 1997); multicultural assessment, particularly process and outcome assessment (Dana, 1993); varied communication and intervention skills; and development of a therapeutic style (Fassinger & Richie, 1997).

Competency Study 5.1 identifies eight essential skills for working with multicultural clients (Giordano & Giordano, 1995).

Skills for Cultural Diversity

- *Assess the importance of ethnicity to patients and families.* To what extent does the patient identify with an ethnic group and/or religion? Is his or her behavior pathological or a cultural norm? Is the patient manifesting "resistance" or is his or her value system different from that of the therapist?
- *Validate and strengthen ethnic identity.* Under great stress an individual's identity can easily become diffuse. it is important that the therapist foster the client's connection to his or her cultural heritage.
- *Be aware of and use the client's support systems.* Often support systems—extended family and friends; fraternal, social, and religious groups—are strained or unavailable. Learn to strengthen the client's connections to family and community resources.
- *Serve as a "culture broker."* Help the family identify and resolve value conflicts. For example, a person may feel pride about some aspects of his or her ethnic background and shame about others, or there may be an immobilizing "tug of war" between personal aspirations and family loyalty.
- *Be aware of "cultural camouflage."* Clients sometimes use ethnic, racial, or religious identity (and stereotypes about it) as a defense against change or pain, or as a justification for half-hearted involvement in therapy. A person who says, "I'm late for our session because I'm on Puerto Rican time" may be trying to avoid a difficult issue.
- *Know that there are advantages and disadvantages in being of the same ethnic group as your client.* There may be a "natural" rapport from belonging to the same

"tribe" as your client. Yet, you may also unconsciously overidentify with the client and "collude" with his other resistance. Unresolved issues about your own ethnicity may be "mirrored" by client families, exacerbating your own value conflicts.

• *Don't feel you have to "know everything" about other ethnic groups.* Ethnically-sensitive practice begins with an awareness of how cultural beliefs influence all our interactions. Knowing your own limitations and ignorance and being open-heartedly curious will help set up a context within which you will have a mutual learning with your clients.

• *To avoid polarization, always try to think in categories that allow for at least three possibilities.* Consider, if you are exploring black and white differences, how a Latina might view it. Consider, if you are thinking of how African Americans are dealing with male–female relationships, how a black lesbian might view it. Consider, when exploring Italian/Irish differences, how an African American might think about them. (pp. 23–24)

In the following sections of this chapter, we cover types of skills, process-stage skill clusters, service delivery and agency linkage, design and implementation, and examples of skill development research.

TYPES OF SKILLS

Skill development is generally process-oriented in social work practice. Social work is seen as a process with a beginning, a middle, and an end, during which the worker exercises skills having to do with engagement, psychosocial assessment, intervention strategy, and termination/ending. These skills are applied to individuals, families, groups, organizations, and communities. Interviewing skills are strongly emphasized since social workers generally conduct the initial intake sessions for mental health and child and family services.

In Competency Study 5.2, Kadushin and Kadushin (1997) list a number of interviewing skills for the culturally sensitive interviewer.

Culturally Competent Interviewing Skills

COMPETENCY STUDY 5.2

1. The culturally sensitive interviewer approaches all interviewees of whatever cultural background with respect, warmth, acceptance, concern, interest, empathy, and due regard for individuality and confidentiality.

2. The culturally sensitive interviewer exerts maximum effort in the early part of the interview when the interviewee's mistrust and suspicion are highest, when the interviewer is apt to be perceived as a stereotype rather than an individual, and in terms of the interviewer's status as a representative of the mainstream culture rather than as a person.

3. Culturally sensitive interviewers strive to develop an explicit awareness that they have a culture as a member of a particular racial or ethnic, gender, age, and occupational group and as such have been socialized to be-

liefs, attitudes, behaviors, stereotypes, biases, and prejudices that affect their behavior in the interview.

4. Having achieved such awareness, culturally sensitive interviewers are comfortably undefensive in their identity as a member of a cultural group.

5. Culturally sensitive interviewers are aware of the cultural factors in the interviewee's background that they need to recognize and accept as potential determinants of the interviewee's decision to come for help, the presentation and nature of the problem the client brings, and the choice of intervention.

6. The culturally sensitive interviewer is ready to acknowledge and undefensively and unapologetically raise for discussion cross-cultural factors affecting the interview.

7. Culturally sensitive interviewers recognize that the great variety of culturally distinct groups makes it impossible to have knowledge of all of them but accepts the obligation to study the cultural background of interviewees most frequently served by their agency.

8. Culturally sensitive interviewers are ready to acknowledge the limitations of their knowledge of an interviewee's cultural background and are ready to undefensively solicit help from the interviewee in learning what they need to know.

9. The culturally sensitive interviewer communicates an attitude that cultural differences are not better or worse but rather legitimately diverse and respects such differences.

10. Culturally sensitive interviewers are aware of indigenous cultures' strengths, culturally based community resources that might be a source of help, and that some kinds of help may be culturally inappropriate.

11. Culturally sensitive interviewers are aware of the problems of disenfranchisement, discrimination, and stigmatization frequently associated with minority group status.

12. Although sensitive to cultural factors that might be related to clients' problems, the culturally sensitive interviewer is aware that such factors may be peripheral to the situation of a particular client, that personality factors may be of more significance than racial or ethnic cultural factors, and that culture does not adequately define the interviewee, who is unique. (pp. 347–348)

Bernard (1979) distinguishes three types of skills in the helping relationship: process skills, conceptualization skills, and personalization skills.

- Process skills refer to the following therapeutic techniques and strategies: opening the interview smoothly; using reflection, probing, restatement, summary or interpretation; helping the client say what is on his or her mind; using nonverbal communication to enhance verbal communication; implementing intervention strategies; and achieving closure.

- Conceptualization skills include deliberate thinking and case analysis abilities: understanding what the client is saying; identifying themes of the client's messages; recognizing appropriate and inappropriate goals; choosing strategies that are appropriate to the client's expressed goals; and recognizing subtle client improvement.

- Personalization skills have to do with learning observable and subtle behaviors, and with the personal growth of the worker, such as communicating authority in the helping relationship and taking responsibility for specialized knowledge and skills; hearing client challenges and feedback without becoming overly defensive; being comfortable with the client's feelings and attitudes; and respecting the client.

Process, conceptualization, and personalization skills are important skills to develop. Generally, process skills are the primary focus of skill building, because they provide the worker with tools to move the client through the helping process.

Conceptualization and personalization skills are generally developed in the student field practicum with agency supervision. An audiotape or a videotape assists the worker and the supervisor with cultivating such conceptualization skills as the analysis of verbal and nonverbal communication, processing of problem themes, goal setting, and selection of the intervention strategy. Careful supervision helps the beginning student worker with the development of conceptualization skills.

Likewise, personalization skills focus on the worker's response to the helping situation. It is important to process how the client affects the worker. "What were you feeling when the client said that she was ready to scream at her mother?" "What was happening to you when the client became angry and said that you were a lousy social worker?" Processing the worker's feelings of insecurity, threat, fear, and uncertainty are examples of developing personalization skills. The focus is to help the worker realize that the client may be projecting feelings intended for someone else. At the same time, the worker must own up to the feelings of the client who may need to confront the worker. Keeping composure and asking "What is going on in this exchange?" helps the worker to maintain an objective perspective in the situation.

The development of process, conceptualization, and personalization skills is essential for cultural competency and requires hours of supervision. In the next section, we turn to five process stages: contact, problem identification, assessment, intervention, and termination. Each stage encompasses a cluster of process, conceptualization, and personalization skills.

PROCESS, CONCEPTUALIZATION, AND PERSONALIZATION SKILL CLUSTERS

Lum's (1996) framework for social work practice with people of color is built around a systematic process-stage approach, following the classic formula of beginning, middle, and end. The beginning process stages are contact and problem identification; the middle stages include assessment and intervention; and the ending stage is termination. This section identifies the process skills necessary to move the multicultural client through these five stages, along with essential conceptualization and personalization skills.

Contact

Contact Process Skills

The establishment of the relationship between the social worker and the multicultural client is basic to the contact stage. Relationship building is the primary requisite for retaining the client. Culturally diverse contact has a skill cluster consisting of understanding the ethnic community, following a relationship protocol, engaging in professional self-disclosure, and developing an effective communication style.

Understanding the ethnic community means that the social worker has a working knowledge of the client community demographic profile. A social worker should be well versed in the history, problems, and profiles of an ethnic community. The worker can consult community study reports, but it is important to walk through a community and observe where people congregate and exchange information. Talking with people living in the community provides valuable knowledge about current issues facing residents. It is important to listen and gain information, while also establishing credibility as a reliable and believable person of integrity.

Relationship protocols are cultural ways of relating to a person of color. A protocol is a code of ceremonial formality and courtesies. In many cultures a relationship protocol is a prelude to conducting business. It may involve a formal greeting, inquiry about the health and well-being of family, and other friendly topics of conversation. It may be considered rude to proceed directly to the main order of business or to the presenting problem without proper protocol conversation. Following a relationship protocol involves the communication of respect and recognition to the head of household, grandparents, and other adults. It is important to practice a relationship protocol regarding the father and mother in a family situation, which means supporting their authority and roles rather than undermining their family influence.

Professional self-disclosure is an extension of the professional use of self, an important social work principle. Rather than hiding behind the professionalism of social work, the worker takes the initiative by disclosing an area of interest shared by the client. The intent is to become a real person and to humanize the relationship.

Finding out about the background of the client may open up appropriate topics of self-disclosure such as travel, children, cars, clothes, shopping, and other areas of common interest. Professional self-disclosure begins to create a sense of community and bonding between the worker and the client.

An effective *communication style* gives a positive message to the multicultural client. The agency environment sets the tone for the initial contact between the worker and the client. A friendly bilingual receptionist, an accessible location, an attractive facility, a private room, comfortable furniture, light refreshments, and a casual approach create a positive atmosphere. Body language, bilingual staff, use of a trained translator or interpreter who is on call, and familiarity with cultural mannerisms and gestures make for effective communication. Active listening responses that vary according to the content of the message and the feelings of the messenger should be used. Supportive, understanding, probing, interpreting, and evaluative (SUPIE) responses are examples of varying listening skills. (See Lum, 1996, Chapter 4 on listening skills.)

Hepworth, Rooney, and Larsen (1997) offer some thoughts on the importance and limitations of empathic communication in Competency Study 5.3.

Empathic Communication Contact Skills

COMPETENCY STUDY 5.3

The importance of knowledge of cultural factors was documented almost 30 years ago by the research findings of Mayer and Timms (1969), who studied clashes of perspectives between clients and social workers. Based on their findings they concluded: "It seems that social workers start where the client is psychodynamically but they are insufficiently empathic in regard to cultural components" (p. 38).

Although empathic communication is important in bridging cultural gaps, it can be used to excess with many Asian Americans and American Indians. Many members of these groups tend to be lower in emotional expressiveness than other client groups and may react with discomfort and confusion if a practitioner relies heavily on empathic communication. Still, it is important to "read between the lines" and to sensitively respond to troubling emotions that these clients do not usually express directly. Like other clients, they are likely to appreciate sensitive awareness by a practitioner to painful emotions associated with their difficulties. (p. 115)

Contact Conceptualization Skills

Ethnographic skills are important to conceptualization in the contact stage. *Ethnography* is derived from *ethnos* (people) and *graphics* (writings, drawing) and literally involves the recording (writing and drawing) of the behavioral culture of a person or a group of people. Ethnography is concerned with the words, thoughts, and feelings of the client from a participant observation stance.

Ethnographic skills have a number of parallels:

- Qualitative inductive survey research begins by framing a research question and interviewing a sample population without a priori assumptions. Likewise, ethnographic skills in the contact stage encourage open-ended questions about the client's family, work, children, and related background areas.
- Social constructionism focuses on life story or narrative and is interested in how a person has constructed his or her life from various pieces of experience. Again, ethnographic skills include the telling of life stories by the person, which is a familiar and nonthreatening way for a multicultural client to open segments of his or her life.

- Emic and etic understanding views the multicultural client from two perspectives. Emic understanding seeks to comprehend the unique particulars of the client in order to understand what sets the person apart from others in his or her culture. Etic understanding is concerned about the link between the client and his or her cultural group. Ethnographic contact skills cover these areas.

Green (1995) offers some practical suggestions about ethnographic interviewing:

- The social work interview must have a mutually accepted purpose and must focus on how the client uses language, what language suggests about the client's state of being and thinking.
- Our concern must be on the salient cultural data bearing on the presenting issue or the cultural context of the problem.
- It is important to understand the perspective of the client and how the client explains the veracity (truthfulness) of cultural expressions and communication.
- The client is our teacher who best explains cultural differences.

Green (1995, p. 146) explains: "The intent of ethnographic interviewing is . . . to recognize ideas, beliefs, and patterns of behavior in the contexts where they are meaningful—all as an aid to informed understanding of people's problems and appreciation of what one will have to do to effectively help resolve them." Contact conceptualization skills enable the worker to learn about the client in an inductive manner.

Contact Personalization Skills

What happens to the worker in the contact stage? The range of subjective feelings on the part of the worker may include normal anxiety and curiosity about the reasons for the client coming for help, positive interest in and empathy for the client, or uneasy feelings about the client due to manipulation, personal attack, racism, and other issues. The worker should constantly check his or her feelings and ask himself or herself: "What am I feeling and sensing as I listen to and interact with this client?" "What is the client's message?" "Am I able to help with the client's problems?" The worker needs to process these feelings and reactions both within himself or herself and with a supervisor or colleague. Subjective reflection about the first impressions of the client is a part of the personalization skills at the contact stage.

Problem Identification

Problem Identification Process Skills

It is crucial to spend as much time as possible cultivating contact in order to retain the multicultural client. However, the present problem eventually emerges

The Hernandez Family: A Case Study

Contact involves the process skills of establishing the relationship between the worker, Mr. Platt, and the Hernandez family as well as employing ethnographic conceptualization skills and reflecting on feelings and reactions as personalization skills. Contact process skills are the foundation of the relationship. The social worker should do the homework of understanding the ethnic community of the client.

In this situation, Mr. Platt should be familiar with the local Latino community. Relationship protocols are important to establish, such as formal greeting, friendly conversation, and respect for each family member. Professional self-disclosure reveals a common point of reference for both parties and is initiated by the social worker.

TASK RECOMMENDATIONS

- State the essential information about the local Latino community that Mr. Platt should know before he meets the Hernandez family.
- Give examples of the use of relationship protocols and professional self-disclosure between Mr. Platt and the Hernandez family.
- Suggest a number of open-ended ethnographic questions about the Hernandez family that Mr. Platt can pose on work, children, and other familiar and nonthreatening topics as beginning subjects for discussion.
- Anticipate the feelings and reactions of the worker after the first session with the family and process them in class.

and the worker must employ problem identification process skills. Among them are problem area disclosure, problem orientation, and identification of racial/ethnic themes.

Problem area disclosure is a skill based on the understanding that a multicultural client may have a difficult time expressing a problem directly to the worker. The client may feel shame and hesitation, and may have a guarded attitude toward disclosing family secrets to a stranger. Hepworth, Rooney, and Larsen (1997) acknowledge this resistance in Competency Study 5.4.

Problem Resistance

Revealing problems to others may be perceived as a reflection of personal inadequacy and as a stigma upon an entire family. The resultant fear of shame may thus impede the development of rapport with clients from this ethnic group (Kumabe, Nishida, & Hepworth, 1985; Lum, 1992; Tsui & Schultz, 1985). African Americans, Native Americans, and Hispanics may also experience difficulty in developing rapport because of distrust that derives from a history of being

COMPETENCY STUDY 5.4

exploited or discriminated against by other ethnic groups (Longres, 1991; Proctor & Davis, 1994).

Clients' difficulties in communicating openly tend to be even more severe when their problems involve allegations of socially unacceptable behavior, such as child abuse, moral infractions, or criminal behavior. In groups, the pain is further compounded by having to expose one's difficulties to other group members, especially in early sessions when the reactions of other members represent the threat of the unknown. (p. 45)

Instead the client may ask indirect questions ("I have this friend who has a problem. How would you help her?"), make oblique or circular comments that approach a problem in a slanted or peripheral way ("I don't know why I am here, but something is bothering me"), or make similar efforts toward problem disclosure. Part of the reason for this communication style may be that the person of color has learned to communicate with cultural understatement. Rather than spelling out all the negative details and unburdening one's self in humiliation, one learns to infer and allude to problem issues. In turn, the worker must read between the lines and piece together the inferences. As a result, it may be culturally more appropriate for the worker to figure out the problem, spell out the details, and ask for comments from the client, who is excused from disgracing himself or herself. A culturally competent social worker is able to pick up on this approach and decipher these indirect messages from the client.

Problem orientation is the core of problem identification. It views the problem as an unsatisfied want or an unfulfilled need (Reid, 1978) and interprets the problem in a positive light. The worker and the client reframe the problem and change the point of reference from negative pathology to positive want satisfaction or need fulfillment. This changes the orientation toward and perspective on the problem in the cognitive mind-set of the client. A problem becomes an opportunity for satisfaction and fulfillment. The culturally competent worker repositions the client and the problem by reframing the problem.

Racial/ethnic themes may be a part of problem identification. The culturally competent worker explores possible problem themes of racism, sexism, and homophobia (ideological beliefs), prejudice (attitude), discrimination (behavior), and expressions manifested in oppression, powerlessness, exploitation, acculturation, and stereotyping. Racism, sexism, and homophobia are related concepts that have similar dynamics: in-group/out-group, superiority/inferiority, domination/submission, power/powerlessness, systemic-institutional and individual. They are cognitive beliefs learned from parents, neighborhood, community, and society. Prejudice is a negative attitudinal and affective response based on prior cognitive belief, while discrimination is the behavioral response expressed as denial, refusal, and rejection. Racism, prejudice, and discrimination result in oppression, powerlessness, exploitation, acculturation, and stereotyping. These five expressions are played out in organizational and interpersonal ways between social institutions and victimized individuals (Lum, 1996). The culturally competent worker looks for racist dynamics that may be a part of the problem set.

CULTURAL COMPETENCY IN ACTION

The Hernandez Family: A Case Study

Problem identification process skills involves problem area disclosure (the particular way that the client may allude to the problem); problem orientation (the reframing of the problem as an unsatisfied want or an unfulfilled need); and the identification of racial/ethnic themes of racism, prejudice, and discrimination, which lead to oppression, powerlessness, exploitation, acculturation and stereotyping.

Problem identification conceptualization skills are concerned about the client's formulation of the problem from his or her cultural and linguistic perspectives. The conceptualization should be inductive and indigenous, arising from the cultural context of the client. Problem identification personalization skills concentrate on the worker's reaction to the problem to determine whether it is appropriate and natural.

The Hernandez family's problems are twofold: (1) Mr. Hernandez's two jobs, long hours, and economic burdens precipitated by having to support two families of in-laws who recently migrated from Mexico, and (2) Ricardo's academic and social problems at school, caused by the unavailability of Mr. Hernandez to help his son with his school work.

Task Recommendations

- Formulate some direct and indirect ways in which Mr. Hernandez might express his problems.
- Reframe the Hernandez family's problem in terms of an unsatisfied want or an unfulfilled need.
- Determine whether racism, prejudice, and/or discrimination are involved in the problem.
- Express how the Hernandez family members may describe the problem rather than a social work problem description.
- Suggest an appropriate personalized response to the problem on the part of the social worker, Mr. Platt.

Problem Identification Conceptualization Skills

Ethnographic problem identification skills involve how the multicultural client formulates the problem. Green (1995) explains his help-seeking behavior model, which relates four principles to problem identification and resolution: the individual's definition and understanding of an experience as a problem; the client's semantic evaluation of a problem from his or her language explanation; indigenous cultural strategies of problem intervention; and acceptable culturally based problem resolution.

These problem identification concepts provide a cultural context for inductive and indigenous problem identification that is not superimposed from the social worker's vantage point. It is important for the culturally competent worker to obtain the client's expression and explanation of the problem.

Problem Identification Personalization Skills

It is important for the worker to determine his or her own reaction to the problem. Does the problem shock the worker in its sensationalism or taboo nature?
Is the problem so overwhelming that the worker privately recognizes that problem resolution is not likely to happen? Is it better to sustain the client through
supportive maintenance than to push for a rapid solution? Is the problem a part
of a problem cluster that will take time to unravel, and should the worker direct
the client toward a series of modest solutions? These are some questions that the
culturally competent worker must consider in the problem identification stage.

Assessment

Assessment Process Skills

Assessment process skills involve a psychosocial perspective that analyzes environment and person (socioenvironmental impacts, psychoindividual reactions),
as well as cultural strengths and the spiritual dimensions of the culture. Assessment ought to uncover the resources available to the client, since *assessment* is
derived from the root word *asset*, which means worth, resources, and value.

The *psychosocial perspective* views the environment as socioenvironmental impacts and the person as psychoindividual reactions. This is especially helpful in
the assessment process, because the worker explains the concept of social/envi-
ronmental stressors impacting the individual and causing psychological stress
reactions (Lum, 1996). Interpreting this view to the client helps the worker to
keep this perspective of the interaction between environment and person. However, people of color experience these stress points in terms of newcomer acculturation, psychosomatic reactions, psychological identity issues, and related
survival adjustment concerns. Imparting this psychosocial perspective helps to
process and interpret assessment in practical terms.

Cultural strengths are a focus of social work assessment in line with the asset
resource understanding advocated by Saleebey (1992) and Cowger (1994). Although cultural strengths per se have not been addressed by Saleebey (1992) and
Cowger (1994), this assessment emphasis discovers internal strengths of the person and external ethnic group strengths from the culture. Examples of cultural
strengths are religious beliefs, historical achievements, ethnic pride, capacities
for endurance and hard work in the family, and related areas.

In Competency Study 5.5, Dupree, Spencer, and Bell (1997) write about the
need to promote resilient coping strategies among African-American children,
which has implications for all people of color.

COMPETENCY STUDY 5.5

African-American Children

Sources of stress, such as poverty and low socioeconomic status, neighborhood
dangers, and daily hassles, which are often prevalent in African American communities but not limited to these communities, reveal an increasing need for

innovative strategies with which to relate to these children and youth. Avoid thinking that the aforementioned factors reflect the experiences of the entire African American community. Similar cultural characteristics may be shared but they are in no way a homogeneous group. In fact, counseling with African American children and youth requires a case-by case, situation-specific approach. One of the goals of counseling with African American children and youth is to promote resilient coping strategies under unique circumstances. Therefore one should avoid using methods that encourage clients to accept their negative environmental circumstances and adapt to such an environment. Methods providing information that promotes the effective use of underutilized resources or resources that are unattainable within their community should be employed. Help-seeking strategies and greater social mobility will enable them to survive in their environment. (p. 258)

The cultural strengths perspective emphasizes the discovery of strengths in the person and the culture, the motivation toward perseverance and change based on inner strength and endurance, and the environment as full of resources at the family, group, and community levels.

The inclusion of cultural and spiritual assessment expands the concept of biopsychosocial assessment beyond the biological, psychological, and social categories to include cultural and spiritual dimensions. African, Latino, Asian, and Native American cultures recognize this interconnectedness. Part of culture is the spiritual and part of spirituality is the culture. Psychiatric cultural assessment (American Psychiatric Association, 1994) addresses cultural identity, cultural explanations of illness, psychosocial environmental levels of functioning, and cultural elements between the worker and the client. Indigenous to ethnic cultures are natural support systems that include significant other persons in families and extended families, as well as neighborhood, church, and ethnic community organizations. Although there may be cases of ethnic clients without natural support systems, these resources are generally available in ethnic community groups. The culturally competent worker should contact cultural network leaders and helping associations and link multicultural clients to them.

Regarding spiritual assessment, linking spirituality and social work is a growing movement in social work education and professional practice (Amato-von Hemert, 1994; Clark, 1994). Part of the movement recognizes the importance of religion and spirituality in people's life, while another part is active in churches and synagogues. From a cultural competency standpoint, it is appropriate to understand and explore past and present spirituality and religious faith in the life of the client. Of course, the worker should ask the client for permission to discuss these areas.

Assessment Conceptualization Skills

A culturally competent social worker must not equate assessment with using the *Diagnostic and Statistical Manual of Mental Disorders*. To do so is to give up the unique perspective of social work psychosocial assessment. Selling this birthright is a capitulation to psychiatric mental health assessment. Culturally sensitive assessment reinterprets and reconceptualizes psychosocial factors as socioenvironmental impacts and psychoindividual reactions; it also acknowledges cultural strengths and includes both the cultural and the spiritual (Lum, 1996). This extension of the conceptual framework used by psychologists should be included in any meaningful discussion of culturally sensitive assessment.

Green (1995, pp. 80–81) has some helpful recommendations for workers attempting to hone their assessment conceptualization skills:

- A worker should think about clients in terms of group characteristics and group strengths as well as clinical pathology and agency protocols of problem resolution.
- A worker should examine group strengths as they are understood by community members themselves, and should view the client as a potential teacher to the worker as well as the recipient of services.
- A worker should openly use indigenous sources of help, which may mean granting credence to lay practitioners from ethnic communities.
- A worker should have a systematic learning style and a supportive agency environment that recognize culturally distinctive modes of behavior and respond to them appropriately.

Assessment Personalization Skills

Psychosocial assessment provides an opportunity to evaluate the positive potential of the client. One must not be trapped into focusing on negative pathology. Cox and Ephross (1998) point out the need for a balanced assessment in Competency Study 5.6.

COMPETENCY STUDY 5.6

Balanced Assessment

Behaviors that could be characterized as pathological, such as viewing a social worker with great suspicion at a first meeting, may be adaptive and quite comprehensible when displayed by a person who has been denied rights or has been the victim of hate violence (Barnes & Ephross, 1995). Social stressors are often intense in minority communities, and people under stress behave in ways that have different meanings that need to be understood. Ethnic clients, in particular, need to be listened to carefully as they define from their perspective the problems they face. Social workers need to be careful, indeed, before assuming a stance that we know better than the client what the client needs.

At the same time, we are concerned that genuine and painful self-destructive pathologies not be concealed beneath a cloak of ethnic diversity. A simple theory of social causation can blind a worker to problems that can be solved and pathology that can be treated.

Effective assessment in social work practice requires balance and joint participation of client and worker to the maximum feasible point, empathic awareness of cultural differences, and the best, most trusting, communication possible. No one of these elements substitutes for another. Using the assumed or supposed characteristics of an ethnic group to solve a worker's own identity confusions or to express a worker's resentments against the majority culture can be harmful to ethnically identified clients. (pp. 35–36)

Assessment ought to mobilize positive resources that support change intervention strategies. In a pathology-oriented assessment, the worker is confronted with an extensive assessment work-up filled with client liabilities. How does one move from pathology assessment to change intervention? It increasingly becomes a dilemma for the social work professional.

In Competency Study 5.7, Hines and Boyd-Franklin (1996) cite the role and dilemma of the African American father.

African-American Fathers

COMPETENCY STUDY 5.7

The identity of African American fathers, regardless of income, is linked to their ability to provide for their families. Success in being a provider, however, often is limited by discrimination. Franklin (1993) introduced the concept of the "invisibility syndrome" to explain the marginalization of African American men. This refers to the paradox that White Americans, while keenly aware of Black Americans' skin color, fear them and treat them as if they were "invisible," thus denying African Americans validation and marginalizing them. Frequently therapists assume that Black fathers are absent and uninvolved, particularly if there has been no formal marriage. It also is not uncommon for therapists to overlook males in the extended family system, including the father's kinship network and the mother's male friends, who may be involved in the children's lives. (p. 69)

A client's strengths and weaknesses are a given reality. However, a conscious effort to focus on positive client potentials and strengths helps to create intervention strategies that draw on these resources. We reframe the problem as an unsatisfied want or an unfulfilled need and the assessment as an evaluation of client potentials and strengths. As a result, intervention builds on these preceding stages in a substantive way. The worker has positive confidence based on these building blocks.

Intervention

Intervention Process Skills

The purpose of intervention is to effect a positive change between the person and the problem situation. Among the intervention process skills are goal setting and agreement, the selection of culturally diverse intervention strategies, and micro/meso/macro levels of intervention. An intervention plan must be based on the needs of the client.

Goal setting and agreement is a cooperative effort between the client and the worker. It involves the detailed formulation of goal outcomes, expected behavioral changes, task objectives, contracting, and task recommendations. (See Lum,

The Hernandez Family: A Case Study

Assessment process skills are concerned with an analysis of person and environment, cultural strengths, and the inclusion of cultural and spiritual dimensions in the biopsychosocial perspective. Person and environment are viewed as interacting, in that socioenvironmental impacts on the person result in psychological reactions. Cultural strengths are essential to the assessment process since the root of the word *assessment* emphasizes the assets or resources of the person. The incorporation of cultural and spiritual assessment expands the notion of biological, psychological, and social levels.

Assessment conceptualization skills focus on recognizing ethnic group characteristics and strengths, indigenous community resources, and culturally distinctive modes of behavior. Assessment personalization skills enable a social worker to evaluate the positive potential of a client. Assessment is a stepping stone toward intervention based on problem reframing and resource potentiality. The natural personal reaction of a social worker is to move in this direction.

Social environmental factors impacting the Hernandez family are the uncertain economic conditions, Mr. Hernandez's need to work two jobs, and the family obligation of assisting two other immigrant families who are relatives. Psychoindividual reactions include Mr. Hernandez's fatigue and neglect of his family, and the determination of the husband and wife to work to meet the financial demands.

TASK RECOMMENDATIONS

- Contrast the socioenvironmental stress impacts and the psychoindividual reactions of Mr. Hernandez and his son, Ricardo, with the internal and external cultural strengths and the cultural and spiritual dimensions available to them and the family.
- Conceptualize the Latino values of hard work, extended family network, and support from indigenous church and ethnic grassroot agencies available to the Hernandez family.
- Evaluate the positive potential of the Hernandez family members from a personal perspective.

1996, pp. 234–235 for a case example of intervention formulation.) These elements comprise the scope of an intervention plan.

Culturally diverse intervention strategies result in liberation, empowerment, parity, maintenance of culture, and unique personhood, the counterparts of oppression, powerlessness, exploitation, acculturation, and stereotyping (Lum, 1996). Relevant intervention strategies address problem themes that are apparent in the client's situation.

The culturally competent worker utilizes intervention skills by selecting relevant *micro, meso, and/or macro strategies* based on the problem identification and assessment work-up of the case. Micro-level interventions include problem solving, crisis intervention, empowerment, existential intervention, family therapy, and working with refugees. Meso-level interventions involve the extended family, the church, and community support systems. Macro-level interventions apply at the level of policy, planning, and administration skills, community organizing, political impact, and legal advocacy. (See Lum, 1996, Chapter 7 for details on these themes.) What makes social work practice unique is the range of change strategies (micro, meso, macro) applicable to client problems. Crafting an intervention plan that addresses all three levels is a practice skill.

Intervention Conceptualization Skills

Intervention strategies should be based on the unique experience of the multicultural client (Ridley, Espelage, & Rubinstein, 1997) and tailored from a broad repertoire of intervention strategies to apply specifically to the client's problem situation. This involves recognizing the unique factors related to the client, the problem, and the social/cultural environment. Particular micro interventions relate to cultural empowerment, structured prescriptive direction, human potential and the freedom to chose, and family systems. Meso interventions use the influential extended family, the minister of a church, or community organizations. Macro interventions may involve a ballot initiative, a class action suit, or corrective legislation (Lum, 1996). The worker conceptualizes a responsive plan with the client.

Another conceptual skill of indigenous interventions involves the client's belief system and culture. Conceptualization of indigenous interventions identifies natural cultural ways of helping and reconciling differences, such as the family group resolution effort in Hawaiian culture called *ho'ponopono*. There are other ways that ethnic groups and communities introduce intervention change. Ron Lewis, a Native American social work educator, asserts that it is important for an Indian with a drinking problem to attend and participate in pow-wows in order to contact his or her Native American culture and tribe. These elements help an Indian person cope with alcoholism. (Ron Lewis, personal conversation with Doman Lum, March 1985). Conceptualizing an indigenous intervention with a particular client offers alternatives.

Intervention Personalization Skills

The culturally competent worker is concerned about intervention implementation. Is the client motivated to make a change? To what extent will the intervention strategy be successful? How can I be a source of encouragement and facilitate the change process? These are some questions of a worker who is going through the intervention stage with a client.

Motivation for change often comes from the pain and suffering experienced by the client as a result of the problem. A person changes when he or she is uncomfortable or has reached a threshold of pain. For example, the best time to reach an alcoholic is when the person has "hit bottom" and is suffering pain, embarrassment, and guilt. These painful moments of suffering are motivators for change. Personalizing the uncomfortable nature of the problem situation and having the client own responsibility are some practical worker skills.

A structured agreement based on specific goals reminds the client about change directions. Daily and weekly task assignments between sessions are structured ways to implement change on a step-by-step basis. The worker assigns homework with a prescriptive list of change actions.

The Hernandez Family: A Case Study

Intervention process skills consist of drawing up goals and an agreement, selecting an intervention strategy, and orchestrating the micro, meso, and macro levels of change. Goal setting and agreement between the worker and the client involve detailing goal outcomes and behavioral tasks in a contract. Intervention strategies entail specific plans to effect change in the psychosocial situation. Micro, meso, and macro levels of intervention, for example, assemble an array of approaches to the Hernandez family case: problem solving and family therapy, church and community support systems, and community organizing.

Intervention conceptualization skills entail the careful selection of an intervention plan that addresses the particular problem situation and fits the belief system and culture of the client.

Intervention personalization skills focus on the reaction of the worker to the client's motivation for change, the potential success of the intervention strategy, and the client's power to make choices. One must consider working with the Hernandez family on the intervention process, conceptualization, and personalization skill levels.

TASK RECOMMENDATIONS

- Suggest a set of goals and an agreement between the social worker, Mr. Platt, and the Hernandez family.
- Select a culturally diverse intervention strategy (one that will result in liberation, empowerment, parity, maintenance of culture, and unique personhood) and micro, meso, and macro levels of intervention.
- Determine whether the intervention plan addresses the particular problem(s) of the Hernandez family and fits their belief system and culture.
- Ascertain whether members of the Hernandez family are motivated toward change and whether the intervention plan has the potential for succeeding.

The worker recognizes that the client has the power to make choices. The worker cannot and should not assume this responsibility. If the worker has structured the necessary means for change, the client has choice in determining the process. Hepworth, Rooney, and Larsen (1997) discuss client involvement in intervention in Competency Study 5.8.

COMPETENCY STUDY 5.8

Client-Selected Intervention

A useful guideline to planning interventions with ethnic minority persons (and other clients, for that matter) is to solicit their views as to what needs to be done to remedy their difficulties. Their suggestions will be in harmony with their beliefs and values. Moreover, their views about essential changes are often on target: they lack only the "know-how" required to accomplish the changes. Deficiencies in the latter are associated with limited knowledge about available resources and about the complexities of our service delivery systems. Determining clients' views enables the practitioner to suggest interventions that clients will perceive as relevant and to couch the rationale for selecting them in terms that make sense to clients. Including clients in the planning of interventive strategies enhances their cooperation, as we noted previously. (p. 370)

Termination

Termination Process Skills

Termination or the ending stage of the social work process is a critical transition time for the client. On the one hand, a meaningful relationship between the worker and the client is ending, but on the other hand, it is crucial to help the client make a transition to coping with the normal problems of living. Among the process skills (Lum, 1996) are the following:

- Helping the client connect with an ongoing support network: family and friends, ethnic community resources, a referral to another agency for follow-up care.
- Conducting retrospective analysis of the problem situation and the growth that has occurred during the helping relationship.
- Ascertaining whether the goals and outcomes agreed upon in intervention planning have been achieved.
- Establishing a sensible plan for follow-up such as periodic phone calls and visits for checking in and rechecks gradually tapering off.

Termination Conceptualization Skills

Termination is a critical stage, but it is least considered in social work practice. Hepworth, Rooney, and Larsen (1997) conceptualize the ingredients for positive termination in Competency Study 5.9

Positive Termination

COMPETENCY STUDY 5.9

Most clients in individual, marital, family, and group therapy experience positive emotions in termination. Benefits of the gains achieved usually *far outweigh* the impact of the loss of the helping relationship. Indeed, clients often report an increased sense of mastery, and both practitioners and clients are likely to experience joy over such accomplishments. This is especially true when practitioners have employed a strength-oriented, problem-solving approach. Furthermore, the participants have experienced mutual enrichment from the deep, personal, and authentic human encounter, and, in a very real sense, the self of each person has been expanded by the contacts with the other.

Until very recent years, the literature on termination reactions has stressed that sadness, loss, ambivalence, apprehension, and other negative reactions are associated with termination on the part of both practitioner and client. Research findings (Fortune, 1987; Fortune, Pearlingi, & Rochelle, 1992), however, have refuted these widely accepted beliefs. These findings indicate that in both open-ended and time-limited treatment the common reactions are positive feelings related to success and progress, positive feelings about the therapeutic experience, increased constructive activities outside of treatment, more free time, more financial resources to spend on other activities, and feelings of pride about accomplishments and/or independence gained through treatment. Negative reactions on the part of both clients and practitioners are not common. (p. 605)

It is important for a worker in an agency to study the termination rates of clients. What is the agency doing to conclude successful client cases? In cases of premature or unsuccessful termination, what are the agency elements that may have contributed to unresolved cases? Follow-up on unsuccessful cases may teach the worker and the agency as much as analyzing successful cases. Exit interview surveys and follow-up on premature termination are important because of the high drop-out rate of multicultural clients. Research and reflection on early termination and clients of color are helpful at this stage.

Termination Personalization Skills

Termination triggers a range of responses on the part of the worker. The caseload number and intensity, along with the stress of unsuccessful resolution of problems take their toll on the social worker. The daily demand on staff is apparent in many service agencies. Many agencies are using case management to broker a network of services for their clients, group treatment with crisis intervention on serious cases, brief treatment with community referral, and other strategies to deal with the volume of clients. As a result, intensive casework with single clients is the exception rather than the rule of service. Short-term treatment with reachable, concrete, and practical goals results in frequent termination and reliance on social services, the family, indigenous community agencies, and ethnic church and community.

CULTURALLY DIVERSE SERVICE DELIVERY

Service delivery deals with structuring programs, facilities, staff, funding, and administration on behalf of serving the needs of client populations in a geographic area. Service delivery design through an ethnic lens is crucial to culturally diverse services. In Competency Study 5.10, Cox and Ephross (1998) discuss the ethnic lens from both the client and the provider perspectives.

**COMPETENCY
STUDY 5.10**

The Ethnic Lens of Service Delivery

Designing social services that are effective in reaching and serving ethnic groups is a major challenge to the profession. The ethnic lens, as it affects clients' per-

---

The Hernandez Family: A Case Study

Termination process skills help the client to connect with a follow-up network (for example, family and friends, ethnic community agency), conduct a retrospective analysis of the problem and the growth achieved, and determine whether goal outcomes have been accomplished. Termination conceptualization skills are concerned with factors surrounding early and premature case drop-outs as well as successful case completions. Conceptualizing about termination assists the social worker with facts and figures to improve the quality of services in an agency. This is a mark of cultural competency from a termination viewpoint.

Termination personalization skills focus on the positive and negative effects of cases on the social worker as a person and a helper. Intensive casework leading to a successful resolution of problems tends to energize a social worker, whereas chronic and complex cases with no closure tend to burn out a worker. If the burnout is compounded by a shortage of staff, heavy caseloads, and mounting paperwork, a social worker reaches a point where personal and professional needs must be nurtured. A culturally competent worker knows when and where to turn for consultation and assistance.

Appropriate intervention strategy for the Hernandez family might involve schoolwork tutoring for Ricardo from a responsible high school senior, the reduction of Mr. Hernandez's workload to allow him to spend more time with his family, and encouraging the personal growth and development of Mrs. Hernandez through her education and community activities. There is a whole array of intervention possibilities based on cultural competency that students are able to devise from this case.

TASK RECOMMENDATIONS

- Propose a termination plan for the Hernandez family that connects them in a continuing helping network, conducts a retrospective analysis of growth and progress, and ascertains the achievement of goals.
- Determine the factors surrounding the Hernandez family that made this a successful case.
- Suggest how Mr. Platt, the social worker, could be debriefed by a social work supervisor on the Hernandez case.

---

ception of services and practitioners' perceptions of clients and their needs, plays a pivotal role in social work's ability to meet this challenge. Consequently, it is incumbent upon agencies to assure that these lenses are free from distortion.

One of the first issues ethnic groups are likely to confront in their perception of the agency is whether the agency is fundamentally "ours" or "theirs," whether it is one that welcomes "people like us" or has staff "like us." Often, this question is not resolvable simply by official policy or statement, because past experiences have frequently taught many ethnic groups that such statements are not reliable. Informal comments, community gossip, rumors, and personal references from former clients can count for much more than stated policies.

Staff persons who are "like us" can make communication easier, due to the histories they share with prospective clients. The terms used to describe the discovery of an Italian-American or African-American staff member are themselves powerful. Reports of a "paisan" or a "brother" among the staff can affect the entire ethnic lens. The agency is transformed into a place that is both welcoming and accommodating to "us." (p. 116)

Service delivery is based on the philosophy of social services reflected in the administrative unit and the board of directors of an agency. It may change as a series of events occurs or as new policies are made that alter how services are organized and delivered to clients. Iglehart and Becerra (1995, pp. 244–245) observe: "Service delivery as a system or organizational process continues to be a dynamic process that is altered by technological, ideological, political, and economic factors. The mode of service delivery has varied from specialization to integrated, comprehensive services." These authors offer the following observations about social service delivery:

- Social service delivery systems are changing as the population of the United States becomes more diverse and as there is an increased challenge to provide services to ethnic minority groups.
- The client-worker relationship is important in the delivery of ethnic-sensitive services, because the client experiences the agency through the worker as the worker interprets the policies of the agency and implements its services.
- In service delivery planning and implementation there is a need to accept and respect the client's ethnicity and culture and to increase sensitivity to the cultures and values of minorities.
- In service delivery arrangements the client is a member of other systems such as groups, communities, and other service delivery systems that are bounded by ethnicity, culture, and community.
- Effective ethnic-sensitive service delivery utilizes and incorporates the client's community and community services in the service delivery process so that the ethnic minority agency is a focal organization with minority staff, services, and access to the minority group and community.
- Service delivery occurs in the context of a system that is shaped by the culture, values, and ideologies of groups and individuals who plan and implement services.
- The ethnic agency captures the interface between a social service delivery system and a client system that blends use of services with community and ethnicity.
- The history of social work reveals racism and exclusion in the charity organizations and settlement house movement, which resulted in disregard for the needs, concerns, and rights of ethnic minority groups and partially explains the current lack of minority clients in these types of agencies.

Lum (1996) has written about the essential characteristics of multicultural service delivery in terms of location and pragmatic services, staffing, community outreach programs, agency setting, and service linkage. The agency should be located in or near areas with a large ethnic population and be accessible to public transportation. It should offer needed and attractive services such as health care, family services, and/or child care. Mental health services may have a social stigma attached in ethnic communities and services should not be advertised as such. There should be bilingual/bicultural staff in a ratio that reflects the ethnic and gender composition of the service population. There should be strong community outreach programs to schools, churches, and family associations in order to build agency/staff credibility and integrity. The agency setting should be friendly and informal with a bilingual receptionist, clean and private offices, and an ethnic-friendly decor. There should be service linkage and a working relationship between ethnic agencies and other organizations that serve the same client population base.

Cox and Ephross (1998) reiterate these principles of service delivery when they discuss availability, accessibility, acceptability, and ethnic staff in Competency Study 5.11.

Ethnic Service Delivery Principles

COMPETENCY STUDY 5.11

Services, regardless of the type of agency offering them, are used when they are available, accessible, and acceptable to the intended population (Wallace, 1990). Availability refers to the location and amount of services provided and whether they are sufficient to meet the group's needs. A clinic located outside of an ethnic community, although on a bus line, may be perceived as unavailable if persons are uncomfortable leaving the boundaries of their particular neighborhood. Obviously, a limited amount of services, such as English classes, can seriously curtail service availability.

Accessibility depends upon persons' knowledge of programs and having the necessary resources, such as finances, insurance, or transportation, needed for utilization. Accessibility is also affected by the degree of coordination or fragmentation among services.

Accessibility also depends upon service providers' ability to reach those in need. Language can be a major barrier to accessibility. Making sure that the person who answers the agency telephone is fluent in the language of the residents is of prime importance, since he or she is often the first contact that the potential client has with the agency. Having workers who speak the same dialects as the residents and assuring that their accents are compatible with the group are important factors in accessibility.

Service accessibility is also dependent upon the effectiveness of the outreach activities. Outreach involves actively informing the community about the service and its goals and making them attractive to the residents. Outreach workers are active in the community describing their services and making them attractive to potential clients. Rather than waiting for persons to come to the agencies, they attend local functions, give talks at community organizations, and meet with people in the neighborhoods. The aim is to encourage service use by demonstrating the accessibility of the program. Involving local leaders such as the clergy, media personalities, and teachers can be important in the success of the outreach activity.

Finally, even the titles of agencies can affect accessibility. Within ethnic communities mental problems are often a source of shame and mental health counseling is not trusted. Consequently, calling a service "Center for Mental Health" is likely to deter access. Instead, a title which emphasizes growth or acceptable concerns such as "healthy living" may encourage persons to seek further information regarding services.

In order for services to be used, they must be acceptable to the ethnic group. Cultural values and traditions as they affect attitudes and behavior are major influences in acceptability. For example, services such as day care, family planning, and mental health counseling may strongly conflict with traditional values. However, as persons become assimilated into the greater society and its values, these traditional values are often modified.

Staff from the same ethnic background as the clients often have an easier time establishing rapport with community members than do those from outside the ethnic group. Persons are less likely to feel that they have to explain or justify themselves to workers from the same background who share the same history and experiences. Language barriers are also reduced, which enables practitioners to obtain a clear understanding of the problem and to more easily discuss with the client possible interventions.

Clients are often suspicious of ethnic group members returning to a neighborhood as agency staff. Because staff have left the traditional community, persons frequently find it difficult to trust them or their motives.

Staff of their own ethnicity may be perceived as less qualified and less competent. In these situations, clients who are compelled to see an ethnic worker are liable to resist the relationship. In fact, the possibilities for misperception in these situations are great. The agency is likely to believe that by providing ethnic clients with an ethnic worker, they are sensitively attempting to meet their clients' concerns. However, the clients may perceive that, by being assigned this worker, they are being stereotyped and are being denied workers of equal worth. (pp. 105–107, 111)

Iglehart and Becerra (1995) identify seven external and five internal forces of agency change to accommodate an ethnic-sensitive service delivery system. The external catalysts for change are the following:

- Changing funding policies with funding regulations that stipulate the inclusion of specific ethnic populations as service beneficiaries.
- Shifting funding priorities to seek new client populations (such as ethnic minority senior citizens) as funding for services to these groups becomes available.
- Out-group protests on behalf of underserved ethnic groups that cause some agency change, inclusion of ethnic populations, and increase of ethnic utilization.
- New constituencies resulting from the creation of new minority voting

districts that elect minority representation who support ethnic-sensitive services.

- New agency leadership (for example, new directors or staff with particular skills and political positions) shifting the agency toward the concerns of clients of color.
- The worker as a change catalyst for the client and the agency.
- Routinization of change where special programs for specific ethnic groups are absorbed as a part of permanent agency structure.

The internal forces for change in agency service delivery include the following:

- The ideology of the agency in terms of ethnic client perception, situational causes, worker and client roles, and desired outcomes.
- The technology of the agency and worker-client activities in terms of process stages, desired outcomes, and client movement.
- The structure of the agency regarding the rules and ethics governing worker-client interaction, agency contact encounters, and agency hierarchy.
- Client inputs about and assessment of services.
- The accountability of the agency in terms of the recognition of the ethnic community as an agency constituency, procedures for ethnic community input about agency services, and agency accountability to the ethnic community.

These external and internal forces offer avenues for introducing change into existing agencies in order to make them more responsive and sensitive to ethnic populations.

AGENCY LINKAGE, DESIGN, AND IMPLEMENTATION

In order to design and implement culturally diverse service delivery, it is important to understand how agency services interrelate. This is called agency linkage or interorganizational relations. Service delivery cooperation and coordination are crucial as funding shrinks or shifts toward specialized needs, ethnic populations increase with new immigrant influx, and qualified ethnic practitioners become scarce resources.

Iglehart and Becerra (1995) offer ten propositions about agency linkage:

- Ethnic agencies are not in competition with mainstream social services for clients but they do receive funding for specialized services to ethnic groups.
- In an interorganizational relationship, the ethnic agency does have access to a particular ethnic population because of its presence in the ethnic community and its relationship with specific target populations.
- Ethnic agencies are participants in alternative service delivery as services are redefined and new interorganizational relations emerge.
- Ethnic agencies will extend more services to special populations due to privatization (purchase of service contracts, contracting).
- Interorganizational relationships are likely to develop between public and

ethnic agencies because public agencies are mandated to meet the needs of the general population, public agencies provide funding and ethnic agencies use the funds to provide services in an exchange relationship, and ethnic agencies with access to ethnic communities have power and bond with public agencies over funding.

- Changing federal funding requirements develop partnerships between mainstream agencies and ethnic agencies.
- The availability of funding governs the interface between mainstream agencies and the ethnic agency in terms of the development of partnerships, reduction in service duplication, and reaching special populations.
- Ethnic agencies are particularly vulnerable to service contract cuts and grants in terms of financial austerity.
- Ideological conflict can occur between the ethnic agency and mainstream agencies.
- The problems of societal race relations may permeate the relations between ethnic and mainstream agencies.

The preceding propositions on service delivery and agency linkage serve as the basis for the design and implementation of culturally diverse service delivery. Service content changes as various ethnic target groups emerge on the scene: the ethnic elderly, legal immigrants, and former welfare recipients. The needs of ethnic and racial groups are defined by public agencies that are the funding source: alcohol and drug abuse, AIDS, gang violence prevention. These trends may be determined by federal and state policies and legislation that cope with social problem areas and include application to ethnic populations. Programs should be derived from the changing needs of the ethnic community, which should influence ethnic-sensitive public social services or ethnic-responsive indigenous community agencies. With decentralization and downsizing of government services, it is politically and fiscally expedient to contract with ethnic agencies that serve ethnic populations.

Agency ideology and philosophy, technology, staffing, and structure may change in light of federal and state funding of ethnic-related programs. Funding requirements and stipulations can transform the service delivery of an agency.

There are five delivery design elements: programs, staffing, facilities, funding, and administration. Programs are based on community research data and public and private grants. Program planning incorporates social planning principles, funding proposals, and social service legislation. Bilingual, bicultural, and gender-balanced staff should reflect the service area population and should meet degree and professional experience requirements. Facilities should be accessible to the service population and should use existing ethnic social service buildings or neighborhood churches. Funding is based on various local, state, and federal public monies as well as private foundation and United Way monies. Program administration is vested in a program director, a community-based board, and a clear chain of command with job descriptions at all levels.

Agency program implementation usually involves a three-year cycle: start up, initial and full implementation, and periodic program evaluation. Agency imple-

CULTURAL COMPETENCY IN ACTION

The Hernandez Family: A Case Study

Practice skill development must be set in the context of a service delivery structure. Our philosophy of delivering services to multicultural clients determines an agency's programs, facilities, staff, funding, and administrative oversight. In turn these structural components impact the lives of clients with problems.

Iglehart and Becerra (1995) and Lum (1996) emphasize a number of service delivery principles:

- That the worker embodies service delivery and that the client experiences the agency through the worker.
- That the ethnic agency is the focal organization that contracts services from the public government sector and is the bridge between the ethnic community and ethnic clients in need.

- That bilingual/bicultural staff should reflect the population's ethnic and gender profile.
- That facilities should be located near the service population in the existing ethnic neighborhood community.

TASK RECOMMENDATIONS

- Design a Latino Family Service Center that addresses the needs of the Hernandez family. Specify location, program services. staffing, community outreach, agency setting, and interagency service linkage.
- Detail a funding plan for the Latino Family Service Center, which could be supported by federal, state, and county monies, private foundations, and ethnic community support.

mentation starts with federal and state regulatory compliance or the terms of the grant. Regional consortiums may pool resources in a cooperative effort. Cooperative projects are the preferred choice for university program training, research evaluation, and/or community-based agencies.

Iglehart and Becerra (1995) discuss agency linkage between ethnic and mainstream agencies:

> A continuum of services seem to unfold in which the ethnic agency may serve as the first line of defense for filling service gaps, for responding to the needs of marginalized groups, and for helping when no other agency does. It may also substitute for public agencies in delivering uniquely packaged and specially tailored services. In the quest for ethnic-sensitive practice, it seems to be a resource that has been underutilized. Mainstream social services and agencies will continue to vary in the degree to which they adopt ethnic-sensitive practice. The variation is due to agency history, ideologies, structure, and technologies. Mainstream agencies are responding to the needs of a mainstream America, and shifts in paradigms do take years to accomplish. (p. 238)

These authors make a strong case for culturally diverse service delivery and agency linkage between ethnic and mainstream agencies.

RESEARCH ON SKILL DEVELOPMENT

Culturally diverse social work practice skills are in constant development. This section describes a number of cultural competence skills that are emerging at the present time, according to research.

Interpersonal Relationship

Among researchers it is generally agreed that the clinician-client interpersonal relationship is an essential part of a dynamic change process. Through the interpersonal relationship, the clinician is a source of support and a bridge for client change. Bordin (1979) explains that initial bonding between the clinician and the client is facilitated by the sensitivity and acumen of the clinician. Clinical process research has developed around the clinical relationship called the therapeutic alliance (Frank & Gunderson, 1990), the helping alliance (Luborsky, 1975), or the working alliance (Bordin, 1979; Horvath & Greenberg, 1994).

There is substantial evidence that the clinical alliance between clients and workers is related to positive outcome (Henggeler, Schoenwald, Pickrel, Rowland, & Santos, 1994). Research findings have reported that the clinical alliance influences compliance with disposition plans (Eisenthal, Emery, Lazare, & Udin, 1979), medication intake (Docherty & Fiester, 1985; Frank & Gunderson, 1990; Waldinger & Frank, 1989), and less premature termination of treatment (Eaton, Abeles, & Gotfreund, 1988; Frank & Gunderson, 1990). Research evidence has also supported the role of the clinical alliance in behavioral and cognitive-behavioral interventions (Raue & Goldfried, 1994). However, almost none of the empirical literature on the alliance has investigated differences in the alliance-outcome relationship by social class, race/ethnicity, or across cultures (Dore & Alexander, 1996).

Personal Styles and Clinical Process

Research has claimed that psychological characteristics (cultural attitudes, emotional well-being, values, attitudes, beliefs, expectations, clinical relationships) of the clinician and the client, and the style match between the two, affect the clinical efficacy and make significant impacts on client change. The subjective personal style differences between the clinician and the client contribute to the dynamics of the clinical process (Bergin & Garfield, 1996).

These personal styles were researched and named "achieving styles" by Lipman-Blumen, Handley-Isaksen, and Leavitt (1983). Subsequently, the Achieving Styles Inventory (ASI) was revised and standardized to assess both individual and organizational styles. Three major sets of domains (direct, instrumental, and relational) contain three related but distinctive styles. Altogether there are nine achieving styles, each of which is a preference pattern for a particular orientation or situation. The concept of personal achieving styles is discussed in business, education, and counseling. Specifically, an achieving style is an individual preference that reflects the behavior, value system, and strategic reasoning of a person. It refers to various learned ways to accomplish tasks or achieve goals regardless of the specific nature of these goals (Lipman-Blumen, Handley-Isaksen, & Leavitt, 1983).

An individual's achieving style is shaped by a his or her attitudes, norms, values, and cultural boundaries (Spence, 1985). On a practical level, it involves an individual's way of thinking, talking, and feeling, particularly as a person acts and interacts with others. These styles are profoundly influenced by the individual's personal experiences and cultural/social context. Beginning in childhood, we learn different ways or strategies to get what we want. These thinking, feeling, and behaving patterns become personal styles for accomplishing tasks or achieving goals. A person uses his or her unique set of achieving styles to project himself or herself, accomplish life goals, and relate to the world. These personal achieving styles seem adequate for accomplishing tasks until we are confronted by a difference or mismatch of interpersonal styles in cross-cultural encounters. An individual is not conscious of his or her achieving styles without a deliberate and conscious examination of himself or herself.

Clinicians often have little awareness of their own personal achieving styles, which closely link and relate to their own clinical practice. Clinicians with direct styles tend to focus their attention on the task and use direct problem-solving approaches. They tend to offer direct advice as a helping authority for clients. Clinicians with instrumental achieving styles frequently use their own credibility, influence, professionalism, or a support system to resolve problems. They rely on clients to assume partial or full responsibility for their actions. Clinicians with relational-cognitive behavioral styles allow clients to select the means and the ends of their goal accomplishments. They use collaborative or contributory approaches to help clients accomplish their own goals through group efforts.

Just as the clinician's choice of skills and intervention strategies is shaped by his or her cultural self, the client comes with his or her culturally contained self. Consequently, an important element of effective cross-cultural clinical practice is the clinician's awareness of this value choice's impact on the clinical process. Recognizing the importance of having styles match is essential for a successful cross-cultural clinical process.

Language Match

Language is an organized learned symbolic system used to represent one's experiences in a cultural community. Language, verbal and nonverbal processes, is the primary means by which a culture transmits its beliefs, values, and norms (Lefley & Pedersen, 1986). Effective communication involves good verbal retention skills, high-level awareness of nonverbal behaviors, and an understanding of the cultural context of language. Some symbolic behaviors (such as time orientation, social distance, spacing, touching, facial expression and gesturing) vary dramatically from culture to culture. Lefley and Pedersen (1986) have identified three aspects of language: (1) linguistic aspects or the manifest context of the consciously spoken word or verbal language; (2) idiosyncratic aspects or the quality of the speaker's voice and nonverbal cues such as facial expression, gestures, body movements; and (3) sociolinguistic aspects or a frame of reference, the context within which the message is interpreted and understood.

Generally, first language (or a regional dialect) is learned at an early age at home and is associated with the values of intimacy, spontaneity, and informality. When clients use their native language or their dialect, their language is more emotionally expressive than that of clients using a second language or standard English (Kochman, 1981). A clinician's use of a native dialect or second language in conjunction with standard English directly affects the client's perception of the clinician's credibility and the degree of the client's change in attitudes and behaviors.

Research is needed to examine language and achieving style congruencies between clinicians and clients and their implications for clinical decisions and alliances. This conceptualization is summarized in the formula *CC=f (LCP, IAS, OS)*: cultural competence (CC) is a function (f) of language/culture proficiency (LCP), the clinician's awareness of individual achieving styles (IAS), and the clinician's awareness of organizational style (OS). Another conceptual formula describes cultural competence and the cross-cultural clinical alliance in the cross-cultural clinical practice: *CCA= f [LC, IP, IAS], [Clinician's (LCP, AS)], (IASC), (OASC)*. That is, at the cross-cultural clinical alliance (CCA) is a function (f) of (1) client variables—level of acculturation (LC), linguistic/culturally indigenous problems (IP), and individual achieving styles (IAS); (2) the clinician's cultural competence—language/culture proficiency (LCP) and achieving styles (AS); and (3) the interactions—the individual achieving styles congruence (IASC) between the client and the clinician and the organizational achieving style congruence (OASC) with the client's indigenous culture.

Creative research on cultural skill development strengthens cultural competency studies and culturally diverse social work practice.

SUMMARY

Culturally competent skill development is the core of a discussion of culturally competent practice, since it affects the worker-client helping relationship. This chapter defines three types of skills—process, conceptualization, and personalization skills—and relates them to the social work practice stages of contact, problem identification, assessment, intervention, and termination. Culturally diverse service delivery was discussed and related to agency linkage, design, and implementation. Research on culturally competent skill development was also discussed.

REFERENCES

Amato-von Hemert, K. (1994). Should social work education address religious issues? Yes! *Journal of Social Work Education, 30*(1), 7–11, 16, 17.

American Psychiatric Association (1994). *Diagnostic and statistical manual of mental disorders* (4th ed.). Washington, DC: Author.

Barnes, A., & Ephross, P. H. (1995). The impact of hate crimes on victims: Emotional and behavioral responses to attacks. *Social Work 39*, 247–251.

Bergin, A. E., & Garfield, S. L. (1996). *Handbook of psychotherapy and behavior change.* New York: John Wiley & Sons.

Bernard, J. M. (1979). Supervisor training: A discrimination model. *Counselor Education and Supervision, 19*, 60–68.

Bordin, E. S. (1979). The generalizability of the psychoanalytic concept of the working alliance. *Psychotherapy: Theory, Research, and Practice, 16*, 252–260.

Clark, J. (1994). Should social work education address religious issues? No! *Journal of Social Work Education, 30*(1), 11–16.

Comas-Diaz, L. (1994). An integrative approach. In L. Comas-Diaz & B. Greene (Eds.), *Women of color: Integrating ethnic and gender identities in psychotherapy* (pp. 287–318). New York: Guilford Press.

Cowger, C. D. (1994). Assessing client strengths: Clinical assessment for client empowerment. *Social Work, 39*, 262–268.

Cox, C. B., & Ephross, P. H. (1998). *Ethnicity and social work practice.* New York: Oxford University Press.

Dana, R. H. (1993). *Multicultural assessment perspectives for professional psychology.* Boston: Allyn & Bacon.

Docherty, J. P., & Fiester, S. J. (1985). The therapeutic alliance and compliance with psychopharmacology. In R. E. Hales and A. F. Frank (Eds.), *Psychiatry Update, 4*, 607–632.

Dore, M. M., & Alexander, L. B. (1996). Preserving families at risk of child abuse and neglect: The role of the helping alliance. *Child Abuse and Neglect, 20*(4), 349–361.

Dupree, D., Spencer, M. B., & Bell, S. (1997). African American children. In G. Johnson-Powell and J. Yamamoto (Eds.), *Transcultural child development: Psychological assessment and treatment* (pp. 237–268). New York: John Wiley & Sons.

Eaton, T. T., Abeles, N., & Gotfreund, M. J. (1988). Therapeutic alliance and outcome: Impact of treatment length and pretreatment symptomatolology. *Psychotherapy, 25*, 536–542.

Eisenthal, S., Emery, R., Lazare, A., & Udin, H. (1979). Adherence and the negotiated approach. *Archives of General Psychiatry, 36*, 393–398.

Fassinger, R. E., & Richie, B. S. (1997). Sex matters: Gender and sexual orientation in training for multicultural counseling competency. In D. B. Pope-Davis & H. L. K. Coleman (Eds.), *Multicultural counseling competencies: Assessment, education and training, and supervision* (pp. 83–110). Thousand Oaks, CA: Sage Publications.

Fortune, A. E. (1987). Grief only? Client and social worker reactions to termination. *Clinical Social Work Journal, 15*, 159–171.

Fortune, A. E., Pearlingi, B., & Rochelle, C. D. (1992). Reactions to termination of individual treatment. *Social Work, 37*, 171–178.

Frank, A. F., & Gunderson, J. G. (1990). The role of the therapeutic alliance in the treatment of schizophrenia. *Archives of General Psychiatry, 47*, 228–236.

Franklin, A. J. (1993, July/August). The invisibility syndrome. *Family Therapy Networker*, pp. 33–39.

Giordano, J., & Giordano, M. A. (1995). Ethnic dimensions in family therapy. In R. Mikesell, D. Lusterman, & S. McDaniel (Eds.), *Integrating family therapy*. Washington, DC: American Psychological Association.

Green, J. W. (1995). *Cultural awareness in the human services: A multi-ethnic approach.* Boston: Allyn & Bacon.

Helms, J. E., & Richardson, T. Q. (1997). How "multiculturalism" obscures race and culture as differential aspects of counseling competency. In D. B. Pope-Davis & H. L. K. Coleman (Eds.), *Multicultural counseling competencies: Assessment, education and training, and supervision* (pp. 60–79). Thousand Oaks, CA: Sage Publications.

Henggler, S. W., Schoenwald, S. K., Pickrel, S. G., Rowland, M. D., & Santos, A. B. (1994). The contribution of treatment outcome research to the reform of children's mental health services: Multisystem therapy as an example. *Journal of Mental Health Administration, 21,* 229–239.

Hepworth, D. H., Rooney, R. H., & Larsen, J. A. (1997). *Direct social work practice: Theory and skills.* Pacific Grove, CA: Brooks/Cole.

Horvath, A. O., & Greenberg, L. S. (Eds.). (1994). *The working alliance: Theory, research, and practice.* New York: John Wiley & Sons.

Hines, P. M., & Boyd-Franklin, N. (1996). African American families. In M. McGoldrick, J. Giordano, & J. K. Pearce (Eds.), *Ethnicity and family therapy* (pp. 66–84). New York: Guilford Press.

Iglehart, A. P., & Becerra, R. M. (1995). *Social services and the ethnic community.* Boston: Allyn & Bacon.

Kadushin, A., & Kadushin, G. (1997). *The social work interview: A guide for human service professionals.* New York: Columbia University Press.

Kochman, T. (1981). *Black and white styles in conflicts.* Chicago: University of Chicago Press.

Kumabe, K., Nishida, C., & Hepworth, D. (1985). *Bridging ethnocultural diversity in social work and health.* Honolulu: University of Hawaii Press.

Lefley, H. P., & Pedersen, P. B. (1986). *Cross-cultural training for mental health professionals.* Springfield, IL: Charles C Thomas.

Lipman-Blumen, J., Handley-Isaksen, A., & Leavitt, H. J. (1983). Achieving styles in men and women: A model, an instrument, and some findings. In J. Spence (Ed.), *Achievement and achievement motives.* San Francisco: Freeman & Company.

Longres, J. F. (1991). Toward a status model of ethnic sensitive practice. *Journal of Multi-Cultural Social Work, 1,* 41–56.

Luborsky, L. (1975). Helping alliance in psychotherapy. In J. L. Claghorn (Ed.), *Successful psychotherapy* (pp. 92–116). New York: Brunner/Mazel.

Lum, D. (1992). *Social work practice and people of color: A process-stage approach.* Pacific Grove, CA: Brooks/Cole.

Lum, D. (1996). *Social work practice and people of color: A process-stage approach* (3rd ed.). Pacific Grove, CA: Brooks/Cole.

Mayer, J., & Timms, W. (1969). Clash in perspective between worker and client. *Social Casework, 50,* 32–40.

Proctor, E. K., & Davis, L. E. (1994). The challenge of racial difference: Skills for clinical practice. *Social Work, 39,* 314–323.

The question of race in America. (1997, June 15). *Sacramento Bee,* p. Forum 4.

Raue, P. J., & Goldfried, M. R. (1994). The therapeutic alliance in cognitive-behavior therapy. In A. O. Horvath & L. S. Greenberg (Eds.), *The working alliance: Theory, research and practice* (pp. 131–152). New York: John Wiley & Sons.

Reid, W. J. (1978). *The task-centered system.* New York: Columbia University Press.

Reynolds, A. L., & Pope, R. L. (1991). The complexities of diversity: Exploring multiple oppressions. *Journal of Counseling and Development, 70,* 174–180.

Ridley, C. R., Espelage, D. L., & Rubinstein, K. J. (1997). Course development in multicultural counseling. In D. B. Pope-Davis & H. L. K. Coleman (Eds.), *Multicultural counseling competencies: Assessment, education and training, and supervision* (pp. 131–158). Thousand Oaks, CA: Sage Publications.

Saleebey, D. (Ed.). (1992). *The strengths perspective in social work practice.* New York: Longman.

Spence, J. T. (1985). Achievement American style: The rewards and costs of individualism. *American Psychologist, 40* (12), 1285–1295.

Tsui, P., & Schultz, G. L. (1985). Failure of rapport: Why psychotherapeutic engagement fails in the treatment of Asian clients. *American Journal of Orthopsychiatry, 55,* 561–569.

Waldinger, R. J., & Frank, A. F. (1989). Clinicians' experiences in combining medication and psychotherapy in the treatment of borderline patients. *Hospital and Community Psychiatry 40,* 712–718.

Wallace, S. (1990). The no-care zone: Availability, accessibility, acceptability in community based long term care. *Gerontologist, 30,* 254–261.

CHAPTER SIX

Inductive Learning

ANDREW BEIN AND DOMAN LUM

This chapter will help you develop competencies in the area of inductive learning.

Generalist level:

- Participation in continuing discussions of multicultural social work practice
- Gathering new information on cultural competency and culturally diverse practice

Advanced level:

- Participation in inductive research on cultural competency and culturally diverse practice
- Participation in writing articles and texts on cultural competency and culturally diverse practice

As a social work educator and practitioner, Ruth G. Dean is concerned about a social worker's evaluation of his or her own practice after completing his or her formal education. Dean (1994) writes:

> As a teacher, supervisor, and clinician I see social workers evaluating and reflecting on their practice all the time. These evaluations are not systematic nor are they written. Sometimes they occur in discussions between colleagues or in supervisory sessions and sometimes they simply occur in the clinician's mind. But a form of evaluation goes on continuously. The challenge is to find the bridge between qualitative methods and the kinds of questions that social workers do ask when they evaluate their practices. If we could pay more attention to these questions and start where the practitioner is, then I think we could integrate qualitative forms of research with practitioners' needs. (pp. 279–280)

I have a similar concern about culturally diverse social work practice. That is, after graduating from a social work program, how does a social work professional evaluate multicultural practice and continue the learning process to explore new information about this field of practice? What questions, issues, and insights from the multicultural client and the cultural diversity–oriented social work practitioner arise in the helping process that might contribute new data to this area? What are the practical qualitative research and practice tools that support inductive learning?

Again, Dean (1994) discusses the changing nature of practice and the need to build on reflective case studies and qualitative analysis:

> Therapeutic methods may shift during the clinical process, the client or client group may change over time, and clinicians' thoughts about cases are also in a continuous process of evolution. Clinicians' reflections on clinical work would be different in the middle of a clinical encounter, if we could stop the action, from reflections occurring days, months, and years later, because ideas about practice shift according to clinicians' interests, studies, readings, experiences, and contexts. Research paradigms and future discussions of case study methods need to more closely reflect the continuously evolving process of practice and reflections on practice. Qualitative methods of analysis, because of their more detailed and individually oriented focus, can incorporate a more accurate sense of practice. (p. 283)

Dean underscores the changes that occur as the social work professional moves through a series of cases and employment experiences. Change is part of the professional development process. It is important to continue the dialogue between teacher and student and between professionals in culturally diverse social work practice.

The purpose of this chapter is to focus on inductive learning, which is a life-long process of continuous discovery about the changing nature of multicultural individual, family, and community dynamics. This chapter starts with a definition of inductive learning and the characteristics of the inductive research approach. It next moves to the inductive learning process, which emphasizes the need for the social worker to continue learning as practitioner and researcher. It makes a case for professional research-oriented practice in the social work tradition. Finally, it argues for qualitative research as an integral part of social work education in the practice and research curriculum. It offers practical suggestions on the task of social work education to wed research-oriented practice and culturally diverse social work practice.

DEFINITION OF INDUCTIVE LEARNING

In the social work competency framework, I was searching for a way that culturally competent social work students might continue to improve their cultural competency as they began their professional practice. The learning process is a part of life and living. At birth, a person begins the process of receiving, processing, and integrating stimuli from significant others (parents, family, friends), events, and experiences. These series of learning experiences become the basis for intelligence, knowledge, and action.

During undergraduate and graduate education, social work educators teach students about social work practice, behavior, policy, research, diversity, populations at risk, values and ethics, and economic and social justice. These social work education areas are introductions to a lifelong series of learning encounters where social workers integrate classroom theory and agency practice. There are constant refinements and applications of new knowledge and experiences in clinical, organizational, and community situations.

Learning, denoting the acquisition of knowledge or skills, has some interesting root meanings. The German word *lernen* means to learn and teach. The connotation is that as one learns, there comes the opportunity to teach what has been learned. In a real sense, the students of today are the teachers of tomorrow. The current social work students are the future social work educators. The Latin word *lira* means track or furrow. The implication is that as one learns, there is imprinted in one's mind a track or furrow or a memory of that learned experience. In an agricultural sense, a furrow is made for planting a seed that grows into a crop. A learning furrow becomes the ground for a seed or an idea to grow into a body of knowledge.

As a social work educator, I hope to teach culturally diverse social work practice and cultural competency so that I will implant seeds of ideas in the minds and hearts of students that will grow and flourish in ways beyond my teaching aspirations and dreams.

The inductive nature of learning has a special meaning for me. In my doctoral social work education, I was trained to conduct survey research. A good social survey researcher is constantly asking questions about areas of concern in an inductive manner. Induction is a part of inductive reasoning that assembles particular facts or individual cases about a subject and draws general conclusions based on findings. There is no hypothesis testing in survey research. A good inductive researcher asks open-ended research questions and draws conclusions based on findings. The inductive method is the opposite of the deductive method. Deduction is a process of reasoning from a known principle that serves as a guide or bench mark to a conclusion that confirms the given. The deductive method may go from the general to the specific or from a premise to a logical conclusion.

From an inductive learning perspective, the social worker begins by ascertaining the background and problems of the multicultural client. Based on careful inquiry and investigation, the social worker learns about the unique issues confronting the client. There may be similarities between multicultural clients. At the same time, there may be unique characteristics that emerge and differ from the existing literature. Inductive learning helps the social worker to become a careful and caring practitioner and offers new insights on emerging information that may differ from the body of knowledge on multicultural clients. This may be especially relevant with new immigrant groups from Eastern European and African countries coming into the United States, where unique cultural knowledge about these people may be lacking.

Inductive learning becomes a linkage between what we know in the present and what we may discover in the future about cultural diversity. As an academician, I am surrounded by students, course outlines, new textbooks, class schedules, committee meetings, student advising, and related university demands. A refreshing experience is to bring practitioners from the field to lecture about current trends and programs. It brings a sense of reality into my ivy tower when there is a town-and-gown cross-fertilization of information. Social work practitioners in the field are rich sources of inductive learning who teach social work educators about problems from the multicultural front lines. They provide new knowledge and skills as they uncover new client information through an open-ended inductive process.

Qualitative research in social work is beginning to reclaim its social work birthright and articulate inductive learning methods for culturally diverse social work practice.

THE INDUCTIVE RESEARCH APPROACH

The inductive research approach fits our concern for inductive learning. Here I will describe several features of inductive research.

Analytic induction is a procedure for verifying theories and propositions based on qualitative data. A hypothesis is tested, revised, and retested case by case across a broad range of cases until the hypothesis adequately explains in all cases the phenomenon being studied (Sherman & Reid, 1994, p. 434). This form of inductive research is useful to test cultural diversity theory.

The grounded theory approach is a type of qualitative inductive research. Its purpose is the discovery of relationships among concepts, processes, and patterns. Grounded theory researchers enter the field with an open inductive mind, pit the emerging empirical findings against new data, and modify findings to fit the data. In short, they practice constant comparison within and across cases. Mizrahi and Abramson (1994, p. 140) explain: The constant comparative method is a process of developing categories, concepts, and broader themes or theory inductively from the data and testing them out at each step by returning to the data to evaluate their fit and appropriateness." This approach combines the openness of induction with the deductive processes of hypotheses testing and cross-validation of empirical findings with the existing literature (Gilgun, 1994).

Ethnography (Fortune, 1994) is another type of qualitative research that utilizes participant observation, family interviewing, autobiographies, and detailed descriptions of the events of all participants. Ethnographic research uses inductive reasoning in its approach. It moves from observation to conceptualization of meaning, with relevance for cross-cultural practice. The ethnographic researcher may ask questions indirectly by implication rather than in a direct way in order to obtain oblique perceptions of the problem or issue at hand.

For example, Lum (1996, pp. 162–165) discusses disclosure of problem areas where ethnic clients may feel a sense of shame and hesitation. Before disclosing the problem, the client might say in an indirect, oblique manner, "I have a friend with a certain problem. What would you suggest if this were the case?" The worker might also respond in an oblique way by offering a helpful and practical suggestion and building trust. Both understand the real circumstances but practice a respectful approach to dealing with the issue in a nonobtrusive manner.

Fortune (1994) further distinguishes between microethnographic and macroethnographic studies. The former deal with individual clients, subgroups, organizations, and programs, and their interactions. The latter are concerned about enhancing knowledge of whole cultures in relation to their setting and perspective.

Monette, Sullivan, & De Jong (1994) suggest that there are four categories to be observed and recorded in ethnographic participant observation research: (1) the setting, or a description of the general physical and social setting being observed by the researcher/practitioner; (2) the people, or a physical and social description of individuals who are the focus (number of people, physical appearance, age, gender, socioeconomic characteristics); (3) individual behavior, or interactions, communications, and behavioral sequences; and (4) group behavior, or the composition, interrelationship, and cliques of groups on the scene.

The theory-building process is an important aspect of qualitative inductive research. Inductive research evolves categories from the data themselves. "What do the data tell us?" is the crucial inductive question posed by the practitioner/ researcher. There is an attempt to work in a reflective manner. One gathers observations (for example, generalizations, similarities and differences) from a range of cases. From these observed themes, the research-oriented practitioner develops conclusions based on findings. Lang (1994, p. 275) explains the inductive pattern of data processing when she suggests that the questions "What do I know from this processing?" and "Therefore, what should I do?" are "the guiding questions of such data processing." Inductive data gathering and processing lead to abstracting or generalizing and later conceptualization.

This line of thinking inductively and generalizing theory from data is a part of the critical mind-set that must be taught to students and practitioners of culturally diverse social work. As social work students graduate and become professional practitioners, it is incumbent on them to establish a research-oriented line of inquiry. Lang (1994, p. 276) explains: ". . . the earliest experiences in class and field for the beginning student practitioner should include inquiry about 'what is' and 'how does it happen,' so that upon entry into the profession, the social work practitioner is habituated to asking questions, thinking about practice, and exploring 'what the practice tells'." In brief, intervention ought to be derived from practice data, which comes from client and community knowledge.

For example, an indigenous cultural practice is the Hawaiian healing method of *ho'oponopono*, which is an interactive, interdependent family and group problem-solving approach. Mokuau (1985) explains the procedure: when a problem is identified, everyone concerned is allowed to speak with minimal confrontation and negative feelings. Resolution occurs in the midst of confessing wrongdoing and seeking forgiveness from family members. There is restitution by wrongdoers. The leader of the *ho'oponopono* session summarizes the process, affirming the family's strength and mutual commitment. Afterward the family prays and offers food to the gods, then shares food together.

In this case, an intervention arises from the culture itself, rather than being imposed by a social worker. Inductive theory building would support the use of *ho'oponopono* because it arises from the culture itself and is a time-honored and time-tested practice for problem resolution among the Hawaiian people. Social work students and practitioners should be sensitized to uncover and understand natural support networks as interventions and use them in culturally diverse practice settings with clients as appropriate. Similar efforts to uncover and understand cultural caring and reconciliation practices pave the way for social work practice to become more oriented to the people of color whom it is serving.

Stern (1994) alludes to this fit when she writes:

> In the process of building knowledge inductively and discovering new practice theory, it is important to recognize existing research knowledge on practice effectiveness and previously validated practice theory so that knowledge building in social work is cumulative. In qualitative research, this typically occurs at the end of the data-processing cycle as part of the contextualizing step where new findings are integrated with previous conceptualizations. The potential value of inductive qualitative methods in knowledge building may also be maximized at times by connecting this approach to the knowledge derived from alternative research methods prior to the end of the data-processing cycle; in this instance, there would be more of an interaction between inductive and deductive data processing. If we value the existence of diverse research methodologies and "ways of knowing," perhaps we can strike a better balance between building on "what we know" and finding the best ways to learn "what we need to know." (pp. 289–290)

Stern reaffirms the need to move from data to theory building; to build knowledge inductively in order to discover new practice theory; and to connect inductive and deductive data processing.

Analytic induction, the grounded theory approach, ethnographic participant observation, and inductive theory building are examples of qualitative research in social work that have relevance for culturally diverse practice. In the next section we discuss inductive social work practice, which integrates the inductive qualitative approach, a strengths perspective, and grounded theory

INDUCTIVE SOCIAL WORK PRACTICE

Inductive approaches are particularly appropriate for cross-cultural social work practice. Practitioners move beyond cultural stereotypes or etic (universal) categorization of psychosocial dynamics when they listen to and appreciate the client's own story. Clients tell social workers about what events, conditions, behaviors, and decisions mean to them, and social workers understand the client's narrative on the client's own terms. When clients *teach* social workers about their lives, clients experience that their voice counts, that they are respected, and that they are not judged.

The nature of inductive understanding is illustrated in Competency Study 6.1.

Inductive Understanding

If, for example, a Latino male adolescent is struggling with behavior problems in a school that is less than 2% Latino, we do not assume or even construct a hypothesis that family and individual ethnic identity issues underlie the youth's struggles. The inductive approach is not about measuring how well a client's experience conforms to an already determined theoretical construct—in this case *ethnic identity confusion*; instead, we build our understanding about this youth's reality upon the family's and the youth's narrative as well as our observations of the youth in various environments

The social worker may learn, for example, that the youth's behavioral struggles are recent and coincide with his learning that his father is terminally ill. We may learn that the youth's mother is, in fact, African American; the youth has comfortably identified himself as African American, and 50% of the school's students are African American.

Theoretical concepts like *ethnic identity confusion* do, however, have some utility. High school students of color may struggle with issues of ethnic identity and these struggles may be significant forces in their lives. An understanding of the potentially destructive consequences of racism also prepares practitioners to tune into elements that may be salient in the client's life. Overall, cross-cultural theory prepares practitioners to hear information related to identity and racism themes, place it within a context, and ask intelligent questions.

However, while the hypothesis-testing, deductive practitioner starts with a theoretical framework (such as identity theory) and tests the theory's utility and relevance for a given client, the inductive practitioner-researcher grounds his or her inquiry on information gleaned from the client's narrative and from observation of the client within his or her ecological system. Theoretical concepts are utilized to sensitize (Glaser & Strauss, 1967; Strauss & Corbin, 1990) workers to possibilities rather than to lock workers into narrow frameworks from which to view clients.

Reactions to the professional golfer Tiger Woods (The question of race in America, 1997) provide a simplistic illustration of inductive and deductive approaches. There are those who strive to categorize Tiger Woods's identity through invoking general sociological theory and proclaim that because of how larger society acts toward him and because of the history of oppression suffered by African Americans within larger society, and in particular, the sport of golf, Tiger Woods (1) is African American, (2) has a social responsibility to declare himself as African American, and (3) is somehow deficient for not declaring himself as African American. Others look at Tiger Woods and state that because he is one fourth Chinese, one fourth Thai, one fourth black, one eighth white and one eighth American Indian, he should have the option of checking a new box labeled "multicultural." Our ultimate goal, however, should be to replace all those racial boxes with just one box: American.

On the other hand, the inductive approach toward understanding Tiger Woods's identity involves asking Tiger Woods to talk about his identity. How does he see himself and define himself and what is significant for him about the various ethnic groups that he mentions? How meaningful is "multicultural"? How important are these identity issues for him? What is it like to have demands placed upon him to identify himself in a certain way? How, in his perception, does his ethnic identity relate to larger social issues involving identity? What kind of family support or stress is present in his life regarding these issues? By answering such questions, Tiger Woods teaches us about his identity. He perhaps raises issues around multicultural or ethnically blended identity for which we are not prepared because there is so little established theory (Root, 1992).

A Strengths Perspective

Students and practitioners who have integrated a strengths perspective (Delgado, 1997; Saleebey, 1992) are best prepared to work with clients in a respectful, open, and nonjudgmental manner. In the absence of a thorough grounding in the strengths perspective, students and practitioners can easily view their clients through a lens distorted either by individual or societal racism or stereotyping or by overly general social psychological theory. The strengths perspective directs practitioners to emphasize clients' strengths, gifts, and talents. It sets the tone for a client-worker *partnership* and orients social workers toward embracing clients and looking for health rather than pathologizing clients and looking for dysfunction. Among other principles in the strengths perspective (see Table 6.1), client knowledge and experience are valued.

The culturally competent practitioner thus combines the inductive researcher's mentality, which involves learning and discovering with clients, asking questions, and observing, with a strengths perspective, which orients the practitioner to embrace clients' behavioral styles, belief systems, and coping patterns. When

TABLE 6.1 *Strengths Perspective Principles*

1. Client knowledge and experience are valued.
2. Client gifts and talents are emphasized.
3. Learned hopefulness is promoted.
4. The practitioner recognizes that people are more successful when moving toward something than when moving away from something.
5. The practitioner avoids labels and the victimizing effects of labels, and uses concepts like resiliency rather than at-risk.
6. Positive expectations are integral to the relationship.
7. In the client-worker relationship, the qualities of openness, clarity of expectations, genuineness, and supportiveness are emphasized.
8. Change in one area reverberates in other areas of life.

CULTURAL COMPETENCY IN ACTION

The Hernandez Family: A Case Study

The inductive process begins with the practitioner's commitment to be a learner and to have the client assume a teacher's role. The practitioner adopts a strengths perspective and sincerely values the client's knowledge, perspectives, and coping strategies. The social worker frames the initial encounter (1) to help manage the anxiety that the individual or family may feel in assuming the teacher role; (2) to orient the client to expect solutions and, thus, help the client maintain hope that the worker's inquiry has a purpose; and (3) to convey respect to the client through asserting that the client's perspectives are valued.

Mr. Platt, the social worker, learns that the Hernandez family is concerned about the disruptive school behavior of 10-year-old Ricardo. He observes the family's reluctance and nervousness during their session and tells himself that these reactions are normal. He informs the family that they will address Ricardo's school situation. However, he would like to first learn about who they are. This approach may be in accordance with a Latino emphasis on *personalismo*, a cultural orientation that emphasizes personal warmth and connectedness. When Mr. Platt learns about Mr. Hernandez's two jobs and willingness to support his extended family, he conveys his admiration of Mr. Hernandez's work ethic and dedication to his family. He inquires about the family's decision to leave Mexico and praises Mrs. Hernandez's courage and her resolve to enhance the economic well-being of her family. Ricardo and his younger siblings are attentive to their parents' words. They are affirmed by the social worker as "respectful, caring children."

Inductive exploration addresses the issue that brought the family for service: Ricardo's school struggles. Mr. Platt works from a strengths perspective and assumes that the parents want Ricardo to experience school success. They have valuable knowledge about Ricardo and Ricardo has valuable knowledge about himself. Mr. Platt addresses the following areas:

What are the issues in school for Ricardo?

What do Ricardo's parents do to prepare him to be successful in school?

What is Ricardo's behavior at home?

What kinds of successes do Mr. and Mrs. Hernandez have with Ricardo and how do they manage to have these successes?

What should Mr. and Mrs. Hernandez tell Ricardo's teacher so that the teacher has a better understanding of Ricardo?

What is the relationship like between the teacher and the Hernandez family?

TASK RECOMMENDATIONS

Inductive inquiry and the strengths perspective are advanced as cornerstones of culturally competent practice. Discussing these questions will clarify the applications and implications of this overall approach:

- How *respectful* is Mr. Platt toward the Hernandez family compared to practitioners you have observed in agencies? What does it mean for a client to feel *respected?*
- What follow-up questions may be helpful to facilitate the collection of more specific data?
- Weick (1992, p. 24) states that "when people's positive capacities are supported, they are more likely

Continued on Next Page

The Hernandez Family: A Case Study (continued)

to act on their strengths." Mr. Platt frequently invokes the metaphors of the family's strong work ethic, courage, and resourcefulness. How can these capacities be mobilized to positively affect Ricardo's academic success?

- How would the social worker's approach be simi-

lar or different if the client or family were in counseling involuntarily?

- Suppose the family presented itself as highly distressed because Ricardo had set a fire at school. How would you modify or not modify Mr. Platt's approach?

---

the inductive and strengths traditions are linked, social workers not only approach clients with an open, inquiring mind, they also sincerely believe that clients are doing things correctly and that clients can teach them about overcoming difficult situations and solving day-to-day dilemmas (see De Jong & Miller, 1995).

Clients shed light and offer new perspectives on how to behave, think, and feel in given social situations; they inform us of psychosocial dynamics that may be useful in our work with similarly situated clients, and that we, as practitioners, have not yet thought about.

The Search for Client Meaning

Grounded Data Collection—Client Narrative

The way in which a client thinks about and comes to understand his or her dilemmas, victories, self-identity, and hopes represents the client's search for meaning. The data collection process is considered *grounded* because it begins with the client's narrative rather than the practitioner-researcher's theoretical constructs or predictions about who the client is or the nature of the client's problems. The practitioner-researcher develops a strong orientation toward learning about the client's unique reality and accepts and embraces the client's perspectives vis-à-vis this reality. It should be noted that acceptance does not imply approval, because some behaviors, beliefs, or values may be the source of the client's struggles and may contribute to why the social worker is involved in the client's life. Acceptance instead is a vehicle for entering the client's world and understanding as completely as possible this person's beliefs, feelings, and behaviors and how these are influenced by this person's cultural and social conditions. When clients interact with practitioner-researchers who incorporate a strengths–inductive learning perspective, the clients feel empowered and that much more prepared to tackle major life issues (Bein, Torres, & Kurilla, 1997).

Figure 6.1 *The Inductive Process for the Practitioner-Researcher*

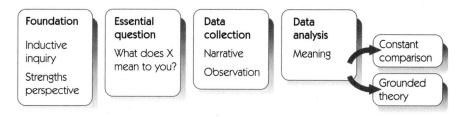

Figure 6.1 illustrates that a strengths–inductive learning orientation serves as a foundation for practitioners-researchers to approach clients with a fundamental question: What does X mean to you? The symbol X can refer to a family or social experience, to feelings, beliefs, or cultural meanings. Social workers address this question through eliciting the client's narrative and through observing the client's behavior in interactions with the worker and in the client's natural environment. The client's narrative deepens when the worker asks open-ended questions and invokes facilitative communication skills (Lum, 1996). Interpretations are offered sparingly to clients and in such a way that clients are free to reject, modify or accept them. Questions such as the following facilitate the development of the client's narrative:

What does having an autistic son mean to you? How do you maintain your strength?

What's it like to have a father who is in jail?

Can you tell me what it's like for you as a Hmong teenager to go to the doctor?

How do you manage to keep your family together when you don't have enough income and you've been homeless?

How is it for you as a Latina to be thinking about leaving your abusive husband?

How does being that angry toward the world affect your life?

What was it like for you to be told by Child Protective Services that you could not take care of your kids? What was it like when the worker came to your house and put your kids in her car?

Out of context, some of these questions may seem insensitive or, perhaps, ineffective. Some clients may be looking for immediate, concrete help and a narrative-generating question that is poorly timed could be interpreted as off-base, insensitive, or indulgent on the worker's behalf. In nearly all cases, however, there is a time and a place for questions of this nature. Clients wish to feel understood, accepted, and respected, and relish opportunities to tell their story to a worker who is eager to learn from them. Most important, this kind of data gathering is likely to yield fruitful results in cross-cultural interactions.

The importance of inductive data gathering is illustrated in Competency Study 6.2.

Inductive Data Gathering

Let us examine alternative approaches that could be used with a Hmong family that is struggling with reports from school that their 12-year-old child is experiencing hearing difficulties and with school personnel who are increasingly frustrated over the family's lack of follow through. On the one hand, working within a task-centered framework (Epstein, 1992), the practitioner would be oriented to set a goal regarding the family's follow through of a medical appointment and hearing screening. Specific tasks leading to the accomplishment of this goal could be explicated and agreed to. Exploration of past non-attendance of clinic appointments may occur in order to identify specific barriers to clinic attendance.

On the other hand, working within an inductive, strengths oriented framework, the practitioner would want to learn how the family perceives the child's progress at school. (This discussion represents an actual case, and the child is a "B" student.) The successes of the family in supporting their daughter would be explored; the family would teach the practitioner how to raise a well-behaved, academically successful child in a mono-lingual, impoverished Hmong home within a high-crime community. The family's impressions regarding their daughter's hearing would be sought, and they would be asked about their beliefs concerning health and illness and what going to a Western health care provider means to them. Joint exploration would occur regarding steps to be taken; the practitioner would respectfully ask permission to provide the family with any feedback regarding the expectations of the school.

Social workers should note that narrative-generating questions do not directly reach for client feelings (Green, 1995). Clients *may* respond to these open-ended questions with feeling statements; however, the social worker should not expect these responses. When one of us asked Latino parents during an Easter Seals support group how they moved forward while having a child who was severely disabled, they consistently mentioned spirituality as a source of coping and resolving existential dilemmas. Spiritual beliefs helped parents make sense of their life circumstances; some believed that raising their special needs child was a higher calling—as if they had "been chosen" to live this difficult life and love this challenging child. As group members mutually revealed that they had all dealt with spiritual questions and had sought spiritual relief, group member intimacy was greatly enhanced. Had group members been asked how they *felt* about raising a severely disabled child, the responses would have been less rich. Reaching for client feelings restricts the variety of responses that clients can provide. In addition, different cultural groups and members within these groups may have more or less willingness and fluency to engage in the language of feelings.

The practitioner-researcher adopts the same spirit of open-ended inquiry with regard to understanding the client's experience of the social work service. The social worker engages the client in *directive narrative consultation*, where the client becomes the expert on the utility of the social worker's involvement. In this

CULTURAL COMPETENCY IN ACTION

The Hernandez Family: A Case Study

The inductive practitioner seeks to understand the meaning of life events and circumstances for the client. The worker's involvement is not based on how Ricardo's teacher constructs the case: Ricardo needs help with his homework and Ricardo's father is working too much"; nor is it based on overly general constructions about how Latinos are supposed to respond in counseling.

Mr. Platt seeks to understand how the parents view their own role in Ricardo's schooling and education. How much is the teacher viewed as the guardian of Ricardo's education and what role do the parents see for themselves? Can the parents imagine a facilitative role that they can play in assisting Ricardo in school? What lessons about life and about their history can the parents impart? What does Ricardo say about his acting-out behavior? How much would he link his behavior to his academic difficulties vs. problems with his teacher or peers? What kinds of school successes has he experienced? What strategies does he have for becoming more successful in school?

TASK RECOMMENDATIONS

Cross-cultural theory sensitizes Mr. Platt to the possibility that parent involvement may have unique meaning to the Hernandez family that is salient to this case. Before establishing a contract regarding Ricardo's completion of homework (perhaps the teacher's desire), the social worker seeks to understand the parents' beliefs about what they can contribute. Mr. Platt is also aware that many people of color, and Mexican immigrants in particular, internalize racist ideology and believe that their life stories and life lessons have little relevance for the education of their children. The parents' narrative regarding these themes deepens Mr. Platt's understanding of what Ricardo's school struggles *mean* to Mr. and Mrs. Hernandez. The exploration is validating for the parents and it provides a fertile environment for a new family paradigm that the worker and Mr. and Mrs. Hernandez jointly construct. For example, Mr. and Mrs. Hernandez have valuable wisdom about Ricardo. They can contribute to his academic success. Their life lessons are powerful educational tools.

Assessment and intervention issues regarding a narrative-generating approach are addressed through the following questions:

- How easy or difficult would it be for you to resist the pressure to impose an immediate solution or condition upon the family (such as a homework contract)? Is this dynamic different if the parents are behaving destructively? Please explain.
- How would you assess the additional resources to be utilized on behalf of the family or Ricardo?
- What questions would you ask the Hernandez family to ascertain their level of satisfaction with your helping effort and the likelihood that they would continue in counseling?
- What interventions with Ricardo's teacher can you suggest that would enhance the probability of positive outcomes?
- What meso-level interventions could assist the school to become more effective with the Hernandez family and with others similarly situated?
- What kinds of observations fortify your data collection process?

role, the client talks with the social worker about what is and is not working, what elements of the social worker's style are appreciated and what elements are not, and what the social worker needs to do in order to facilitate gains. One client may state that he or she needs direct advice; the social worker is not clear enough and needs to play an expert role. Another client may state that the social worker is pushing too hard in a particular direction; the client wants to feel more supported regardless of his or her decisions and wants the social worker to be more active in setting up employment opportunities.

The social worker should learn about the client's past involvement with helping professionals and nonprofessionals and develop a sense of the client's expectations for the present helping encounter. This area of inquiry frames the present helping encounter as fluid and open to client input.

Grounded Data Collection-Client Observation

In addition to client narrative, grounded data collection also involves observation. A child, for example, may not discuss his or her peer relationships in much detail; however, when you observe the child in various interactions, the child appears withdrawn. Through child, family, or teacher interviews you want to learn about the meaning of this withdrawn behavior. Again, rather than forming a quick hypothesis regarding the etiology of the withdrawn behavior (the child does not feel accepted because of his or her ADD; because he or she is in foster care; because of inadequate social skills), the social worker learns "from the ground up" the meaning of this behavior. The worker wants to see whether there are instances where the child is not withdrawn and identify the differences. He or she wants to understand how the child experiences being removed from others and what staying alone represents.

Grounded Data Analysis and Theory Building

When the practitioner-researcher works with individual clients, families, or systems, he or she relies on narrative or observational data to develop an understanding of the client's reality. The worker does not seek higher-level theoretical constructs when working with the individual client; instead, the worker attempts to weave gathered data into useful, data-driven themes. The social worker discusses these themes with the client so that the client can confirm them, build upon them, or reject them.

Inductive data gathering and theory building are illustrated in Competency Study 6.3.

COMPETENCY STUDY 6.3

Inductive Data Gathering and Theory Building

The social worker in the earlier Hmong example reflected with family members upon the difficulty of interacting with a medical system that was largely distrusted by the family and the Hmong community and then discussed and explored the dilemmas that were presented by living in a society that made unaccustomed demands upon them. The parents wanted to do the best for their child and give her the greatest opportunity for success, but they were not always sure what doing the best meant. These themes were presented to the parents (through a translator) and the themes resonated with the parents' experience. The parents decided after two home visits by the social worker to have their daughter fitted for a hearing aid.

In order to build grounded theory and higher-order theoretical constructs, the practitioner-researcher compares this Hmong family with other Hmong families facing medical issues. Narratives and observed situations generate data that the practitioner-researcher *conceptualizes*. For example, mistrust becomes a *name* that the practitioner-researcher assigns to common phenomena he/she observes in the community or hears about from similarly situated clients. The properties and nature of mistrust are developed through the study of more cases. Higher-level concepts are developed and become categories.

The grounded theorist may realize, for example, that mistrust is manifested differently within the Hmong community and is dealt with in various ways by medical entities that interact with the Hmong community. Grounded in observation and client narrative, the theorist concludes that Hmong mistrust is dealt with either by: (1) medical provider coerciveness/insensitivity; (2) medical provider directiveness/pseudosensitivity; or (3) medical provider partnership orientation. The grounded theorist develops these three higher-order categories by constantly comparing cases until the themes and properties of the categories are saturated (Strauss & Corbin, 1990).

The constant comparison process assures that the grounded theorist does not attempt to explicate theory based upon a few cases; in fact, the grounded theorist makes an extensive search to uncover exceptions to the developing categories. Ultimately, the grounded theorist realizes that no matter how elegant the theory and all-inclusive it appears to be (for example, Kübler-Ross's 1969 theory that people who successfully deal with death proceed through various stages: denial, anger, bargaining, sadness, acceptance), it is actually fluid and subject to revision (Gilgun, 1994).

For example, social workers now realize, based on work with many AIDS patients, that many patients acquire a functional, positive, "I'm going to beat this thing" approach that deserves to be respected, protected, and honored; this mental attitude, rather than being labeled as denial, can be seen as a vehicle for AIDS patients to "live as though they were going to beat AIDS." As Green and Sherr (1989, p. 209) observe, "Such patients often appeared happier and more energetic in dealing with their condition. It is hard to believe that what was objectively an irrational view could be anything but beneficial for them."

Cross-cultural social work theory at its core has always taken exception to the universal categorization of complex phenomena (such as a healthy process of dying) and argued for an emic or more client- and culture-specific understanding of issues (Devore & Schlesinger, 1996; Green, 1995; Lum, 1996). A grounded approach to data collection makes sense even where established theory exists and especially makes sense when theory is undeveloped (for example, regarding identity issues for mixed-ethnicity individuals, PTSD recovery for Southeast Asian refugees, successful coping patterns for families affected by welfare reform).

A classroom study illustration on the inductive strengths perspective is shown in Competency Study 6.4.

Inductive Strengths Perspective

If social work faculty members are to teach students to become inductive, strengths-oriented practitioners-researchers, then they themselves need to model this approach in their treatment of students. Being new to California and relatively unexposed to its many Asian communities and to Asian students, I adopted an inductive, strengths-oriented approach to learning about Asian cultures and about particular issues facing Asian social work students. I soon noticed that in large and small group discussions and activities, many Asian students would defer to non-Asian students and would, generally, remain relatively quiet throughout small and large group discussions. I, however, valued class participation and believed that students needed to develop assertiveness skills in order to be effective client and community advocates.

An etic or universal approach to addressing this dilemma would have been to: (1) define assertiveness skills as the ability to verbally "express oneself boldly or forcefully . . . (and) to defend or maintain one's rights" (*Webster's* II, 1994) and assume that these skills are valuable; (2) scan the classroom environment and conclude that many Asian students were "low assertive"; (3) assess that many Asian students were "deficient" in group activities; (4) admonish various Asian students to participate more.

Rather than follow these steps, I adopted an inductive, strengths-oriented approach. I assumed that Asian students had a lot to teach me about the nature and origin of different styles of participation. I became committed to observing participation differences and to engaging in one-to-one discussions with students and faculty members regarding my observations (*inductive inquiry*).

My inquiry was not framed along the lines of "what's wrong with these students and how can they participate more," but with the belief that style differences reflected deep traditions built around cultural successes. I believed that lessons from these traditions were potential gifts for me, the social work class members, and, ultimately, for clients (*strengths perspective*).

When I met with some Asian students, I shared my perceptions. One person experienced my perception sharing as overly stereotyping. I began asking some students, in one form or another, about being in groups and the values, expectations, and self-assessment that was part of their group experiences. I asked some Asian students how they believed their cultural background affected the nature of their group participation (*"Tell me about what X—being in a classroom group—means to you"*). Various Asian students stated that giving others the opportunity to speak was viewed as respectful and was valued. Students consistently told me that though they were listening and not talking, they were very *involved* in group discussions; involvement did not imply talking.

In fact, it was considered polite not to talk, and talking a lot about one's self was a sign that one lacked humility. Although some students in other cultural groups were very comfortable and, perhaps, indulgent when discussing their own lives, this characteristic was not viewed as necessarily positive. Finally, even when a person's behavior was monopolizing, ineffective, or simply annoying, it could have been disrespectful to point out these shortcomings *(grounded data collection—narrative)*.

As mentioned, I observed that many Asian students waited until others spoke *before* they did. However, if an exercise involved a format such as systematically going around in a circle, then Asian students responded verbally and nearly to the same degree as non-Asian students *(grounded data collection—observation)*.

Although some Asian students and a faculty member can identify cultural patterns that predict lower verbal involvement in class groups (respect, deference, nonindulgence, nonconfrontation), Asian students and faculty clearly are in a position to instruct non-Asian students and faculty concerning how to listen and how to be respectful. Listening is a highly valued form of participation in Asian culture; however, it is not highly regarded in the dominant society. Some Asian students stated that they knew that social work demanded that they increase their behavioral repertoire and have greater willingness to become verbally assertive. In situations that demanded verbal participation—"going-around-the-circle" exercises—Asian students had opportunities to rehearse verbally assertive behavior *(meaning of group participation for Asian students in social work classes)*.

The development of grounded theory concerning these processes is still in progress. I have not systematically examined the roles that English language proficiency, acculturation, or Asian ethnicity plays in this phenomenon. I am also investigating how all students acquire a greater range of communication styles. Because I initially addressed this issue with a foundation in inductive inquiry and strengths, I am seeking to develop and study a cross-cultural classroom environment where

- valuable communication lessons are to be learned across ethnic and cultural groups—non-Asians from Asians, Asians from non-Asians;
- social work students work from the premise that the wider one's communication repertoire is, the more opportunities a practitioner will have for success; and
- the primary learning challenge is to experiment with different communication styles.

Within this classroom environment, narrative and observational data needs to be systematically collected, both within the Asian student body and between Asians and non-Asians *(constant comparison)*. After data collection, analysis needs to occur that uncovers a *useful story* (Glaser & Strauss, 1967) linking major conceptual categories and themes (Strauss & Corbin, 1990) concerning the meaning of Asian participation in small groups within social work classes *(grounded theory)*.

The Hernandez Family: A Case Study

The inductive practioner-researcher relies on collection of the client's narrative and his or her own observations to build an understanding of the client's reality. Data-driven themes are discussed with the client so that the client can confirm, reject, or further construct them. The culturally competent social worker maintains a researcher's mentality when working with the individual client or family; eventually the practitioner-researcher assigns conceptual names to what is happening in the client's environment.

School officials and teachers frequently admonish parents to play a larger role in their child's education. This admonishment is well-intentioned and is based on the well-established correlation between parent involvement and child academic success. However, the Hernandez family has been accustomed to having the teacher and the school be responsible for their child's education. They do not perceive a role for themselves. If anything, the parents feel ashamed about their lack of formal education and their Spanish monolingualism.

TASK RECOMMENDATIONS

Working within the grounded theory tradition, Mr. Platt compares the Hernandez case with other cases regarding parent involvement issues. After conducting qualitative interviews with Latino parents of other underachieving children, he realizes that (1) parents do not see themselves as the primary "authors" of their child's education and their child's future; (2) parents believe that their lack of English and math skills severely limits their ability to help;

(3) parents do not know what "doing well" means for their early-age school child; (4) parents have limited time to help their child (Garcia & Dyer, 1996).

Mr. Platt uses these findings to theoretically sensitize himself in his work with other families. He does not mechanically apply these newfound concepts to each family with whom he works. Rather, he maintains an inductive, strengths-based posture, then compares the new family's narrative with the already existing categories. New data contribute either to the enriched description of existing categories, to the explication of exceptions to existing categories, or to the emergence of new categories. He uses emergent knowledge to plan interventions and conducts case studies to document the effectiveness of various efforts.

Mr. Platt prepares the Hernandez family to meet with Ricardo's teacher. He talks with them about the value of their information and prepares the teacher to listen to the parents and validate them. Mr. Platt talks to Mr. and Mrs. Hernandez about a successful social worker whom he knows whose Latino parents were monolingual farm workers. Mr. Platt's story describes how these parents monitored their child's homework and gained the support of other potentially helpful adults in order to contribute to his childhood academic success. The social worker talks to Mr. and Mrs. Hernandez about an available homework group that exists on the school grounds.

- Researcher bias is a potential pitfall in grounded theory building. The practitioner-researcher may superimpose initial impressions and analysis on

The Hernandez Family: A Case Study (continued)

subsequent cases. How do you guard against this tendency?

- What is the difference between approaching a case with "theoretical sensitivity" and approaching a case with a formulated hypothesis to be tested about the client's problems and intervention strategies?

- How much do Mr. Platt's approaches flow from the inductive assessment of the case's dynamics?
- How can processes involving inductive knowledge building or systematic research become incorporated into a social service site?
- What dynamic or topic can you imagine systematically investigating with an inductive approach?

Inductive social work practice is part of the inductive learning experience, which needs to be taught in the repertoire of social work interventions. In the next section we propose an inductive learning process that can be used in the practice and research classroom and later translated to the social work agency.

THE INDUCTIVE LEARNING PROCESS

We have made a case for inductive learning and qualitative inductive practice and research. We have surveyed various types of qualitative research and qualitative inductive practice and have argued for the need to prepare social work students and practitioners in culturally diverse research-oriented practice. In this section we explain Lang's three-stage model of integrating practice and research.

Lang (1994) pushes for the needed integration between the data processing of qualitative research and social work practice in order to advance the practitioner as knowledge builder. She maintains an emphasis on the practitioner as primary and qualitative research in social work practice as secondary, while at the same time comparing and contrasting the varying research and practice methodologies. Her emphasis is on the research-oriented practitioner which agrees with my perspective. That is, culturally diverse social work should educate practitioners to work with multicultural clients and also do clinical and community ethnic research.

Lang's threefold model encompasses data gathering, data processing and data transformation, and integration of qualitative research and social work practice. These three stages should be taught in social work practice and research classes. They also become the structure for professional social work practice in social service agencies.

Data Gathering

Data-gathering strategies consist of firsthand observation and writing down those observations in process descriptions that record important client-worker verbal and nonverbal interactions.

The social work practitioner is concerned about the following questions: What is discovered? How does it happen? What needs to be done? How can I contribute? The practitioner must uncover information from observation and must also determine a course of action. Observation is used to develop practice directives. Practitioner observations occur at critical junctures in the helping process: at the beginning of a new client relationship, at various stages of the relationship, and when a client terminates.

The written description of observations captures significant details and constitutes the data for practice analysis and directives. The emphasis is on self-supervision through scrutinizing practice records. Lang believes that it is important to record practice sessions as material for qualitative research: "The promotion of and provision for large-scale process recording by numerous practitioners as a professional requirement would enable the profession to enter an era in which qualitative research methods could become widely use for theory-building purposes" (p. 268). Lang's suggestion underlines the need to bring together social work education programs and social work agencies on a local level. The creation of a multicultural study and discussion group consisting of multicultural social work educators, students, and practitioners is an opportunity to discuss multicultural cases that have implications for learning and to implement social work practice and qualitative research methodologies.

The Lang model suggests a focus group that would meet to discuss systematic ways to conduct uniform data gathering of multicultural case material. Hardcastle, Wenocur, & Powers (1997, p. 172) explain that a focus group is "a small number of individuals meet[ing] together with a trained facilitator to discuss a narrow topic in a detailed, guided way." Its purpose is to air ideas, to react to each other, and to refine opinions.

A focus group has the atmosphere of a study group. It provides valuable information and insights into issues, describing ways in which people react to areas of concern. It also tests the waters and may provide themes and key concepts for formulating an area of concern. Finally, a focus group provides specialized assessment of some subject matter, tasks to be pursued, and the population under study. Members of a focus group could gather various theoretical and clinical/community case study data in completing Lang's first stage.

Data Processing and Data Transformation

The first level of data processing consists of abstracting and generalizing. Abstracting primary features and characteristics from the data has a twofold effect: reducing the data by selection and transforming the data into an abstracted, generalized form. Generalizing involves linking similar features and making connections in the data. Categorizing and sorting comparable items and naming them as a class is the next step after abstracting and generalizing. It begins to focus and elaborate the inquiry to a higher level of abstraction. It creates the beginning of a classification scheme or typology. Next there is conceptualizing into a profile, model, or paradigm. Finally there is contextualizing, where the new theory is placed in the context of relevant existing theories.

Two emerging patterns of data processing are the action-focused and knowledge-focused patterns. The action-focused pattern derives appropriate interventions for immediate practice implementation. It is motivated by the demand for action in the immediate helping situation. Lang (1994, p. 270) explains: "Thus the practitioner in the action-focused pattern may run on a short cycle of inductive data processing limited to the first level of abstraction and generalization, followed by a deductive process involving interpretation of data in the light of theory, derivation of action, and a return to the concrete." The knowledge-focused pattern involves the matching of previous and current data into knowledge building and developing. The practitioner evolves classifications and conceptualizations and turns quickly to theory for an immediate explanation. The issue is to know what to do and what action to take.

A focus group consisting of social work educators, students, and practitioners can become a force committed to processing and transforming data. This involves, for example, working on a major area of multicultural study and abstracting concepts and findings that are selected and related to each other. This task is best done by a group of persons who are familiar with the existing body of knowledge and skill relating to a major aspect of culturally diverse practice. Cultural competencies in the classroom are enlarged and strengthened through participating in the focus group.

Generalizing, conceptualizing, and contextualizing involve creative effort by academicians who are able to develop theory and clinicians who understand the relationship between theory development and skill application. On a local or regional level, such a focus group would have to be highly committed to a major undertaking that involves many hours, weeks, and months of steady work and creative data refinement.

Integration of Qualitative Research and Social Work Practice

Lang (1994) calls for social work educators and professionals to commit themselves to qualitative research methodologies in social work practice. This involves the development of a social work curriculum requirement to teach qualitative research methodology. At the same time, the role of the social work practice professional is to participate in the inductive pattern of data processing and abstracting and generalizing from qualitative research data.

The social work practitioner is involved in process recording so that knowledge is retained and practice theory is generated from data. Lang (1994, p. 277) points out: "We have not thought of the practitioner as knowledge builder, yet no social worker is in practice very long before accumulating expert knowledge from practice experience. We recover only a fraction of this knowledge because it may not be articulated or formulated into a transmittable, shareable state and because our emphasis in practice is on doing." In the end, Lang believes that we must integrate the practice and research methodologies of data processing. It must start with the education of social work students in research-oriented practice.

In the meantime, a focus group consisting of social work educators, social work students with research skills, and social work practitioners should work on short-term research-oriented practice projects involving cultural diversity. Such a group needs three ingredients for the integration of qualitative research and social work practice: social work educators who are familiar with social work practice literature, course material, and research trends; social work students who are learning about social work practice and research and who have assignments in these areas; and social work practitioners who have past and current clinical cases, notions about clients and their problems, and practical experiences. Together they are a formative force for investigation, discussion, and integration.

Tools for Student Learning 6.1 outlines five phases of integrating practice and research based on Lang's model. They are: (1) getting started; (2) gathering the data; (3) processing the data; (4) categorizing, classifying, and contextualizing the data; and (5) integrating qualitative research and social work practice. This exercise uses the focus group as the discussion and investigatory vehicle.

TOOLS FOR STUDENT LEARNING 6.1

Structuring the Inductive Learning Process

The purpose of this group exercise is to implement Lang's three-stage model of integrating practice and research in social work classes. This exercise clarifies how a group might process qualitative research data and apply it to social work practice in order to build knowledge about cultural diversity. It further supports the interchange between research-oriented practice and practice-oriented research. It outlines the entire inductive learning process and can be spread over a series of sessions that might actually occur over weeks and months.

Phase I: Getting Started

1. The creation of a focus group is crucial to bringing together various key members who have theoretical, didactic, clinical, and research interests and experiences in culturally diverse social work practice issues. Describe the composition of such a focus group with members' specific qualifications.

_____

_____

_____

2. Data gathering begins with sharing firsthand observations from experiences of culturally diverse practice. List various clinical and community
   experiences with clients of color that members of the focus group come
   up with.

_____

_____

_____

_____

_____

3. Lang suggests that in order to concentrate on specific topics and issues,
   the focus group should answer certain general questions. Lum adds a
   multicultural perspective to these questions:

   - What have I discovered about working with clients of color?
   - Have these observations and experiences about this client group been a
     part of my practice?
   - What needs to be done to uncover and develop further knowledge
     about a specific theme that emerges from my discovery?
   - How can I make a contribution to refine a multicultural topic that
     interests me?

_____

_____

_____

_____

_____

4. After an initial discussion, list the range of topics on the board and select a
   single area of interest based on group consensus.

   - Why did the group focus on this particular theme?
   - Why did the group agree that this area was worthy of further investiga-
     tion and development?
   - What particular aspect of the social work practice process involving
     people of color does this theme relate to—contact, problem identifica-
     tion, assessment of client/environmental strengths, intervention, or
     termination?

_____

_____

_____

_____

_____

Phase 2: Gathering the Data

5. What basic observations does the focus group have about its selected area of interest based on case experiences, readings, review of the literature, professional insights, classroom discussion, and other avenues of knowledge?

_____

_____

_____

_____

_____

6. Are there any case process recordings from the practitioner group members, articles or chapters of books from the academic group members, or research material uncovered by the student group members on this topic? Are there any local experts who could speak to the group about the topic under investigation?

_____

_____

_____

_____

_____

Phase 3: Processing the Data

7. Which persons in the group are able to select material that could be assessed in a thoughtful way, arranged into subcategories, and interpreted to the whole group?

_____

_____

_____

8. Based on Lang's guidelines, answering the following questions is crucial to processing the data:

   - What features and characteristics can be abstracted from the data?
   - What linkages (similarities, connections) can be made among features and characteristics to arrive at generalizations about the data?
   - What action-focused areas of the data lend themselves to immediate application with clients?
   - What knowledge-focused areas of the data make a contribution to theory building and understanding?

Phase 4: Categorizing, Classifying, and Contextualizing the Data

9. The group is moving into data transformation, where systematic arrangement of the data takes place. Can the group build a framework, model, or paradigm around the categories of material? Various group members might take leadership roles in the creation of a conceptual scheme that brings together components of the topic in a logical and meaningful way.

10. The initial framework may need refinement based on individual scrutiny and group review. Initial drafts of the model should be given to group members for critical analysis, further discussion, and revision.

11. After building consensus, the new model should be assessed in light of how it fits into the current literature on social work practice and people of color.

Phase 5: Integrating Qualitative Research and Social Work Practice

12. As a follow-up to the focus group, there should be an effort to ensure that qualitative research methodologies are taught in social work programs. There should be content on practice-oriented research and research-oriented practice. The focus group is an excellent resource to interact with social work research classes and to share their deliberations and results. This would provide an illuminating example of how academicians, professionals, and students can work together on a joint project committed to qualitative research.

QUALITATIVE RESEARCH AND SOCIAL WORK EDUCATION

There is a strong case for qualitative research as an integral part of social work education. Cultural competency hinges on research-oriented practice and practice-oriented research in multicultural settings from the inductive learning perspective. In this chapter we have discussed how qualitative approaches enhance our multicultural practice and knowledge base. Examples have illustrated how inductive qualitative approaches help social workers to construct an emic (culture-specific) understanding of client reality and lead students, educators, and practitioners to learn from clients and help them feel accepted, respected, and heard in the learning and helping process.

The inductive qualitative approach to research is especially consonant with social work's emphasis on "starting where the client is" (Gilgun, 1994). Not only is this a practice dictum but it is also an inductive learning principle for research. Rather than initiating client or research interviewee contact with a preformed hypothesis about client or interviewee dynamics, the inductive researcher-practitioner establishes rapport, tunes into client or interviewee strengths, and utilizes communication skills in guiding the process and letting the client's or the interviewee's story unfold. The storytelling process becomes an empowering event: an interviewee in a research project becomes a *teacher* rather than a *subject* and experiences a sense of contribution and connectedness (Bein, 1994). Ultimately, the inductive practitioner-researcher seeks to minimize "the extent to which constraints are placed on output(s)" (Patton, 1990, p. 41). Rather than asking a client or interviewee to respond "never," "sometimes," or "always" to a given question framed by the practitioner-researcher's theoretical orientation, the practitioner-researcher engages the client or interviewee in a joint process of discovery where an infinite number of data possibilities are present.

Stories and themes that emerge from qualitative inquiry in many instances yield even in evaluation research more powerful insights and findings than statistical data. For example, Patton (1990) discusses the power of direct quotations in evaluation research and offers a compelling example of his qualitative evaluation of a teacher accountability system in Kalamazoo, Michigan. Teacher responses to closed-ended questions concerning the accountability system produced similar findings for each question. For instance, 90% of the teachers disagreed with the administration's official statement that the system was "designed to personalize and individualize education." Patton (1990, p. 21) reported: "When the school officials and school board members rejected the questionnaire data, rather than argue with them about the meaningfulness of teacher responses to the standardized items, we asked them to turn to the pages of open-ended teacher comments and simply read at random what teachers said." As board members read through 373 teacher comments they found statements like:

> Fear is the word for accountability as applied in our system. My teaching before accountability is the same as now. Accountability is a political ploy to maintain power. Whatever good there may have been in it in the beginning has been destroyed by the awareness that our educational system has at its base a political

motive. Students get screwed. . . . The bitterness and hatred in our system is incredible. What began as noble has been destroyed. You wouldn't believe the new layers of administration that have been created just to keep the monster going. Our finest compliment around our state is that the other school systems know what is going on and are having none of it. Lucky people. Come down and visit in hell sometime. (teacher response 251, p. 22)

In 10 years of teaching, I have never ended a school year as depressed about education as I have this year. . . . The Kalamazoo accountability system must be viewed in its totality . . . it is oppressive and stifling. (teacher response 244, p. 21)

Qualitative inquiry allowed for the teachers' voices to emerge, and the collective intensity of their responses served as a basis for renewed dialogue and the forced resignation of the district superintendent (Patton, 1990). Although this example involves data collected from service providers (teachers), it is instructive of qualitative research issues.

The empowerment and social justice traditions embedded in social work demand that practitioner-researchers provide opportunities for clients to "give voice" to their experiences. Hartman (1994) exhorts the social work profession to enhance our opportunities for knowledge; to listen to the stories that arise out of practice with clients and to learn about their wisdom, lived experience, and vision of the world.

SUMMARY

This chapter provided a framework for learning based on a foundation of inductive research and respect for cultural strengths. This framework was then applied to social work practice, and a process of inductive practice was advanced. The practitioner-researcher's tasks within this process were discussed, and case examples were provided. Finally, it was argued that qualitative research makes an important contribution to the social work knowledge base and is consonant with social work perspectives emphasizing client uniqueness and empowerment. The culturally competent practitioner-researcher may want to consult the literature cited in this chapter to gain a deeper understanding of various qualitative research traditions.

REFERENCES

Bein, A. (1994). *Early termination of outpatient counseling among Hispanics.* Unpublished doctoral dissertation, University of Illinois at Chicago.

Bein, A., Torres, S., & Kurilla, V. (1997). The repelled Latino client: Re-examination of issues in cross-cultural practice. Article submitted for publication to *Journal of Multicultural Counseling and Development.*

Dean, R. G. (1994). Commentary: A practitioner's perspective on qualitative case evaluation methods. In E. Sherman & W. J. Reid (Eds.), *Qualitative research in social work* (pp. 279-284). New York: Columbia University Press.

De Jong, P. , & Miller, S. (1995). How to interview for client strengths. *Social Work, 40,* 729-736.

Delgado, M. (1997). Strengths-based practice with Puerto Rican adolescents: Lessons from a substance abuse prevention project. *Social Work in Education, 19,* 101-112.

Devore, W., & Schlesinger, E.G. (1996). *Ethnic-sensitive social work practice.* Boston: Allyn & Bacon.

Epstein, L. (1992). *Brief treatment and a new look at the task-centered approach.* New York: Macmillan.

Fortune, A. E. (1994). Commentary: Ethnography in social work. In E. Sherman & W. J. Reid (Eds.), *Qualitative research in social work* (pp. 63-67). New York: Columbia University Press.

Garcia, E., & Dyer, L. (1996). *Exploring issues of academic success among Latino students and families.* Unpublished master's thesis, California State University, Sacramento.

Gilgun, J. F. (1994). Hand into glove: The grounded theory approach and social work practice research. In E. Sherman & W. J. Reid (Eds.), *Qualitative research in social work* (pp. 115-125). New York: Columbia University Press.

Glaser, B. G., & Strauss, A. L. (1967). *The discovery of grounded theory: Strategies for qualitative research.* New York: Aldine de Gruyter.

Green, J. W. (1995). *Cultural awareness in the human services.* Boston: Allyn & Bacon.

Green J., & Sherr, L. (1989). Dying, bereavement and loss. In J. Green & A. McCreaner (Eds.), *Counseling in HIV infection and AIDS* (pp. 207-223) Oxford: Blackwell Scientific Publications.

Hardcastle, D. A., Wenocur, S., & Powers, R. (1997). *Community practice: Theories and skills for social workers.* New York: Oxford University Press.

Hartman, A. (1994). Setting the theme: Many ways of knowing. In E. Sherman & W. J. Reid (Eds.), *Qualitative research in social work* (pp. 459-463). New York: Columbia University Press.

Lang, N. C. (1994). Integrating the data processing of qualitative research and social work practice to advance the practitioner as knowledge builder: Tools for knowing and doing. In E. Sherman & W. J. Reid (Eds.), *Qualitative research in social work* (pp. 265-278). New York: Columbia University Press.

Lum, D. (1996). *Social work practice and people of color: A process-stage approach* (3rd ed.). Pacific Grove, CA: Brooks/Cole.

Mizrahi, T., & Abramson, J. S. (1994). Collaboration between social workers and physicians: An emerging typology. In E. Sherman & W. J. Reid (Eds.), *Qualitative research in social work* (pp. 135-151). New York: Columbia University Press.

Mokuau, N. (1985). Counseling Pacific Islander-Americans. In P. Pedersen (Ed.), *Handbook of cross-cultural counseling and therapy.* Westport, CT: Greenwood Press.

Monette, D. R., Sullivan, T. J., & DeJong, C. R. (1994). *Applied social research: Tool for the human services.* Fort Worth, TX: Harcourt Brace.

Patton, M. (1990). *Qualitative evaluation and research methods* (2nd ed.). Newbury Park, CA: Sage.

The question of race in America. (1997, June 15). *Sacramento Bee,* p. Forum 4.

Root, M. P. (Ed.). (1992). *Racially mixed people in America.* Newbury Park, CA: Sage Publications.

Saleeby, D. S. (Ed.). (1992). *The strengths perspective in social work practice.* New York: Longman.

Sherman, E., & Reid, W. J. (Eds.). (1994). *Qualitative research in social work.* New York: Columbia University Press.

Stern, S. B. (1994). Commentary: Wanted! Social work practice evaluation and research-All methods considered. In E. Sherman & W. J. Reid (Eds.), *Qualitative research in social work* (pp. 285-290). New York: Columbia University Press.

Strauss, A., & Corbin, J. (1990). *Basics of qualitative research: Grounded theory procedures and techniques.* Newbury Park, CA: Sage Publications.

Weick, A. (1992). Building a strengths perspective for social work. In D. Saleebey (Ed.), *The strengths perspective in social work practice* (pp. 18-26). New York: Longman.

CHAPTER SEVEN

Some Reflections on Culturally Competent Practice

This chapter summarizes the themes of the book and points you toward increasing effectiveness in culturally competent social work practice.

Culturally competent practice is emerging as an integral part of social work practice and education. It is a journey whose time has come in a number of ways. The Council on Social Work Education has taken a leadership role in Evaluative Standard 1: Program Rationale and Assessment, by asking each social work program to have clear outcome measures and measurement methods and to indicate actual outcomes of the education program. Accredited social work programs are required to measure and evaluate program and curriculum functions and outcomes. Program and curriculum measurement instruments and findings on competencies are the natural results of this accreditation mandate. Student progress in courses on social work practice, human behavior and the social environment, social policy, social research, diversity, populations at risk, values and ethics, and social and economic justice, and in the field practicum must be identified, measured, and evaluated.

This mandate quickens the emergence of competencies in general, and cultural competencies in particular, as models are sought for teaching, learning, and evaluation purposes. Not only is the accreditation requirement reasonable, but the need for instructors to evaluate their teaching effectiveness and for students to ascertain their learning are important reasons to build competencies into curriculum and course work.

This text has defined *cultural competency* and *cultural competencies* and has offered a measurement instrument and a social work cultural competencies framework. As a result, I hope that social work educators who teach in related curriculum areas will identify competencies and create measurement instruments in social work practice, behavior, policy, research, fieldwork, and other areas.

The purpose of this closing chapter is to highlight the major themes of this book and to foster the growth of cultural competency. In my estimation, much will be written about cultural competency from a social work perspective in the coming years.

THE MEANING OF CULTURAL COMPETENCY

In the Cultural Competence Series published by the Office for Substance Abuse Prevention, Health Resources and Services Administration, Bureau of Primary Health Care, Orlandi (1992) defines *cultural competence* as

> a set of academic and interpersonal skills that allow individuals to increase their understanding and appreciation of cultural differences and similarities, within, among, and between groups. This requires a willingness and ability to draw on community-based values, traditions, and customs and to work with knowledgeable persons of and from the community in developing focused interventions, communications, and other supports. (p. 3–4)

In this book we detail and distinguish cultural competence even more than Orlandi's understanding.

Cultural competency and *cultural competencies* are defined in a specific sense to establish a division of labor among and between the terms. Cultural competency is the subject area that relates to the experiential awareness of the worker about culture, ethnicity, and racism; knowledge about historical oppression and related multicultural concepts; development of skills to deal effectively with the needs of the culturally diverse client; and inductive leaning, which heuristically processes new information about this area. These definitions focus on the worker's interpersonal and academic understanding of self, others, and the information needed to become culturally competent. That is, the social worker must become aware of his or her own sense of culture and ethnicity, his or her racism/prejudice/discrimination, and his or her contact with other ethnic/racial groups and individuals before working with multicultural clients. Next the worker participates in academic social work education to gain knowledge about people of color and develop skills for working with clients in a helping relationship. Finally, the worker develops a methodology of inquiry and investigation that is applied to multicultural case studies so that clinical and community data result in new knowledge and skills.

Cultural competency is the result of a number of processes: individual and social reflection, academic education, career development, skill mastery, and continued contributions in multicultural practice. Cultural competency is a process and an arrival point for the social worker. The worker achieves cultural competency after developing cultural awareness, mastering knowledge and skills, and implementing an inductive learning methodology. In the midst of this, the social worker has reflected on self-awareness, cultural awareness, and the social trends affecting people in our society; gone through an academic educational program in social work; incorporated aspects of culturally diverse social work practice in career development; honed multicultural skills with clients; and sought to make a professional contribution to culturally diverse social work practice through a case study insight, a professional conference presentation, or an article.

Cultural competencies are a series of related behavioral outcomes that are observable and measurable and demonstrate effective multicultural practice.

Cultural competencies are systematically identified and measured through a checklist or an instrument that tells the student, the instructor, the worker, and/or the supervisor that cultural competency has been fully achieved, partially achieved, slightly achieved, or not achieved.

An alternative way to understand cultural competency is from a micro, meso, and macro perspective. Micro cultural competency involves the client of color and the social worker. The client acquires cultural competency from personal background and development. The client has the task of sorting culture of origin and elements of the dominant culture to achieve bicultural integration and bicultural competency. Likewise, the worker develops expertise and skills through education and through working with culturally diverse clients. Cultural competency presupposes adequate course offerings in culturally diverse social work, the inclusion of multicultural social work texts and articles in course reading assignments, the recruitment and development of qualified multicultural social work educators, and the nurturing of social work doctoral students who are interested in multicultural research and provide a new supply of social work faculty members.

Meso cultural competency addresses the organizational level to determine whether an institution has a culturally competent system of care. Cross, Bazron, Dennis, & Isaacs (1989) explain six anchor points along a cultural competency continuum with regard to an organizational system of care:

1. *Cultural destructiveness* represents a set of attitudes, practices, and/or policies that promote the superiority of the dominant culture and attempt to eradicate the inferior and different culture.
2. *Cultural incapacity* refers to a set of attitudes, practices, and/or policies that adhere to separate but equal treatment and tend toward segregated institutional practices.
3. *Cultural blindness* refers to a set of attitudes, practices, and/or policies that have an unbiased view of undifferentiated elements of culture and people and treat all people as assimilated.
4. The *culturally open organization* has attitudes, practices, and/or policies that are receptive to the improvement of cultural services through staff hiring practices, training on cultural sensitivity, and minority board representation.
5. The *culturally competent agency* has attitudes, practices, and/or policies that respect different cultures and people by seeking advice and consultation from ethnic/racial communities and is committed to incorporating these practices into the organization.
6. *Cultural proficiency* is a set of attitudes, practices, and/or policies that are sensitive to cultural differences and diversity, improve cultural quality of services through cultural research, disseminate research findings, and promote diverse group cultural relations.

Meso-level interaction takes place between the system of care, the worker, and the client along the continuum of cultural competency.

Macro cultural competency refers to large system efforts to address cultural competency issues and programs. Multicultural counseling psychologists have established national cultural competency practice, research, and training criteria to impact the accreditation standards of the American Psychological Association. Two major texts address these issues on a macro professional level (Ponterotto, Casas, Suzuki, & Alexander, 1995; Pope-Davis & Coleman, 1997). The U.S. Public Health Service's Office for Substance Abuse Prevention launched a series of monographs that integrate cultural competence, alcohol and drug abuse treatment programs, and ethnic groups and community (Orlandi, Weston, & Epstein, 1992). This interface between ethnic target groups, major problem areas, and cultural competency for treatment workers further illustrates how macro cultural competency can be expressed.

I hope there will be continuing dialogue on the meanings of cultural competency and cultural competencies. Culturally diverse social work must build on these concepts and also facilitate a growth and action process to increase our understanding of culturally competent practice.

THE SOCIAL WORK CULTURAL COMPETENCIES FRAMEWORK

The core of this book has been the social work cultural competencies framework, which draws on the contributions of the Association for Multicultural Counseling and Development (AMCD). The AMCD explained cultural competencies as a three-characteristics × three-dimensions matrix (Sue, Arredondo, & McDavis, 1992). Cultural competency worker characteristics are: an awareness of personal assumptions about human behavior, values, biases, preconceived notions, and personal limitations; understanding of the culturally different client without negative judgments; and development and practice of appropriate, relevant, and sensitive intervention strategies and skills in working with culturally different clients. These characteristics never reach an end point, because cultural competency is a constant growth process on the part of the worker.

The social work cultural competencies model addresses generalist and advanced levels in the areas of cultural awareness, knowledge theory, skill development, and inductive learning. The generalist practice level emphasizes beginning professional relationships, knowledge, values, skills, and process stages. The advanced practice level covers breadth and depth of knowledge and skills and advanced content areas. This framework serves as a guide for developing a social work curriculum on cultural competency. The essential elements of the framework are reviewed in the following pages.

Cultural Awareness

The first component of the framework is cultural awareness, which is the gatekeeper of the model. The social worker cannot be effective with clients of color unless the worker makes an accounting of his or her self-awareness about persons of other races and/or ethnicities. This self-awareness arises from past impressions, personal experiences, learned beliefs, stereotypes, and factual realities regarding African, Latino, Asian, and Native Americans. There is also the worker's consciousness about his or her own ethnicity and racism. To what extent does the worker regard himself or herself as an ethnic and cultural individual, and to what extent has the worker dealt with his or her own racism, prejudice, and discrimination? Culture, ethnicity, and racism have a strong impact on the professional social worker's attitude, perception, and behavior toward clients of color. How the worker relates to the culturally different client has a lasting impact on his or her effectiveness.

Cultural awareness starts with the social worker's awareness of his or her life experiences as a person related to a culture. Family heritage, family and community events, beliefs, and practices serve as a baseline for an understanding of one's own culture. Next the worker explores his or her range of contacts with individuals, families, and groups of other cultures and ethnicities to determine his or her perceptions and impressions of various cultural groups. Of particular concern are positive and negative experiences with cultural/ethnic persons and events. Often these experiences contribute to beliefs, feelings, and behaviors of the worker and feed into racism, prejudice, and discrimination. The worker must become aware of his or her own racism, prejudice, and discrimination. Uncovering, discovering, and dealing with these dynamics is painful, but the worker becomes a more effective helper with a client of color rather than masking over this aspect.

On the advanced level, the worker assesses his or her involvement with people of color in his or her childhood, adolescence, young adulthood, and adulthood, taking a longitudinal view of the various developmental stages. The social work student reviews present and future course work, fieldwork experiences, and research projects on culturally diverse clients and groups. Part of cultural awareness is to establish an educational and professional career continuum involving the development of cultural competency.

Knowledge Acquisition

Knowledge encompasses a range of information, facts, principles, and social work practice concepts. Knowledge acquisition influences the refinement of theory into a series of systematically arranged principles and categories.

On the generalist level, a beginning step is to understand basic terminology: *ethnicity, minority, culture, multiculturalism,* and *diversity.* These terms must be understood since they are widely used and applied in multicultural social work theory. Demographic knowledge provides a baseline of statistical data and alludes to client and problem profiles. Cultural/ethnic demographics report the rapid and steady growth of ethnic/racial populations and the precipitating causes of immigration and birthrate. Critical thinking develops theory and problem analysis and assessment and applies several principles to culturally diverse practice models. Critical thinking as a part of knowledge building and development is an important tool for social work education.

The history of oppression of African, Latino, Asian, and Native Americans is related to economic and social exploitation, removal from land and/or restriction to geographic ghettos, social and geographic segregation and barriers to equal opportunities, the struggle for civil and human rights, and poverty/family fragmentation/social dysfunction. Historical knowledge provides the student with a necessary background about what has already happened and how to anticipate better results in the present and future.

Knowledge about cultural values is rooted in ethnic, religious, and generational beliefs, traditions, and practices. A respect for cultural values helps the social worker to better understand the lives and actions of multicultural clients. Among the range of culturally diverse values are family, respect, harmony, spirituality, and cooperation. Values reflect core cultural beliefs, practices, and behaviors, which come from ethnic traditions. Culturally competent social workers must understand and respect these cultural values, which are essential to the well-being of people of color.

On the advanced level, culturally diverse knowledge draws on social work practice theories. Systems theory, psychosocial theory, role theory, family theory, and conflict theory are representative of micro, meso, and macro practice applications. Clinical practice has embraced problem-solving/task-centered, existential, crisis, empowerment, and related individual-oriented theories. An emerging theory is social constructionism, which is an inductive indigenous approach focusing on cultural story or narratives. Qualitative research-oriented social work practice is attuned to social constructionism. Ethnicity, culture, minority status, and social class are essential themes in theories of cultural diversity. Ethnicity and culture are positive themes which draw on strengths and a historical perspective, while minority status and social class point to the struggle to cope with negative determinism, transcend minority and social barriers. and move toward social equality and social justice.

Courses in social work practice, behavior, policy, research, values and ethics, diversity, populations at risk, and economic and social justice, and the social work practicum have thrived on social science theory. Social work has encompassed a wide range of theories because social work practice serves diverse target population groups with many needs. The culturally competent social worker should be well read and educated in the broad social sciences. A liberal arts background for social work education includes courses in psychology, sociology, anthropology, government, history, ethnic and women's studies, economics, and related areas. There is continuous application of social science theory to the field of social work.

Skill Development

Skill development refers to the acquisition of a helping repertoire that can readily be used at the professional discretion of the worker. Skill is the practical application of cultural awareness and knowledge at the actual helping interface between the social worker and the multicultural client. Whether the worker has a set of culturally sensitive and responsive skills determines whether the worker can be regarded as culturally competent.

Three types of skills in the helping relationship were identified: process skills, conceptualization skills, and personalization skills (Bernard, 1979). Process skills refer to therapeutic techniques and strategy; conceptualization skills include deliberate thinking and case analysis abilities; and personalization skills relate to the learning, the observable and subtle behaviors, and the personal growth of the worker.

Contact, problem identification, assessment, intervention, and termination are the five stages (Lum, 1996) that were identified with the process, conceptualization, and personalization skills they each involve. Contact process skills center on understanding the ethnic community, relationship protocols, professional self-disclosure, and communication style (Lum, 1996). Contact conceptualization skills focus on the words, thoughts, and feelings of the client from an ethnographic point of view. Contact personalization skills involve the subjective feelings and reactions of the worker in the initial sessions. Problem identification process skills are problem area disclosure, problem orientation perspective, and racial/ethnic theme analysis (Lum, 1996). Problem identification conceptualization skills involve Green's (Green, 1995) four principles: the client's definition and understanding of an experience as a problem, the client's semantic evaluation of a problem, indigenous strategies of problem intervention, and culturally based problem resolution. These procedural steps have been helpful in conceptualizing how to lead a client through a problem-solving process. Problem identification personalization skills focus on the worker's own reactions to the problem.

Assessment process skills include psychosocial perspective analysis (assessing socioenviromnental impacts and the psychoindividual reactions), assessment of cultural strengths, and the inclusion of cultural and assessment (Lum, 1996). Assessment conceptualization skills focus on cultural/ethnic group strengths, use of indigenous sources of help, and a supportive learning approach to assessing clients. Assessment personalization skills evaluate the positive potential of the client, which mobilizes positive resources to support change intervention strategies.

Intervention process skills implement goal setting and agreement, the selection of culturally diverse intervention strategies, and micro/meso/macro levels of intervention (Lum, 1996). A wide range of intervention possibilities on multiple levels have been identified for the culturally competent worker who consults with the multicultural client. Intervention conceptualization skills involve careful selection of intervention strategies based on unique cultural factors related to the client, the problem, and the social/cultural environment. Particular micro interventions relate to indigenous strategies such as empowerment or traditional approaches, which range from structure and boundaries to freedom and human potential. Meso intervention may use extended-family members or the minister of a church, while macro intervention may mean campaigning for a ballot initiative or working with an attorney to file a class action suit to address an issue in court. The culturally competent worker crafts with the multicultural client a responsive and meaningful intervention plan. Intervention personalization skills explore the worker's concerns about client change, client decision making, and defining a change procedure.

Termination is a critical transition time for the client. Termination process skills involve destination, or a connection to a support network; recital, or a retrospective analysis of the problem situation; and completion, or goal attainment/outcomes appraisal (Lum, 1996). Termination conceptualization skills entail a follow-up plan and the study of premature and successful termination. Termination personalization skills help the worker to use short-term treatment with reachable, concrete, and practical goals. The worker relies on referral to appropriate social service resources, indigenous community agencies, and the ethnic church and community.

On the advanced level, service delivery deals with the structure of programs, facilities, staff, funding, and administration to serve the needs of the client population in a geographic area. Social service delivery systems are changing as populations in the United States become diversified due to immigration and birthrates. Service delivery changes as a series of events or as new policies alter program emphases (Iglehart & Becerra, 1995). The growth of welfare rolls, negative public opinion toward welfare recipients, and a conservative Republican Congress with a Democratic President running for re-election were major factors in the 1996 welfare reform legislation. Time-limited and program-restricted welfare reform changed the delivery system from federal entitlement income maintenance for parents and dependent children to state-operated employment readiness and referral.

Lum (1996) has written about the characteristics of multicultural service delivery: location and nature of services, staffing, community outreach programs, agency setting, and service linkage. Iglehart and Becerra (1995) identified internal and external factors of agency change and service delivery related to funding, external pressure groups, agency and worker leadership, agency ideology and technology, and client inputs. These aspects of service delivery shape agency linkage or interorganizational relations, especially program design and implementation. The ethnic social service agency is the link between mainstream service organizations and ethnic communities and is the key mediator in multicultural service delivery.

Research on cultural skill development uncovers new data on how to work effectively with multicultural clients. For example, the worker-client interpersonal relationship is an essential part of the dynamic process of change. Bordin (1979) explains the importance of initial bonding between the worker and the client. The clinical relationship has developed around the concept of the therapeutic alliance (Frank & Gunderson, 1990) or the working alliance (Horvath & Greenberg, 1994), which has a direct effect on positive outcome (Henggeler, Schoenwald, Pickrel, Rowland, & Santos, 1994). This area of research is an example of how social class, race and ethnicity, and cross-cultural factors add a multicultural dimension to skill development.

Inductive Learning

Inductive learning deals with the question of how a social work professional continues to evaluate his or her multicultural practice and carries out the learning process of exploring new information about this field after graduation. Dean (1994) suggests the importance of reflecting on case studies and conducting qualitative analysis in informal ways with supervisors and staff. Inductive learning is a lifelong process of continuous discovery about the changing nature of multicultural families and communities.

On the generalist level, inductive reasoning assembles particular facts or individual cases about a subject and draws general conclusions based on findings. The social work student learns about inductive and deductive reasoning in the social work foundation research class. Inductive learning becomes a linkage between what we know in the present and what we may discover in the future about cultural diversity. Social work practitioners (graduates of social work programs) gain new knowledge and skills as they use an open-ended inductive process to uncover new data about multicultural clients.

Inductive social research is an important tool to teach students, because it shapes open-ended questions and allows the data to tell us about clients. One gathers observations and information from a range of cases. Lang (1994, p. 275) talks about the importance of asking "What do I know from this processing?" and "Therefore, what should I do?" These questions capture the essence of inductive data gathering and processing, which lead to abstracting or generalizing and later conceptualization. This critical mind-set should be taught to social work students in practice-oriented research and research-oriented practice so that they will always ask "What does the data tell us?" As social work students graduate and become professional practitioners, it is incumbent on them to establish a research-oriented line of inquiry that can be applied throughout their social work career.

On the advanced level, there is a relationship between inductive learning and qualitative inductive research. Lang (1994) argues for the needed integration between the data processing of qualitative research and social work practice in order to advance the practitioner as knowledge builder. Her model involves data gathering, data processing and data transformation, and integration of qualitative research and social work practice. Data-gathering strategies consist of first-hand observation and writing down those observations in process-recording descriptions of important client-worker verbal and nonverbal interactions. Data processing consists of abstracting features and characteristics that are primary in the data into categories that can be linked. Data transformation takes these categories and translates them into a framework, model, or paradigm. The product is placed in the context of relevant existing theories about a subject. There are implications for cultural competency in the generation of new knowledge and skills.

The integration of qualitative research and social work practice is a three-way partnership with social work educators, practitioners, and students. Social work educators are familiar with social work practice literature, course material, and research tools. They are able to conceptualize new material for cultural competency. Social work practitioners have a knowledge about past and current clinical cases, notions about clients and their problems, and practical experiences. They are the pragmatic realists of the group. Social work students are learning about social work practice and research and have assignments in these areas. They are motivated, by and large, by the requirements of writing and researching materials to complete courses and their degree. Together, social work educators, practitioners, and students form the basis for focus groups to work on short-term inductive learning and research-oriented practice projects involving cultural diversity. These discussion and work-oriented groups have the potential of identifying baseline data on cultural competency and culturally diverse social work based on culturally oriented research methodologies and resulting in the publication of articles and texts in the field.

THE SOCIAL WORK CULTURAL COMPETENCIES SELF-ASSESSMENT INSTRUMENT

In Chapter 1 you were asked to complete the Social Work Cultural Competencies Self-Assessment instrument as a pretest that measured your level of cultural competence at the start of a course on culturally diverse social work practice. Now it is important for you to take a posttest to determine the extent of your cultural competency at the end of the course.

The cultural competency areas may have been foreign and unfamiliar to you at the beginning of this book. I hope that the lectures, discussions, exercises, and assignments have contributed to your understanding of cultural competency and cultural competencies and to an enthusiastic passion for culturally diverse social work practice.

As you complete the Social Work Cultural Competencies Self-Assessment instrument (Tools for Student Learning 7.1) for the second time, compare your levels of competency as indicated by the pretest and the posttest scores. Write a two-page analysis comparing the results of your pretest and posttest. Indicate the particular items where your score made a significant difference and where there were no changes.

CULTURAL COMPETENCY STANDARDS IN SOCIAL WORK EDUCATION

Social work education is concerned with the development of cultural competency and cultural competencies, which are benchmark indicators of the diversity and populations-at-risk content areas in the Council on Social Work Education's Curriculum Policy Statement. No doubt there will be a steady stream of articles and books on social work cultural competency.

TOOLS FOR STUDENT LEARNING 7.1

Social Work Cultural Competencies Self-Assessment

Introduction

This instrument measures your level of cultural competency at the beginning and end of the semester. The results of this self-assessment will be evaluated by your social work instructor. Strict confidentiality is observed regarding the results of the self-assessment.

Rate yourself on your level of competency on a scale of 1–4: 1=Definitely; 2=Likely; 3=Not very likely; and 4=Unlikely. Circle the appropriate number.

Name: *Course:*   *Campus:*

Cultural Awareness

1. I am aware of my life experiences as a person related to a culture (e.g., family heritage, household and community events, beliefs, and practices).

Definitely	*Likely*	*Not very likely*	*Unlikely*
1	*2*	*3*	*4*

2. I have contact with individuals, families, and groups of other cultures and ethnicities.

Definitely	*Likely*	*Not very likely*	*Unlikely*
1	*2*	*3*	*4*

3. I am aware of positive and negative experiences with persons and events of other cultures and ethnicities.

Definitely	*Likely*	*Not very likely*	*Unlikely*
1	*2*	*3*	*4*

4. I know how to evaluate the cognitive. affective, and behavioral components of my racism, prejudice, and discrimination.

Definitely	*Likely*	*Not very likely*	*Unlikely*
1	*2*	*3*	*4*

5. I have assessed my involvement with cultural and ethnic people of color in childhood, adolescence, young adulthood, and adulthood.

Definitely	*Likely*	*Not very likely*	*Unlikely*
1	*2*	*3*	*4*

6. I have done or plan to do academic course work, fieldwork, and research on culturally diverse clients and groups.

Definitely	*Likely*	*Not very likely*	*Unlikely*
1	*2*	*3*	*4*

7. I have or plan to have professional employment experiences with culturally diverse clients and programs.

Definitely	*Likely*	*Not very likely*	*Unlikely*
1	*2*	*3*	*4*

8. I have assessed or plan to assess my academic and professional work experiences with cultural diversity and culturally diverse clients.

Definitely	*Likely*	*Not very likely*	*Unlikely*
1	*2*	*3*	*4*

Knowledge Acquisition

9. I understand the following terms: *ethnic minority, multiculturalism, diversity, people of color.*

Definitely	*Likely*	*Not very likely*	*Unlikely*
1	*2*	*3*	*4*

10. I have a knowledge of demographic profiles of some culturally diverse populations.

Definitely	*Likely*	*Not very likely*	*Unlikely*
1	*2*	*3*	*4*

11. I have developed a critical thinking perspective on cultural diversity.

Definitely	*Likely*	*Not very likely*	*Unlikely*
1	*2*	*3*	*4*

12. I understand the history of oppression and of multicultural social groups.

Definitely	*Likely*	*Not very likely*	*Unlikely*
1	*2*	*3*	*4*

13. I know about the strengths of men, women, and children of color.

Definitely	*Likely*	*Not very likely*	*Unlikely*
1	*2*	*3*	*4*

14. I know about culturally diverse values.

Definitely	*Likely*	*Not very likely*	*Unlikely*
1	*2*	*3*	*4*

15. I know how to apply systems theory and psychosocial theory to multi-cultural social work.

Definitely	*Likely*	*Not very likely*	*Unlikely*
1	*2*	*3*	*4*

16. I have knowledge of theories on ethnicity, culture, minority identity, and social class.

Definitely	*Likely*	*Not very likely*	*Unlikely*
1	*2*	*3*	*4*

17. I know how to draw on a range of social science theory from cross-cultural psychology, multicultural counseling and therapy, and cultural anthropology.

Definitely	*Likely*	*Not very likely*	*Unlikely*
1	*2*	*3*	*4*

Skill Development

18. I understand how to overcome the resistance and lower the communication barriers of a multicultural client.

Definitely	*Likely*	*Not very likely*	*Unlikely*
1	*2*	*3*	*4*

19. I know how to obtain personal and family background information and determine the extent of his or her ethnic/community sense of identity.

Definitely	*Likely*	*Not very likely*	*Unlikely*
1	*2*	*3*	*4*

20. I understand the concept of ethnic community and practice relationship protocols with a multicultural client.

Definitely	*Likely*	*Not very likely*	*Unlikely*
1	*2*	*3*	*4*

21. I use professional self-disclosure with a multicultural client.

Definitely	*Likely*	*Not very likely*	*Unlikely*
1	*2*	*3*	*4*

22. I have a positive and open communication style and use open-ended listening responses.

Definitely	*Likely*	*Not very likely*	*Unlikely*
1	*2*	*3*	*4*

23. I know how to obtain problem information, facilitate problem area disclosure, and promote problem understanding.

Definitely	*Likely*	*Not very likely*	*Unlikely*
1	2	3	4

24. I view a problem as an unsatisfied want or an unfulfilled need.

Definitely	*Likely*	*Not very likely*	*Unlikely*
1	2	3	4

25. I know how to explain problems on micro, meso, and macro levels.

Definitely	*Likely*	*Not very likely*	*Unlikely*
1	2	3	4

26. I know how to explain problem themes (racism, prejudice, discrimination) and expressions (oppression, powerlessness, stereotyping, acculturation, and exploitation).

Definitely	*Likely*	*Not very likely*	*Unlikely*
1	2	3	4

27. I know how to find out problem details.

Definitely	*Likely*	*Not very likely*	*Unlikely*
1	2	3	4

28. I know how to assess socioenvironmental stressors, psychoindividual reactions, and cultural strengths.

Definitely	*Likely*	*Not very likely*	*Unlikely*
1	2	3	4

29. I know how to assess the biological, psychological, social, cultural, and spiritual dimensions of a multicultural client.

Definitely	*Likely*	*Not very likely*	*Unlikely*
1	2	3	4

30. I know how to establish joint goals and agreements with the client that are culturally acceptable.

Definitely	*Likely*	*Not very likely*	*Unlikely*
1	2	3	4

31. I know how to formulate micro, meso, and macro intervention strategies that address the cultural and special needs of the client.

Definitely	*Likely*	*Not very likely*	*Unlikely*
1	2	3	4

32. I know how to initiate termination in a way that links the client to an ethnic community resource, reviews significant progress and growth, evaluates goal outcomes, and establishes a follow-up strategy.

Definitely	*Likely*	*Not very likely*	*Unlikely*
1	2	3	4

33. I know how to design a service delivery and agency linkage and culturally effective social service programs in ethnic communities.

Definitely	*Likely*	*Not very likely*	*Unlikely*
1	2	3	4

34. I have been involved in services that have been accessible to the ethnic community.

Definitely	*Likely*	*Not very likely*	*Unlikely*
1	2	3	4

35. I have participated in delivering pragmatic and positive services that meet the tangible needs of the ethnic community.

Definitely	*Likely*	*Not very likely*	*Unlikely*
1	2	3	4

36. I have observed the effectiveness of bilingual/bicultural workers who reflect the ethnic composition of the clientele.

Definitely	*Likely*	*Not very likely*	*Unlikely*
1	2	3	4

37. I have participated in community outreach education and prevention that establish visible services, culturally sensitive programs, and credible staff.

Definitely	*Likely*	*Not very likely*	*Unlikely*
1	2	3	4

38. I have been involved in a service linkage network to related social agencies that ensures rapid referral and program collaboration.

Definitely	*Likely*	*Not very likely*	*Unlikely*
1	2	3	4

39. I have participated as a staff member in fostering a conducive agency setting with a friendly and helpful atmosphere.

Definitely	*Likely*	*Not very likely*	*Unlikely*
1	2	3	4

40. I am involved or plan to be involved with cultural skill development research in areas related to cultural empathy, clinical alliance, goal-obtaining styles, achieving styles, practice skills, and outcome research.

Definitely	*Likely*	*Not very likely*	*Unlikely*
1	2	3	4

Inductive Learning

41. I have participated or plan to participate in a study discussion group with culturally diverse social work educators, practitioners, students, and clients on cultural competency issues, emerging cultural trends, and future directions for multicultural social work.

Definitely	*Likely*	*Not very likely*	*Unlikely*
1	2	3	4

42. I have found or am seeking new journal articles and textbook material about cultural competency and culturally diverse practice.

Definitely	*Likely*	*Not very likely*	*Unlikely*
1	2	3	4

43. I have conducted or plan to conduct inductive research on cultural competency and culturally diverse practice, using survey, oral history, and/or participatory observation research methods.

Definitely	*Likely*	*Not very likely*	*Unlikely*
1	2	3	4

44. I have participated or will participate in the writing of articles and texts on cultural competency and culturally diverse practice.

Definitely	*Likely*	*Not very likely*	*Unlikely*
1	2	3	4

Compare the levels of competency in the pretest and the posttest regarding score changes and particular items.

_____

_____

_____

_____

Write a brief two-page analysis comparing the results of the pre- and posttests.

Indicate the particular items in which you scored and made a significant difference and where there were no changes.

_____

_____

_____

_____

_____

Please count up your scores on the 44 self-assessment items and rate your level of cultural competency: Circle the appropriate level and write your raw score in one of the following levels:

Level 1: Definitely (scores 43–95)

Level 2: Likely (scores 96–128)

Level 3: Not Very Likely (scores 129–171)

Level 4: Unlikely (scores 172 and over)

Thank you for your cooperation on this self-assessment instrument. You have made a significant contribution to our research on social work cultural competency.

What is needed is a strategy of development to explore new dimensions of cultural competency for social work education. An interesting case study is to examine how a group of multicultural counseling psychologists began to influence the accreditation process of the American Psychological Association toward multicultural content and cultural competency. It was a grassroots strategy to write and present a series of position papers on multicultural counseling, to introduce the concept of cultural competencies, and to create a theory base for multicultural counseling psychology. It is ironic that social work educators in general and culturally diverse social work practice educators in particular now face a top-down strategy rather than the bottom-up strategy of the multicultural psychologists. That is, the Council on Social Work Education through its Commission on Educational Policy and its Commission on Accreditation has asked social work programs for cultural diversity content (diversity and populations at risk) and outcome measurements. Both commissions are comprised of peer social work educators who meet periodically for two related reasons. The Commission on Educational Policy is charged with the revision of the Curriculum Policy Statement and related accreditation standards and procedures every four years. Revision drafts are forwarded to the Board of Directors of the Council on Social Work Education and distributed to the general membership for peer review and comments. The Commission on Accreditation is mandated to implement the final agreed-upon Curriculum Policy Statement and related standards and procedures as it reviews new candidate schools and accredited schools that are in the process of reaffirmation of full accreditation. It has a heavy load of reviewing social work programs at various stages of accreditation and meets three times each year to process program self-studies, site visitor reports, and interim program reports. It is the major body granting accreditation to social work programs in the United States and represents the Council on Social Work Education on accreditation matters.

The social work education commitment to cultural diversity has been present in specific mandates to teach content on people of color, women, and gays and lesbians. The accreditation program and individual membership provide grassroots inputs related to these areas to the accreditation administrative level. Likewise, the Commission on Educational Policy and the Commission on Accreditation, comprised of recognized peer social work educators, endorse and implement these standards. Nevertheless, social work education has much to learn about the development of cultural competency from their multicultural counseling psychology counterparts.

THE GROWTH AND DEVELOPMENT STRATEGY OF MULTICULTURAL COUNSELING PSYCHOLOGY

An academic and professional movement begins with a nucleus of key players who influence a discipline through their teaching, writing, and political inroads. Multicultural clinical and counseling psychology have drawn together such persons as Paul Pedersen, Stanley Sue, Derald Wing Sue, Allen Ivey, Richard Brislin, Anthony Marsella, Joseph Ponterotto, and Charles Ridley. These individuals have written in the field of multicultural psychology, which has been termed the fourth force by Pedersen (insight-oriented, behavioral, and existential psychologies are the three other forces), and have held high offices in the American Psychological Association. From academic publication and professional bases they have been able to influence the discipline of psychology and to shape a number of doctoral training programs in counseling psychology with multicultural curriculum and training requirements.

From an organizational perspective, the American Psychological Association in 1980 adopted a professional competent practice requirement and recognized the importance of cultural competence as an essential element (American Psychological Association, 1980). The adoption of cultural competence meant the acceptance of the concept, which required detailing of particular cultural competencies in educational programs. During the mid-eighties and into the early nineties, discussions occurred around Criterion II of the American Psychological Association's accreditation standards (American Psychological Association, 1986). This particular section incorporated multicultural content and experience in faculty recruitment and promotion, student recruitment and evaluation, curriculum, and field training (Altmaier, 1993). There was resistance among the majority of clinical and counseling psychology faculty in doctoral programs, who lacked sufficient commitment, interest, and academic background in multicultural psychology.

In 1982 a major position paper on cross-cultural counseling competencies was presented that specified multicultural knowledge, awareness, and skill areas in counseling psychology. This represented a watershed in the movement; since then, there has been a steady stream of material on cultural competency concepts and their application in practice, research and training, and instrumentation. As a result, multicultural counseling competencies have been addressed in counseling practice, research, and training (Casas, Ponterotto, & Gutierrez, 1986; Ibrahim & Arredondo, 1986). Measurement instrumentation in the form of a number of cultural competencies self-report measures was developed in the mid-eighties to the early nineties: the Multicultural Awareness-Knowledge-Skills Survey (MAKSS), the Multicultural Counseling Inventory (MCI), and the Multicultural Counseling Awareness Scale—Form B: Revised Self-Assessment (MCAS-B) (Pope-Davis & Dings, 1995). These instruments tested and measured cultural competency variables and established an empirical data base in this area.

By 1992, Sue, Arredondo, and McDavis (1992) had identified a set of 38 cultural competencies and listed them under multicultural awareness, knowledge, and skills categories in a conceptual framework. The results of a follow-up study on this model were reported several years later (Arredondo et al., 1996). A related concern was supervision and training in multiculturalism. Multicultural counseling supervision has been categorized according to multicultural awareness, knowledge, and skills (D'Andrea & Daniels, 1997). Some progress has been made toward infusing multicultural content into graduate programs. A multicultural counseling program training checklist reported initial findings in counseling psychology doctoral programs (Ponterotto, 1997). At least one multicultural course on the doctoral level and a doctoral-level faculty member with interest and expertise in multicultural psychology are required. However, much remains to be developed in terms of faculty and student minority recruitment and presence, curriculum, research and supervision, and cultural setting. On the course level, learning objectives have been identified that address cultural competency behavior, knowledge, skill, theory, self-awareness, and group and cultural differences (Ridley, Mendoza, & Kanitz, 1994). Two significant texts have been published that explain cultural competency (Ponterotto, Casas, Suzuki, & Alexander, 1995; Pope-Davis & Coleman, 1997).

By 1993 the American Psychological Association had committed itself to multicultural competency with ethnic, linguistic, and culturally diverse populations (American Psychological Association, 1993).

The contributions of core multicultural counseling psychologists are evident in the recognition of cultural competency in applied social science disciplines such as psychology and social work. This book is an effort to bring preliminary material together so that social work students, educators, and practitioners can begin a process of incorporating cultural competency in social work. The gathering of social workers who are teaching, writing, and practicing in cultural competency is a starting place for a national clearinghouse of material (course work, instruments, articles) and thoughtful ideas for the future. Please contact me on email at lumd@csus.edu regarding your interest and work in cultural competence.

CLOSING THOUGHTS

As social work education and culturally diverse social work practice enter the 21st century (the new millennium), cultural competency is an emerging topic that can catalyze new growth and development in curriculum. Cultural competency points toward the future of social work education and practice: outcome-based knowledge and skills, measurement accountability, and mastery of culturally competent practice with people of color. The basic concepts of ethnic-sensitive, culturally/aware, and culturally diverse social work practice have been clearly articulated and accepted by the social work education and practice communities.

It is now time to move ahead with cultural competency, which fits into the profession's emphasis on competency-based practice. As a social work educator I have had and will have the good fortune to have taught and written about cultural competency in both centuries. I look forward to the new century as I interact with my social work education colleagues and students about this vital area of cultural competency.

REFERENCES

Altmaier, E. M. (1993). Role of Criterion II in accreditation. *Professional Psychology: Research and Practice, 24*, 127–129.

American Psychological Association, Educational and Training Committee of Division 17. (1980, September). *Cross-cultural competencies: A position paper.* Paper presented at the annual meeting of the American Psychological Association, Montreal, Canada.

American Psychological Association. (1986). *Accreditation handbook.* Washington, DC: Author.

American Psychological Association. (1993). Guidelines for providers of psychological services to ethnic, linguistic, and culturally diverse populations. *American Psychologist, 48*, 45–48.

Arredondo, P., Toporek, R., Brown, S. P., Jones, J., Locke, D. C., Sanchez, J., & Stadler, H. (1996). Operationalization of the multicultural counseling competencies. *Journal of Multicultural Counseling and Development, 24*, 42–78.

Bernard, J. M. (1979). Supervisor training: A discrimination model. *Counselor Education and Supervision, 19*, 60–68.

Bordin, E. S. (1979). The generalizability of the psychoanalytic concept of the working alliance. *Psychotherapy: Theory, Research, and Practice, 16*, 252–260.

Casas, J. M., Ponterotto, J. G., & Gutierrez, J. M. (1986). An ethical indictment of counseling research and training: The cross-cultural perspective. *Journal of Counseling and Development, 64*, 347–349.

Cross, T. L., Bazron, B. J., Dennis, K. W., & Isaacs, M. R. (1989). *Toward a culturally competent system of care.* Washington, DC: Georgetown University Child Development Center.

D'Andrea, M., & Daniels, J. (1997). Multicultural counseling supervision: Central issues, theoretical considerations, and practical strategies. In D. B. Pope-Davis & H. L. K. Coleman (Eds.), *Multicultural counseling competencies: Assessment, education and training, and supervision* (pp. 290–309). Thousand Oaks, CA: Sage Publications.

Dean, R. G. (1994). Commentary: A practitioner's perspective on qualitative case evaluation methods. In E. Sherman & W. J. Reid (Eds.), *Qualitative research in social work* (pp. 279–284). New York: Columbia University Press.

Frank, A. F., & Gunderson, J. G. (1990). The role of the therapeutic alliance in the treatment of schizophrenia. *Archives of General Psychiatry, 47,* 228–236.

Green, J.W. (1995). *Cultural awareness in the human services: A multiethnic approach* (2nd ed.). Boston: Allyn & Bacon.

Henggeler, S. W., Schoenwald, S. K., Pickrel, S. G., Rowland, M.D., & Santos, A. B. (1994). The contribution of treatment outcome research to the reform of children's mental health services: Multisystem therapy as an example. *Journal of Mental Health Administration, 21,* 229–239.

Horvath, A. O., & Greenberg, L. S. (Eds.). (1994). *The working alliance: Theory, research, & practice.* New York: John Wiley & Sons.

Ibrahim, F. A., & Arredondo, P. M. (1986). Ethical standards for cross-cultural counseling: Counselor preparation, practice, assessment, and research. *Journal of Counseling and Development, 64,* 349–352.

Iglehart, A. P., & Becerra, R. M. (1995). *Social service and the ethnic community.* Boston: Allyn & Bacon.

Lang, N. C. (1994). Integrating the data processing of qualitative research and social work practice to advance the practitioner as knowledge builder: Tools for knowing and doing. In E. Sherman & W. J. Reid (Eds.), *Qualitative research in social work* (pp. 265–278). New York: Columbia University Press.

Lum, D. (1996). *Social work practice and people of color: A process-stage approach* (3rd ed.). Pacific Grove, CA: Brooks/Cole.

Orlandi, M. A. (1992). The challenge of evaluating community-based prevention programs: A cross-cultural perspective. In M. A. Orlandi, R. Weston, & L. G. Epstein (Eds.), *Cultural competence for evaluators: A guide for alcohol and other drug abuse prevention practitioners working with ethnic/racial communities* (pp. 1–22). Rockville, MD: U.S. Department of Health and Human Services, Office for Substance Abuse Prevention.

Orlandi, M. A., Weston, R., & Epstein, L. G. (Eds.). (1992). *Cultural competence for evaluators: A guide for alcohol and other drug abuse prevention practitioners working with ethnic/racial communities.* Rockville, MD: U.S. Department of Health and Human Services, Office for Substance Abuse Prevention.

Ponterotto, J. G. (1997). Multicultural counseling training: A competency model and national survey. In D. B. Pope-Davis & H. L. K. Coleman (Eds.), *Multicultural counseling competencies: Assessment, education and training, and supervision* (pp. 290–309). Thousand Oaks, CA: Sage Publications.

Ponterotto, J. G., Casas, J. M., Suzuki, L. A., & Alexander, C. M. (Eds.). (1995). *Handbook of multicultural counseling.* Thousand Oaks, CA: Sage Publications.

Pope-Davis, D. B., & Coleman, H. L. K. (Eds.). (1997). *Multicultural counseling competencies: Assessment, education and training, and supervision.* Thousand Oaks, CA: Sage Publications.

Pope-Davis, D. B., & Dings, J. G. (1995). The assessment of multicultural counseling competencies. In J. G. Ponterotto, J. M. Casas, L. A. Suzuki, & C. M. Alexander (Eds.), *Handbook of multicultural counseling* (pp. 287–311). Thousand Oaks, CA: Sage Publications.

Ridley, C. R., Mendoza, D. W., & Kanitz, B. E. (1994). Multicultural training: Reexamination, operationalization, and integration. *The Counseling Psychologist, 22,* 227–289.

Sue, D. W., Arredondo, P., & McDavis, R. J. (1992). Multicultural counseling competencies and standards: A call to the profession. *Journal of Counseling and Development, 70,* 477–486.

Index

Credits

TO THE OWNER OF THIS BOOK:

We hope that you have found *Culturally Competent Practice: A Framework for Growth and Action*, useful. So that this book can be improved in a future edition, would you take the time to complete this sheet and return it? Thank you.

School and address: _____

Department: _____

Instructor's name: _____

1. What I like most about this book is: _____

_____

_____

2. What I like least about this book is: _____

_____

_____

3. The name of the course in which I used this book is: _____

_____

4. Were all of the chapters of the book assigned for you to read? _____

   If not, which ones weren't? _____

5. In the space below, or on a separate sheet of paper, please write specific suggestions for improving this book and anything else you'd care to share about your experience in using the book.

_____

_____

_____

_____

_____

_____

Optional:

Your name: _____ Date: _____

May Brooks/Cole quote you, either in promotion for *Culturally Competent Practice: A Framework for Growth and Action,* or in future publishing ventures?

Yes: _____ No: _____

Sincerely,

Doman Lum

IN-BOOK SURVEY

At Brooks/Cole, we are excited about creating new types of learning materials that are interactive, three-dimensional, and fun to use. To guide us in our publishing/development process, we hope that you'll take just a few moments to fill out the survey below. Your answers can help us make decisions that will allow us to produce a wide variety of videos, CD-ROMs, and Internet-based learning systems to complement standard textbooks. If you're interested in working with us as a student Beta-tester, be sure to fill in your name, telephone number, and address. We look forward to hearing from you!

In addition to books, which of the following learning tools do you currently use in your counseling/human services/social work courses?

_____ **Video** _____ in class _____ school library _____ own VCR

_____ **CD-ROM** _____ in class _____ in lab _____ own computer

_____ **Macintosh disks** _____ in class _____ in lab _____ own computer

_____ **Windows disks** _____ in class _____ in lab _____ own computer

_____ **Internet** _____ in class _____ in lab _____ own computer

How often do you access the Internet? _____

My own home computer is:

_____ Macintosh _____ DOS _____ Windows _____ Windows 95

The computer I use in class for counseling/human services/social work courses is:

_____ Macintosh _____ DOS _____ Windows _____ Windows 95

If you are NOT currently using multimedia materials in your counseling/human services/social work courses, but can see ways that video, CD-ROM, Internet, or other technologies could enhance your learning, please comment below:

_____

_____

_____

Other comments (optional): _____

_____

Name _____ Telephone _____

Address _____

School _____

Professor/Course_____

You can fax this form to us at (408) 375-6414; e:mail to: info@brookscole.com; or detach, fold, secure, and mail.

FOLD HERE

- -

BUSINESS REPLY MAIL
FIRST CLASS   PERMIT NO. 358   PACIFIC GROVE, CA

POSTAGE WILL BE PAID BY ADDRESSEE

ATT: *Lisa Gebo*

**Brooks/Cole Publishing Company
511 Forest Lodge Road
Pacific Grove, California 93950-5098**

- -

FOLD HERE